Garfield hogs the spotlight

BY JIM DAVIS

Ballantine Books • New York

2018 Ballantine Books Trade Paperback Edition

Copyright © 2000, 2018 by PAWS, Inc. All rights reserved.
"GARFIELD" and the GARFIELD characters are trademarks of PAWS, Inc.

Published in the United States by Ballantine Books, an imprint of Random House,
a division of Penguin Random House LLC, New York.

BALLANTINE and the HOUSE colophon are registered trademarks of Penguin Random House LLC.

Originally published in slightly different form in the United States by Ballantine Books,
an imprint of Random House, a division of Penguin Random House LLC, in 2000.

ISBN 978-0-425-28574-9
Ebook ISBN 978-0-425-28575-6

Printed in China on acid-free paper

randomhousebooks.com

9 8 7 6 5 4 3 2 1

First Colorized Edition

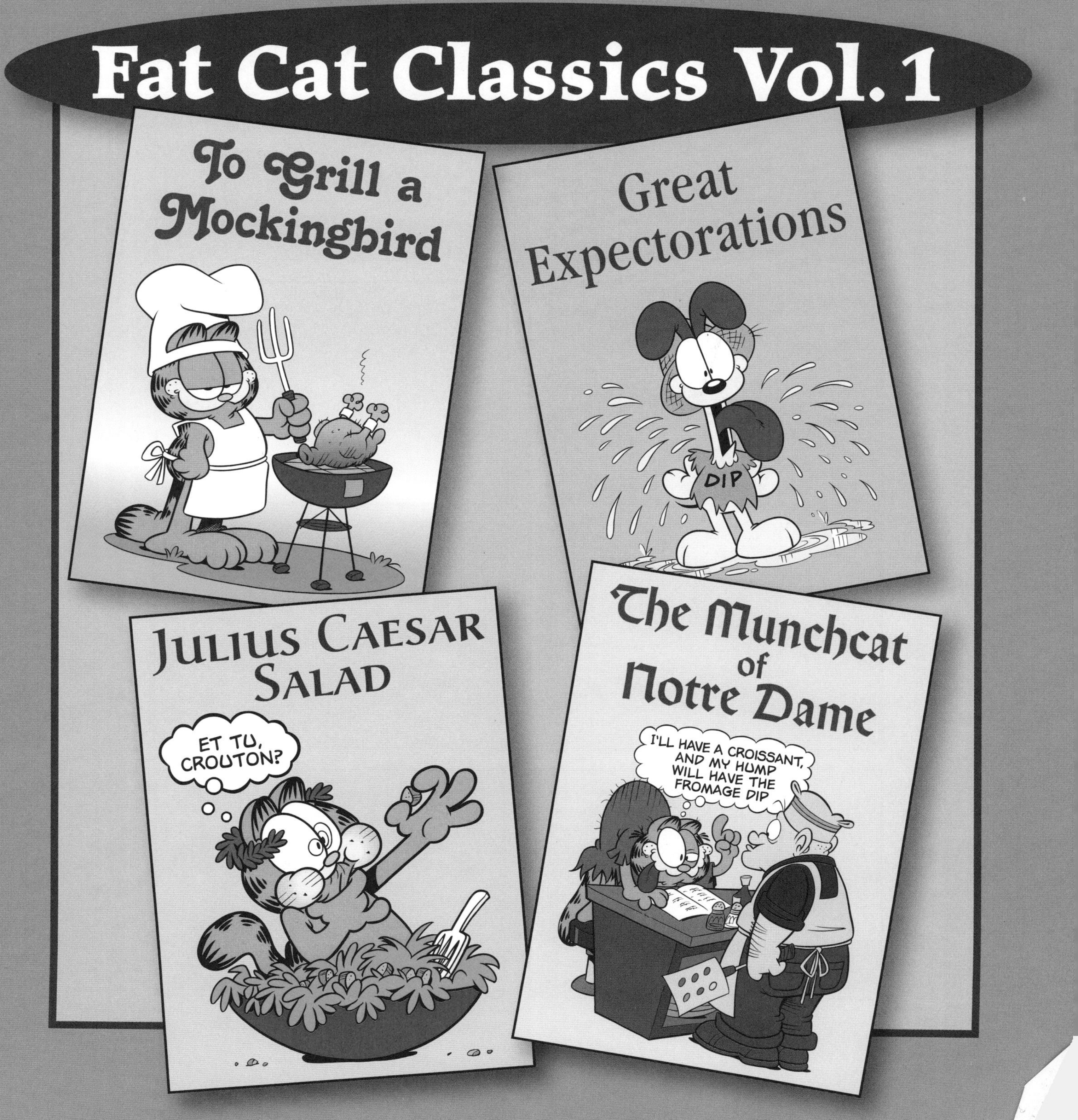
Fat Cat Classics Vol. 1
To Grill a Mockingbird
Great Expectorations
DIP
Julius Caesar Salad
ET TU, CROUTON?
The Munchcat of Notre Dame
I'LL HAVE A CROISSANT, AND MY HUMP WILL HAVE THE FROMAGE DIP

GARFIELD
PAT PAT
UH-OH
© 1999 PAWS, INC. All Rights Reserved.
JIM DAVIS 2-14

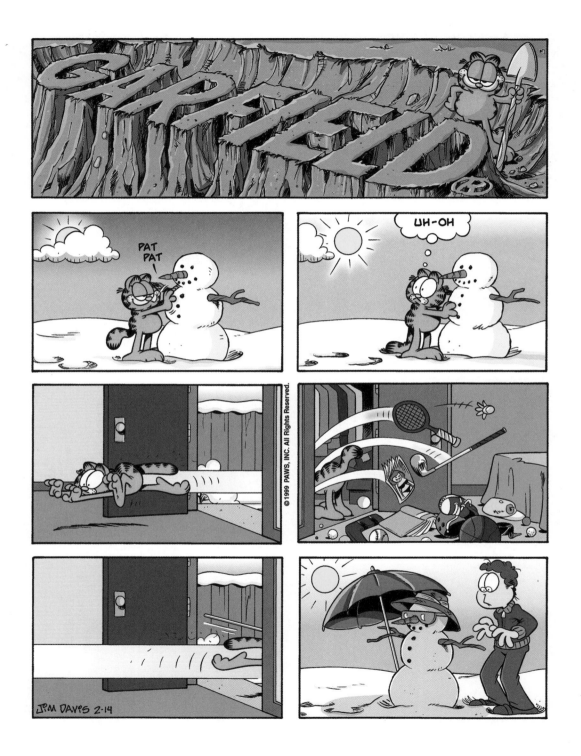

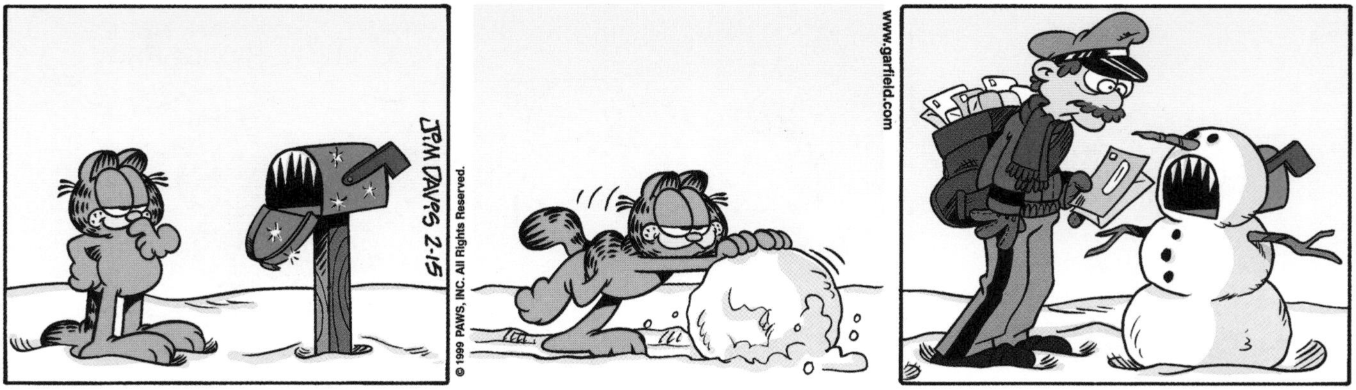
JIM DAVIS 2-15
© 1999 PAWS, INC. All Rights Reserved.
www.garfield.com

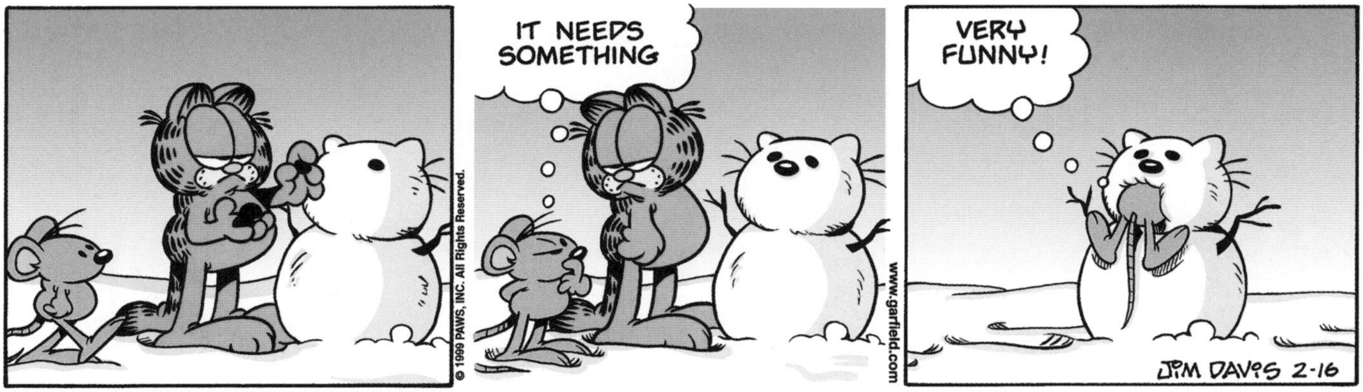
© 1999 PAWS, INC. All Rights Reserved.
IT NEEDS SOMETHING
www.garfield.com
VERY FUNNY!
JIM DAVIS 2-16

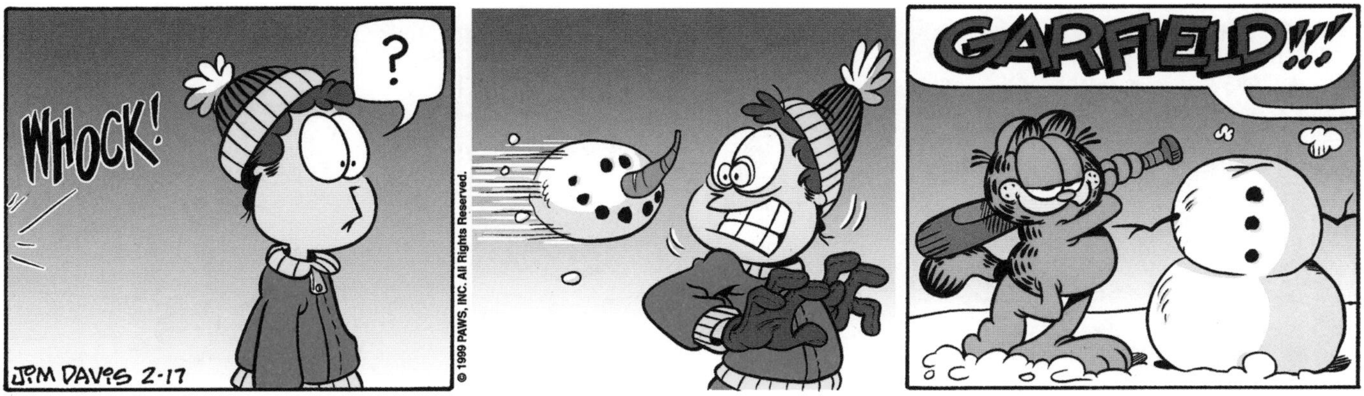
WHOCK!
?
JIM DAVIS 2-17
© 1999 PAWS, INC. All Rights Reserved.
GARFIELD!!!

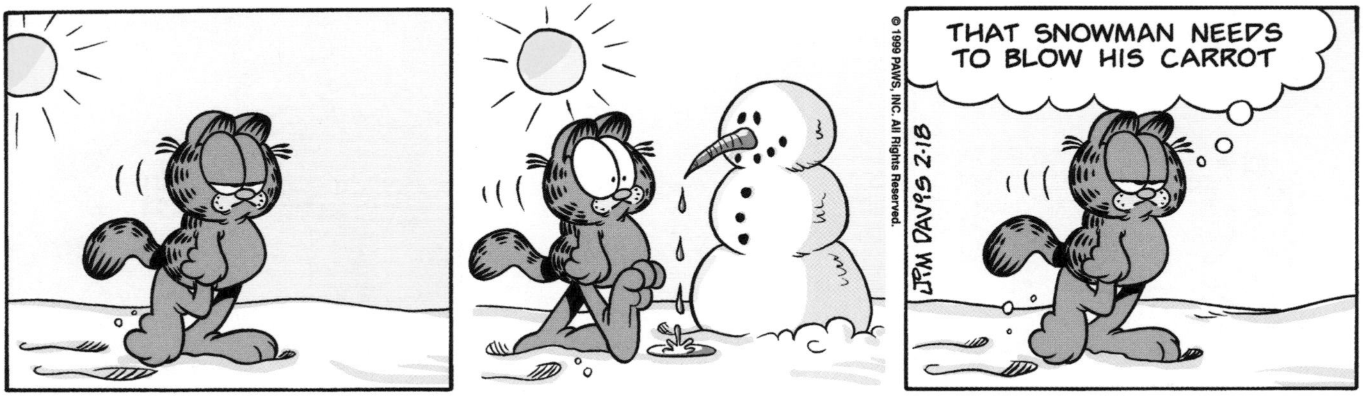
© 1999 PAWS, INC. All Rights Reserved.
JIM DAVIS 2·18
THAT SNOWMAN NEEDS TO BLOW HIS CARROT

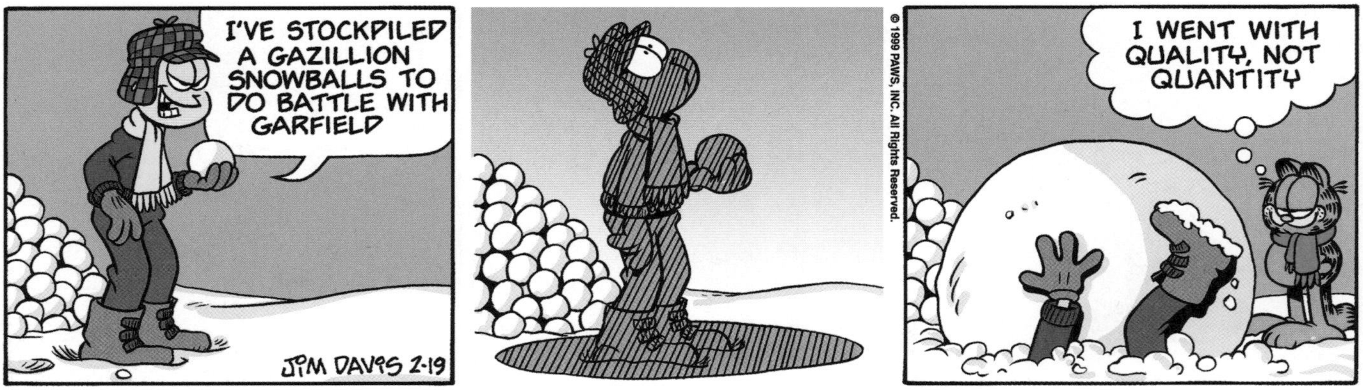
I'VE STOCKPILED A GAZILLION SNOWBALLS TO DO BATTLE WITH GARFIELD
JIM DAVIS 2-19
© 1999 PAWS, INC. All Rights Reserved.
I WENT WITH QUALITY, NOT QUANTITY

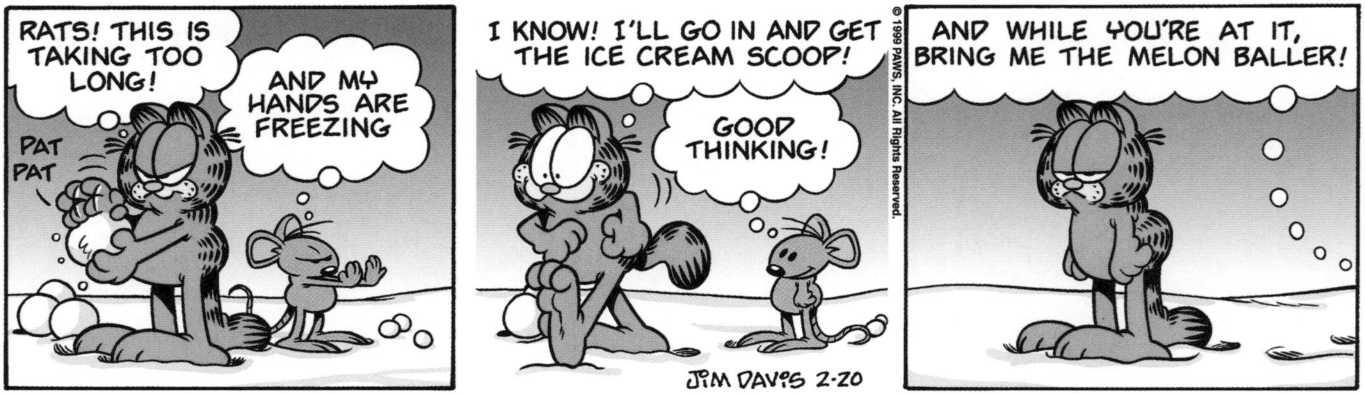
RATS! THIS IS TAKING TOO LONG!
AND MY HANDS ARE FREEZING
PAT PAT
I KNOW! I'LL GO IN AND GET THE ICE CREAM SCOOP!
GOOD THINKING!
JIM DAVIS 2-20
© 1999 PAWS, INC. All Rights Reserved.
AND WHILE YOU'RE AT IT, BRING ME THE MELON BALLER!

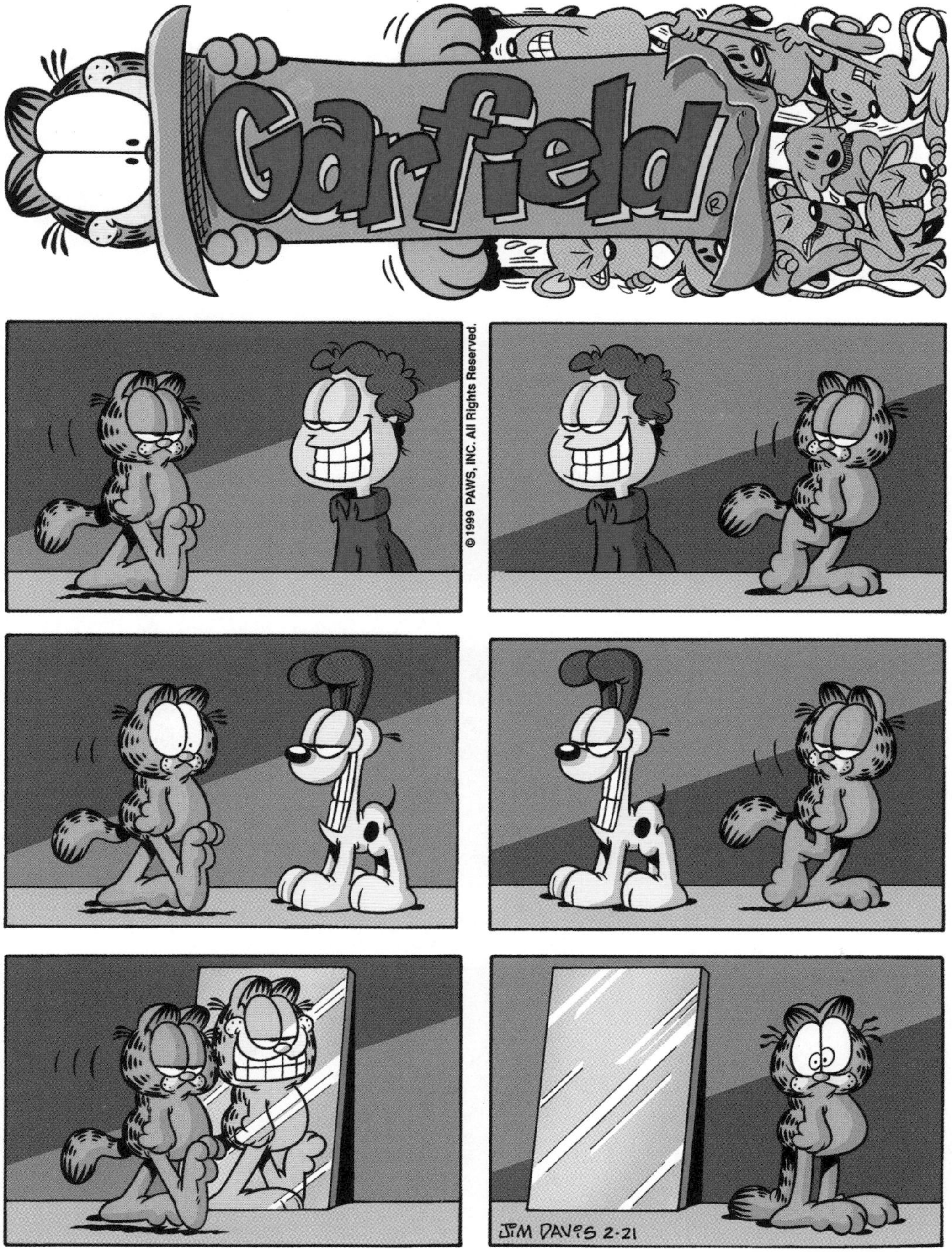
Garfield
©1999 PAWS, INC. All Rights Reserved.
JIM DAVIS 2-21

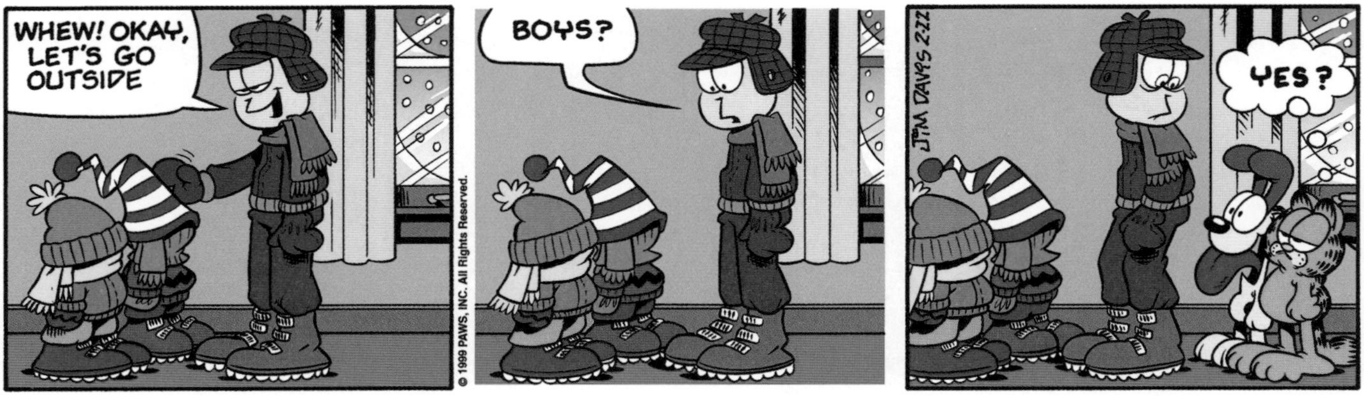
WHEW! OKAY, LET'S GO OUTSIDE
© 1999 PAWS, INC. All Rights Reserved.
BOYS?
JIM DAVIS 2-22
YES?

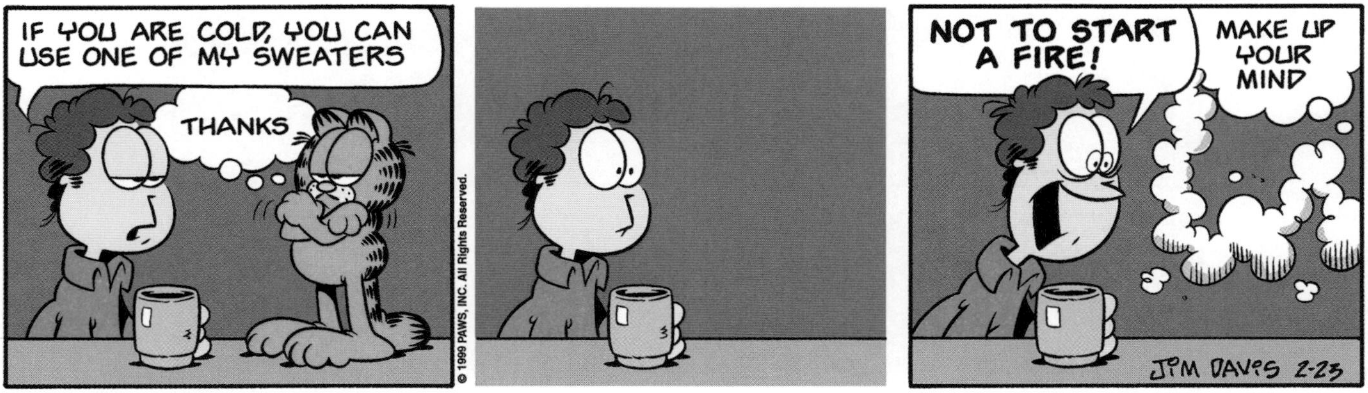
IF YOU ARE COLD, YOU CAN USE ONE OF MY SWEATERS
THANKS
© 1999 PAWS, INC. All Rights Reserved.
NOT TO START A FIRE!
MAKE UP YOUR MIND
JIM DAVIS 2-23

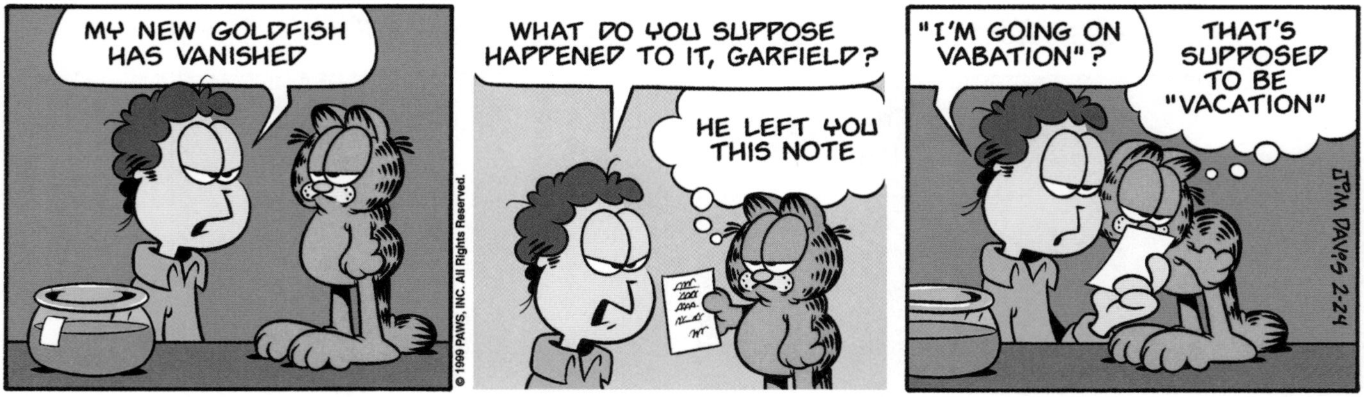
MY NEW GOLDFISH HAS VANISHED
© 1999 PAWS, INC. All Rights Reserved.
WHAT DO YOU SUPPOSE HAPPENED TO IT, GARFIELD?
HE LEFT YOU THIS NOTE
"I'M GOING ON VABATION"?
THAT'S SUPPOSED TO BE "VACATION"
JIM DAVIS 2-24

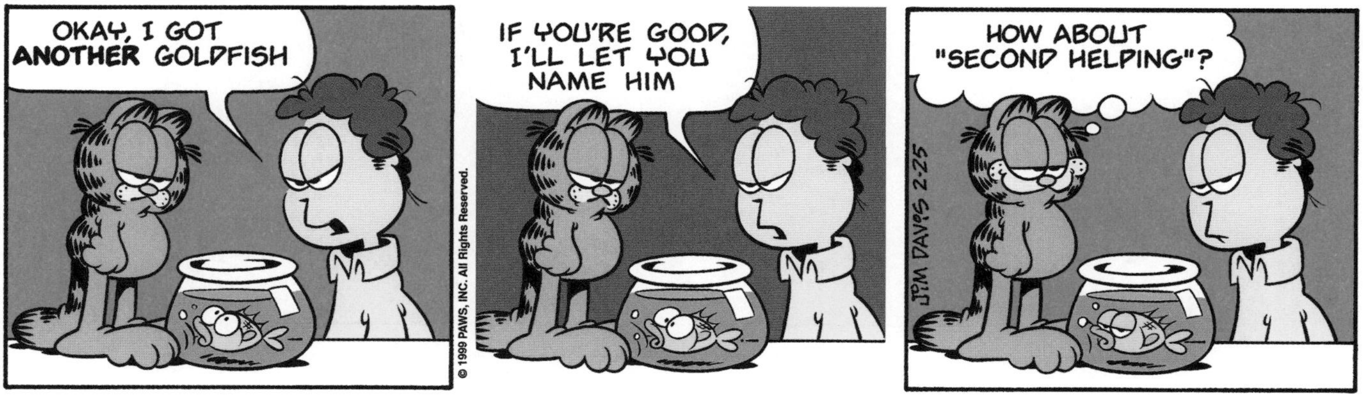
OKAY, I GOT **ANOTHER** GOLDFISH
IF YOU'RE GOOD, I'LL LET YOU NAME HIM
HOW ABOUT "SECOND HELPING"?
JIM DAVIS 2-25

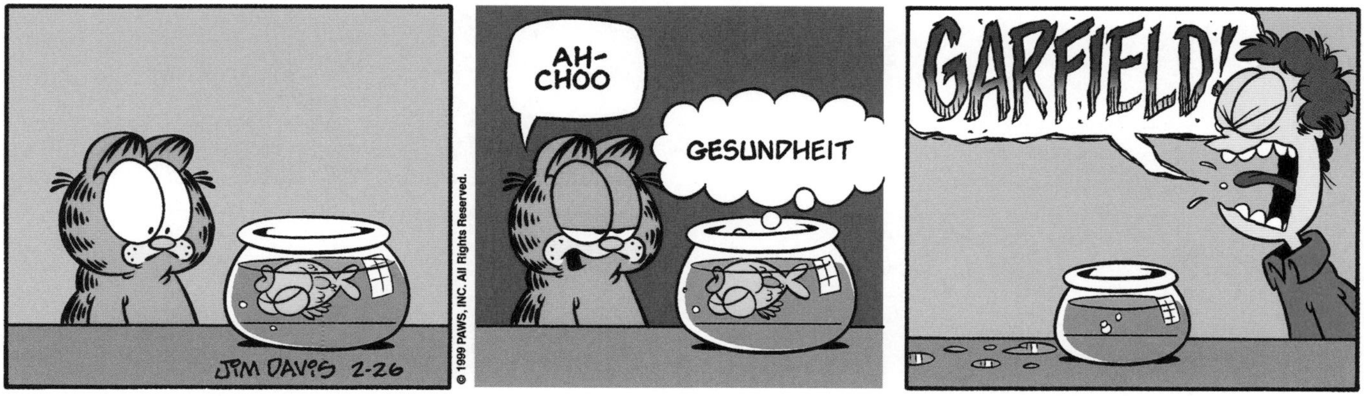
JIM DAVIS 2-26
AH-CHOO
GESUNDHEIT
GARFIELD!

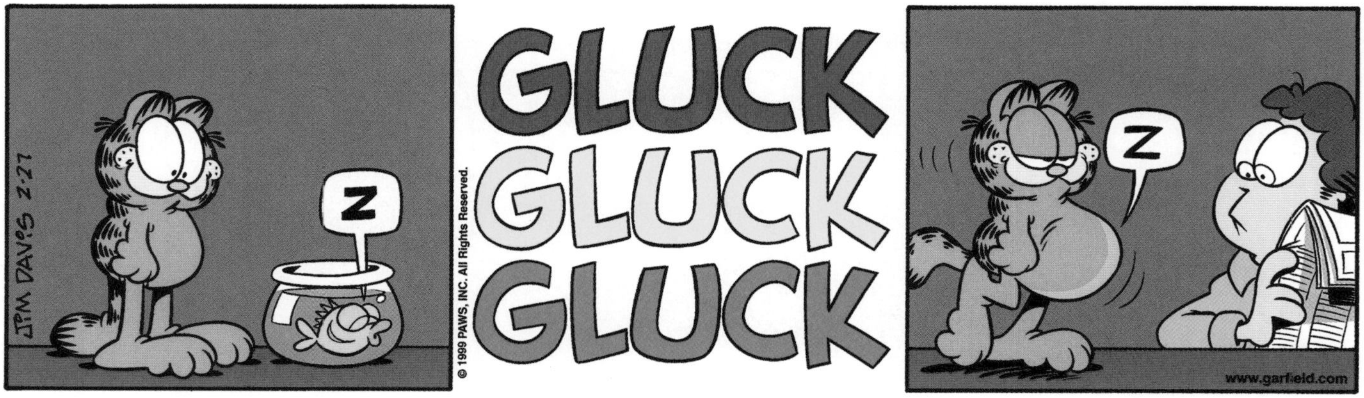
JIM DAVIS 2-27
Z
GLUCK
GLUCK
GLUCK
Z

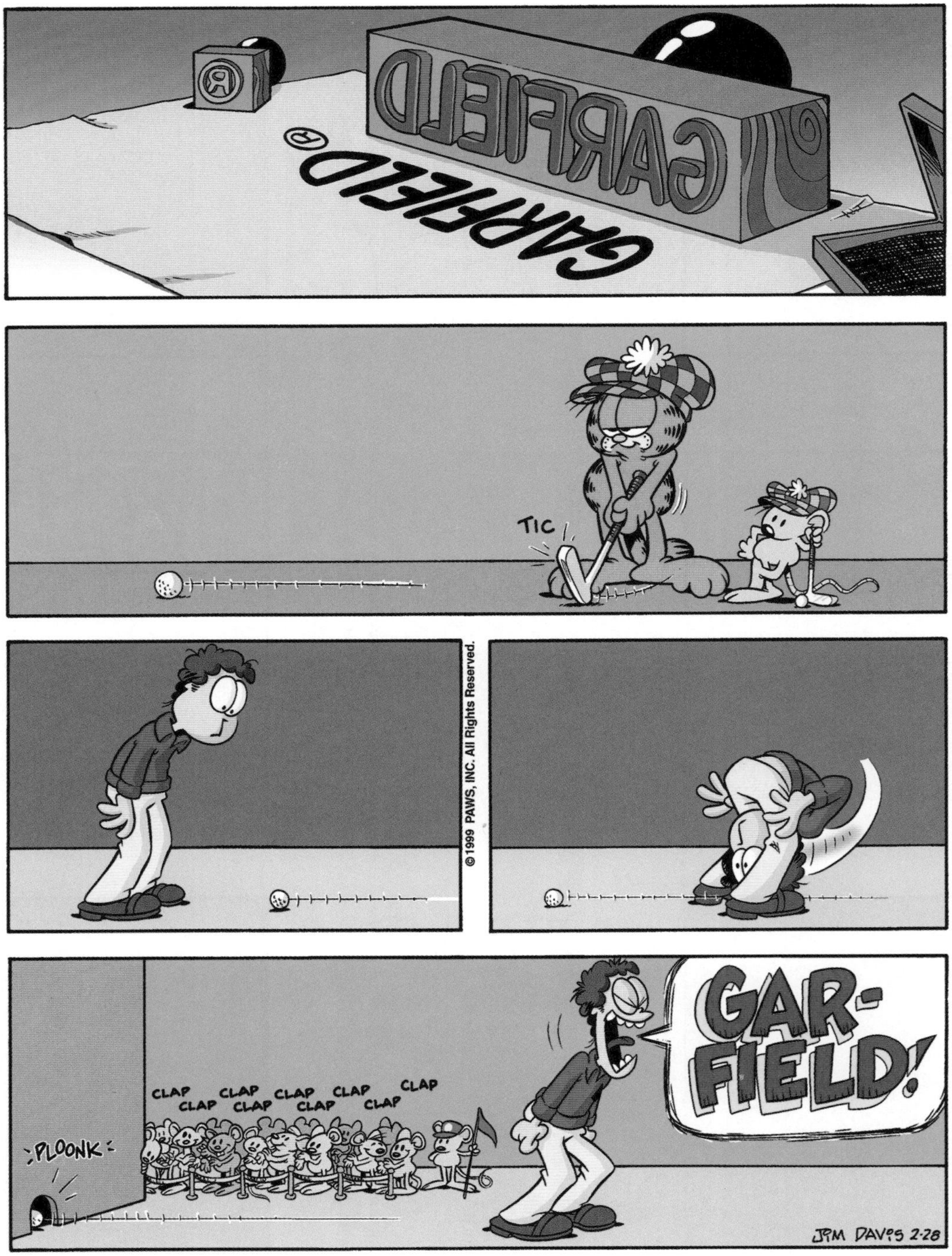

GARFIELD
TIC
CLAP CLAP CLAP CLAP CLAP CLAP CLAP CLAP CLAP
PLOONK
GAR-FIELD!
JIM DAVIS 2-28

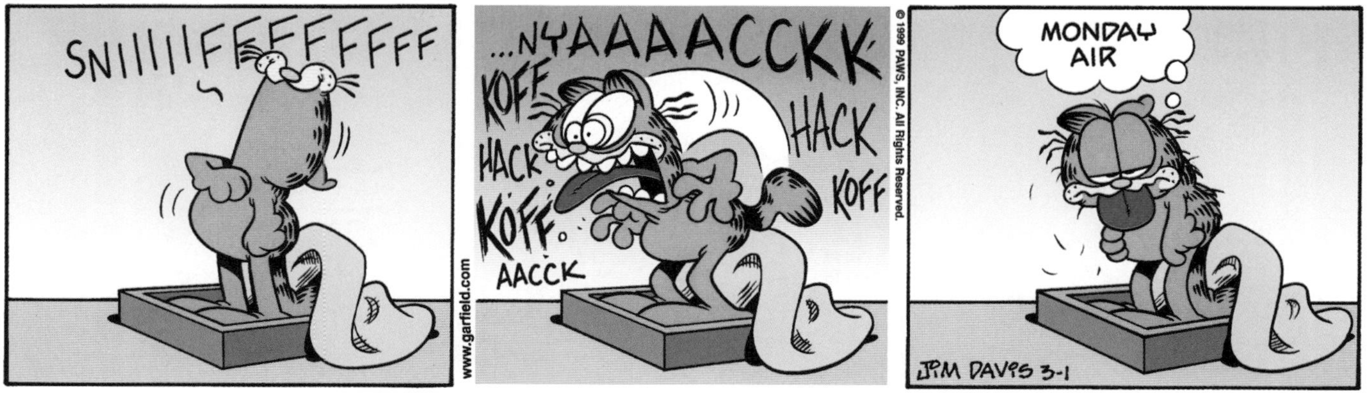
SNIIIIIFFFFFFFFF
www.garfield.com
...NYAAAACCKK
KOFF
HACK
KOFF
AACCK
HACK
KOFF
© 1999 PAWS, INC. All Rights Reserved.
MONDAY AIR
JIM DAVIS 3-1

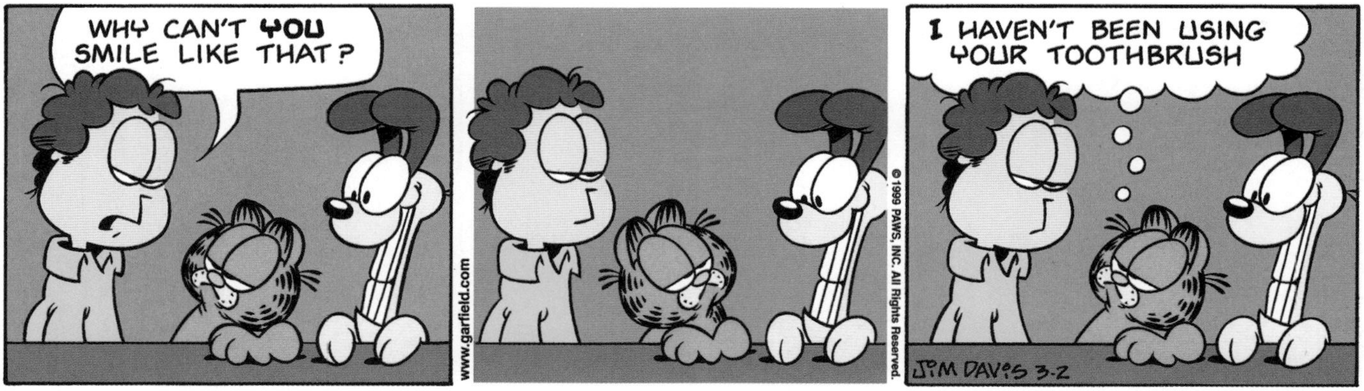
WHY CAN'T **YOU** SMILE LIKE THAT?
www.garfield.com
© 1999 PAWS, INC. All Rights Reserved.
I HAVEN'T BEEN USING YOUR TOOTHBRUSH
JIM DAVIS 3-2

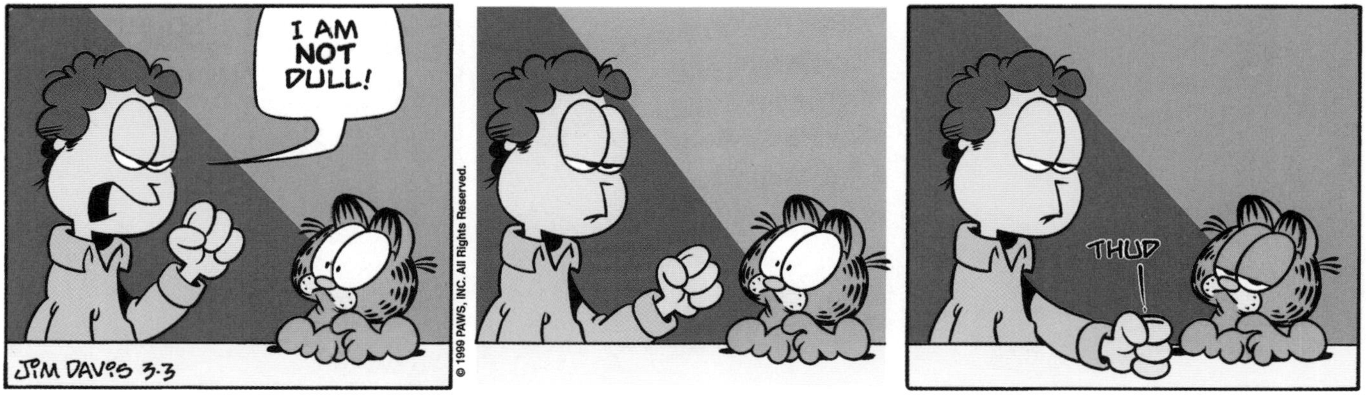
I AM **NOT** DULL!
JIM DAVIS 3-3
© 1999 PAWS, INC. All Rights Reserved.
THUD

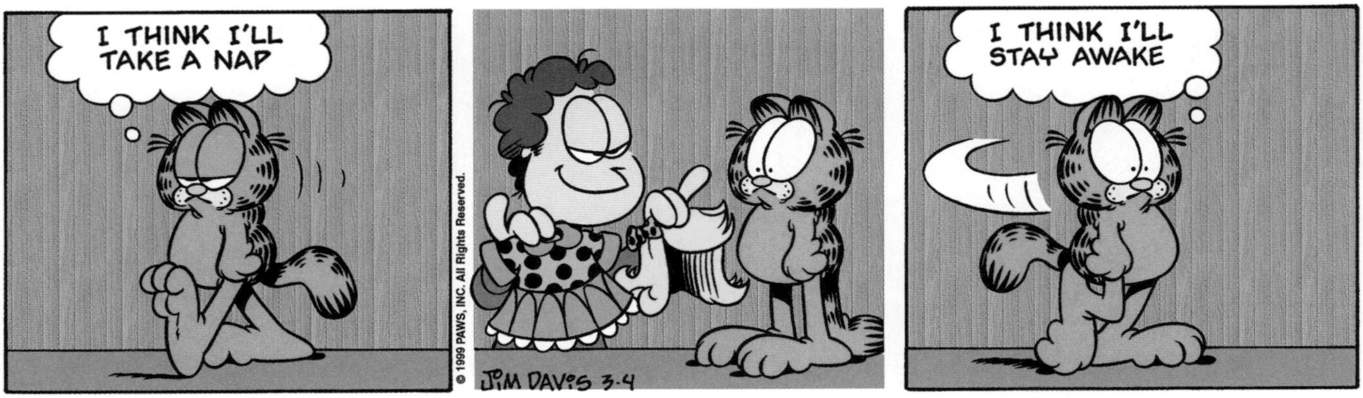
I THINK I'LL TAKE A NAP
© 1999 PAWS, INC. All Rights Reserved.
JIM DAVIS 3-4
I THINK I'LL STAY AWAKE

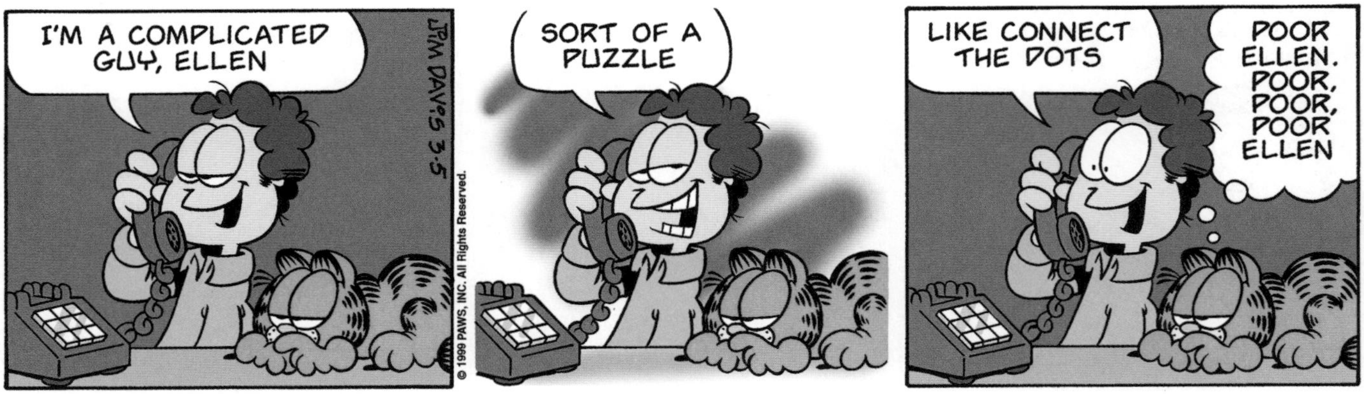
I'M A COMPLICATED GUY, ELLEN
JIM DAVIS 3-5
© 1999 PAWS, INC. All Rights Reserved.
SORT OF A PUZZLE
LIKE CONNECT THE DOTS
POOR ELLEN. POOR, POOR, POOR ELLEN

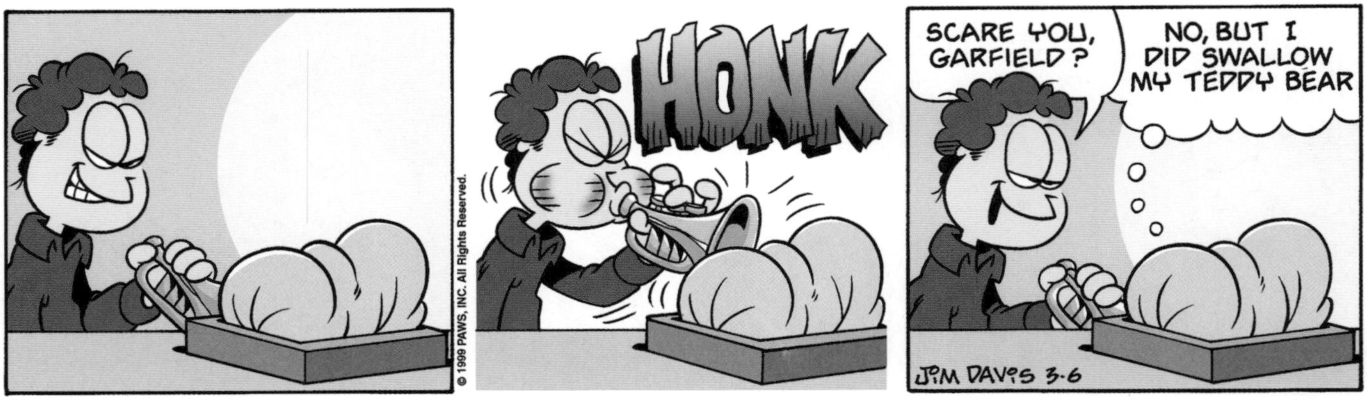
© 1999 PAWS, INC. All Rights Reserved.
HONK
SCARE YOU, GARFIELD?
NO, BUT I DID SWALLOW MY TEDDY BEAR
JIM DAVIS 3-6

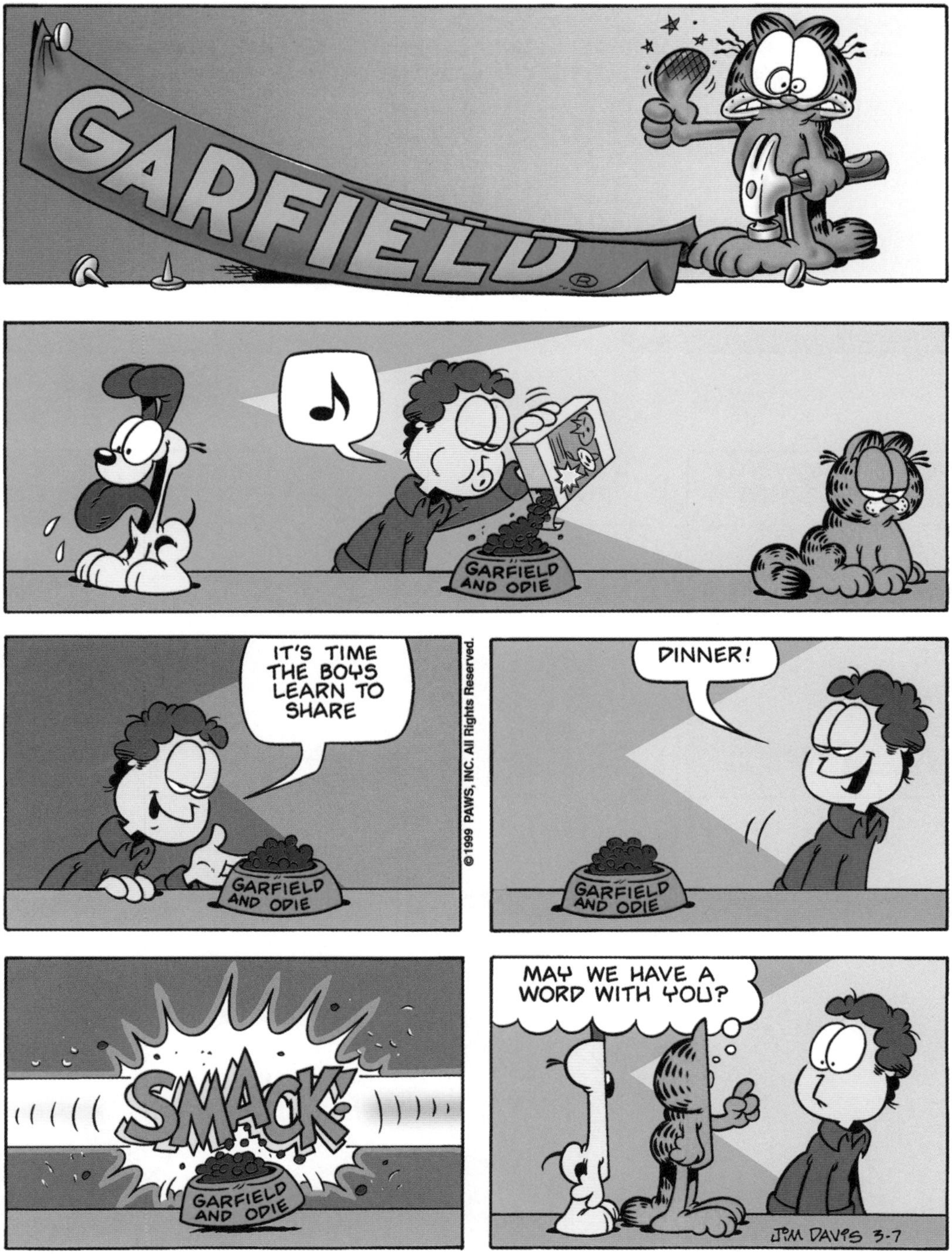
GARFIELD®
GARFIELD AND ODIE
IT'S TIME THE BOYS LEARN TO SHARE
DINNER!
SMACK!
MAY WE HAVE A WORD WITH YOU?
JIM DAVIS 3-7

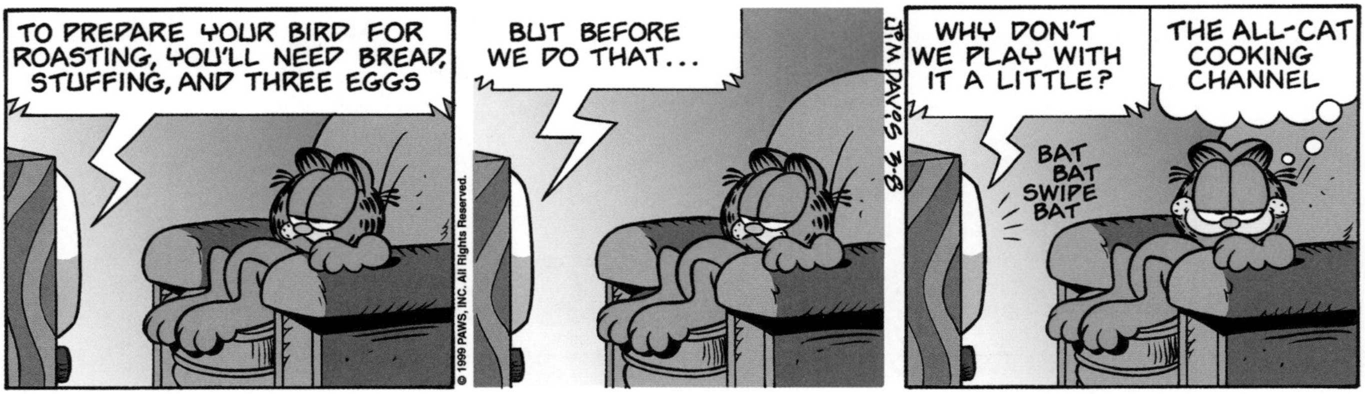
TO PREPARE YOUR BIRD FOR ROASTING, YOU'LL NEED BREAD, STUFFING, AND THREE EGGS
© 1999 PAWS, INC. All Rights Reserved.
BUT BEFORE WE DO THAT...
JPM DAVPS 3-8
WHY DON'T WE PLAY WITH IT A LITTLE?
BAT BAT SWIPE BAT
THE ALL-CAT COOKING CHANNEL

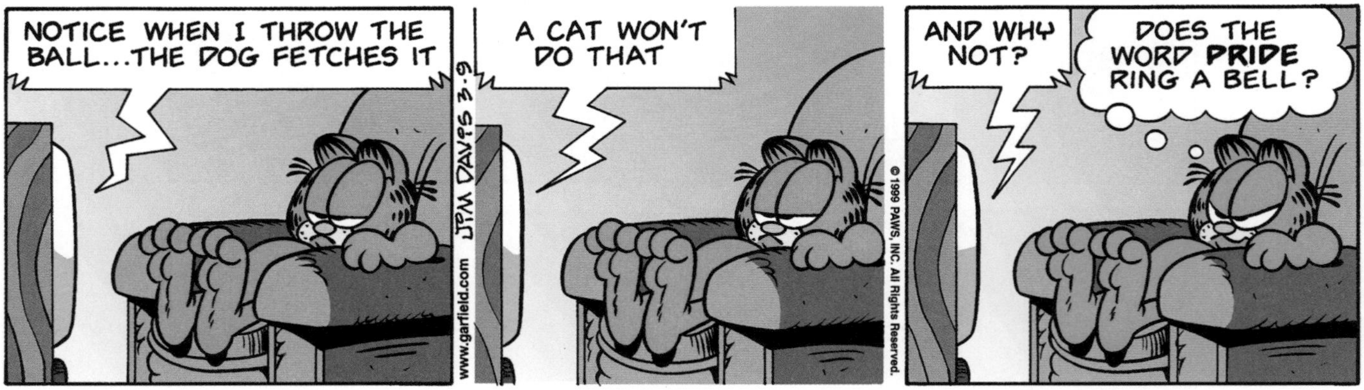
NOTICE WHEN I THROW THE BALL...THE DOG FETCHES IT
JPM DAVPS 3-9
www.garfield.com
A CAT WON'T DO THAT
© 1999 PAWS, INC. All Rights Reserved.
AND WHY NOT?
DOES THE WORD **PRIDE** RING A BELL?

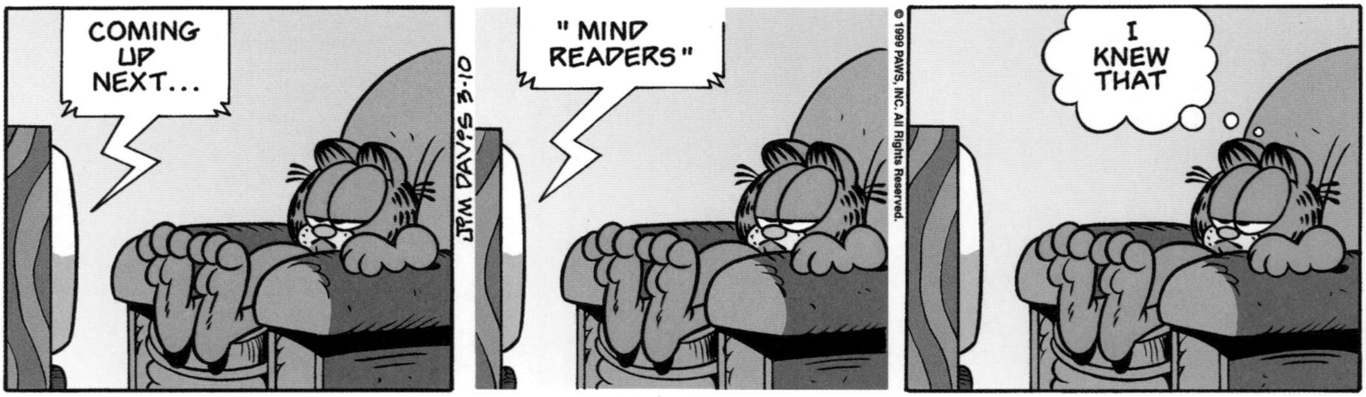
COMING UP NEXT...
JPM DAVPS 3-10
"MIND READERS"
© 1999 PAWS, INC. All Rights Reserved.
I KNEW THAT

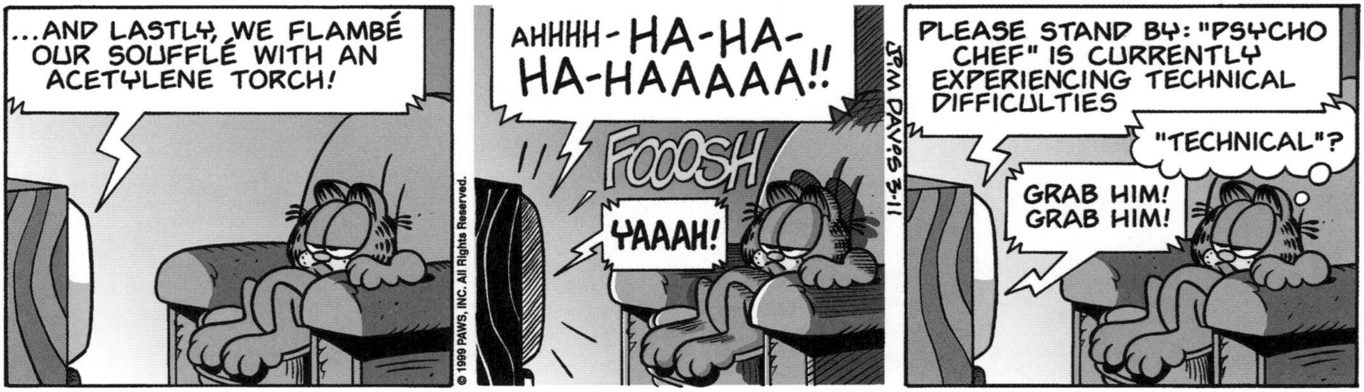
...AND LASTLY, WE FLAMBÉ OUR SOUFFLÉ WITH AN ACETYLENE TORCH!
© 1999 PAWS, INC. All Rights Reserved.
AHHHH-HA-HA-HA-HAAAAA!!
FOOOSH
YAAAH!
JPM DAVPS 3-11
PLEASE STAND BY: "PSYCHO CHEF" IS CURRENTLY EXPERIENCING TECHNICAL DIFFICULTIES
"TECHNICAL"?
GRAB HIM! GRAB HIM!

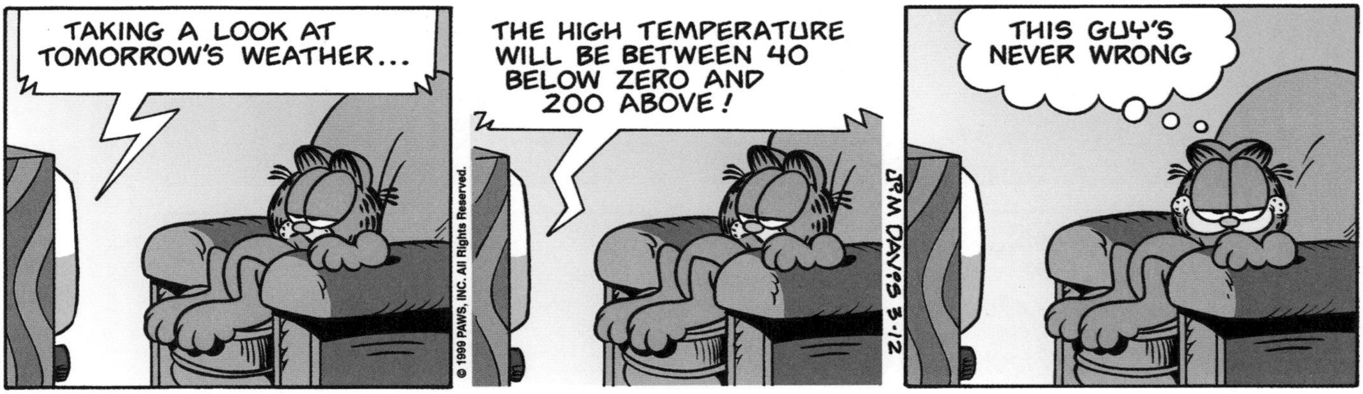
TAKING A LOOK AT TOMORROW'S WEATHER...
© 1999 PAWS, INC. All Rights Reserved.
THE HIGH TEMPERATURE WILL BE BETWEEN 40 BELOW ZERO AND 200 ABOVE!
JPM DAVPS 3-12
THIS GUY'S NEVER WRONG

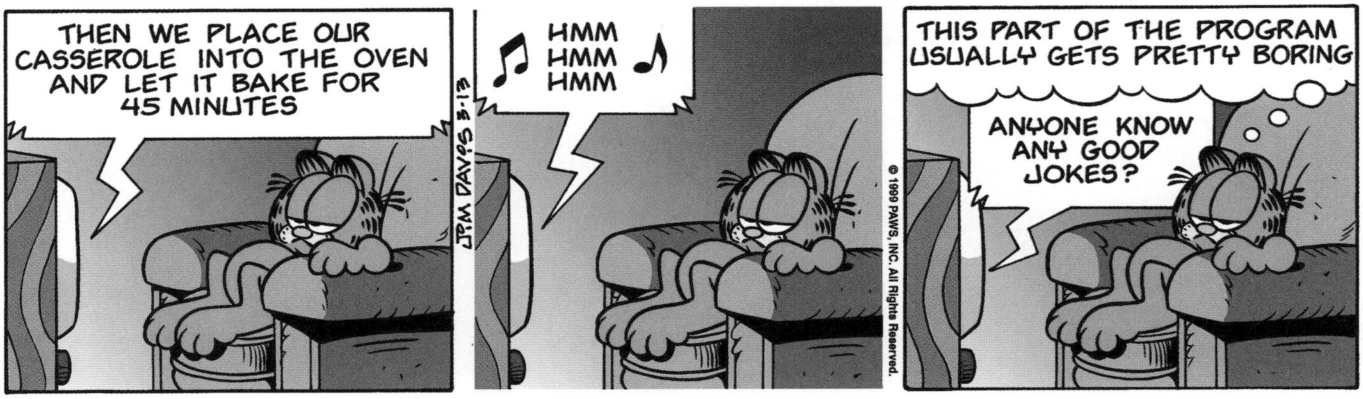
THEN WE PLACE OUR CASSEROLE INTO THE OVEN AND LET IT BAKE FOR 45 MINUTES
JPM DAVPS 3-13
HMM HMM HMM
© 1999 PAWS, INC. All Rights Reserved.
THIS PART OF THE PROGRAM USUALLY GETS PRETTY BORING
ANYONE KNOW ANY GOOD JOKES?

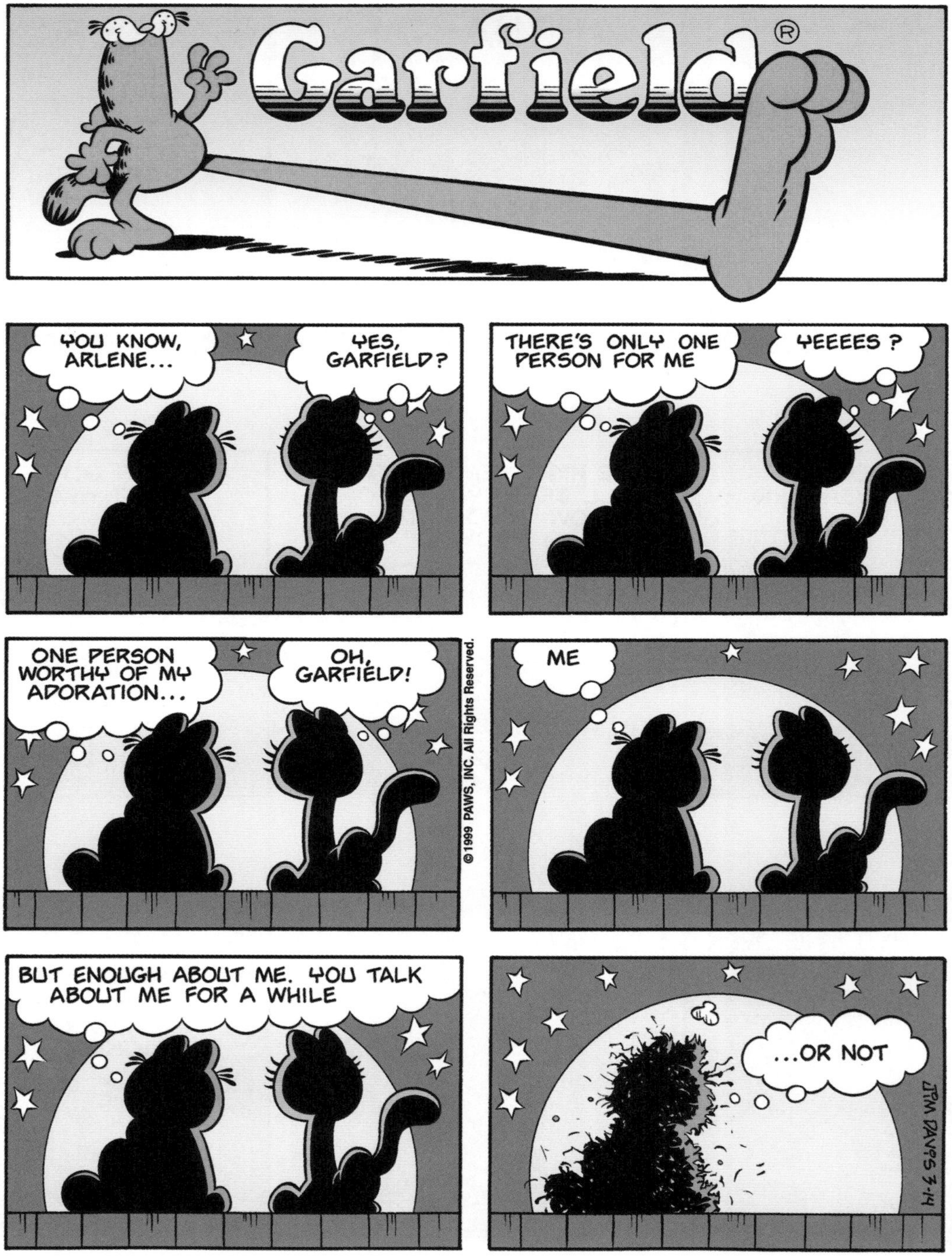
Garfield®
YOU KNOW, ARLENE...
YES, GARFIELD?
THERE'S ONLY ONE PERSON FOR ME
YEEEES?
ONE PERSON WORTHY OF MY ADORATION...
OH, GARFIELD!
© 1999 PAWS, INC. All Rights Reserved.
ME
BUT ENOUGH ABOUT ME. YOU TALK ABOUT ME FOR A WHILE
...OR NOT

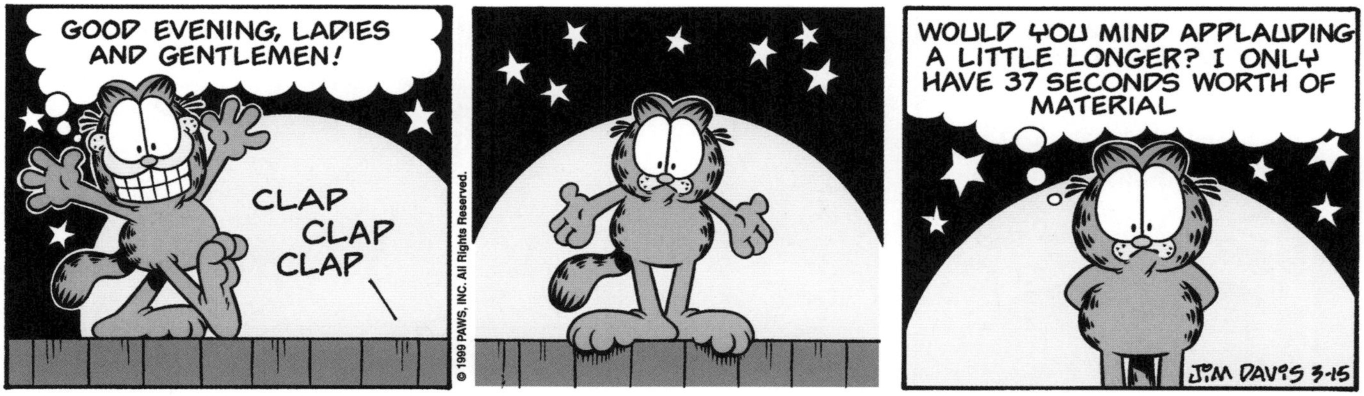
GOOD EVENING, LADIES AND GENTLEMEN!
CLAP CLAP CLAP
© 1999 PAWS, INC. All Rights Reserved.
WOULD YOU MIND APPLAUDING A LITTLE LONGER? I ONLY HAVE 37 SECONDS WORTH OF MATERIAL
JIM DAVIS 3-15

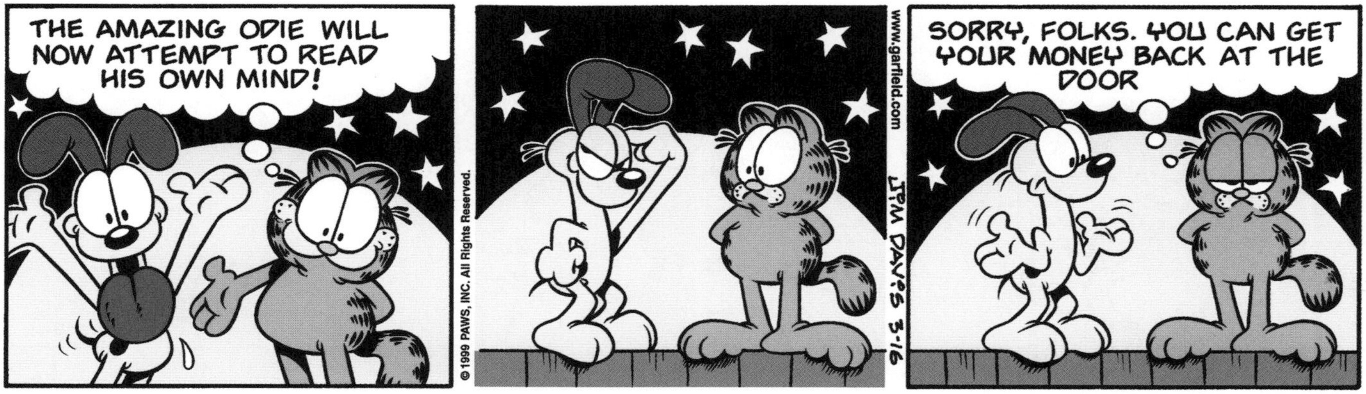
THE AMAZING ODIE WILL NOW ATTEMPT TO READ HIS OWN MIND!
© 1999 PAWS, INC. All Rights Reserved.
www.garfield.com
JIM DAVIS 3-16
SORRY, FOLKS. YOU CAN GET YOUR MONEY BACK AT THE DOOR

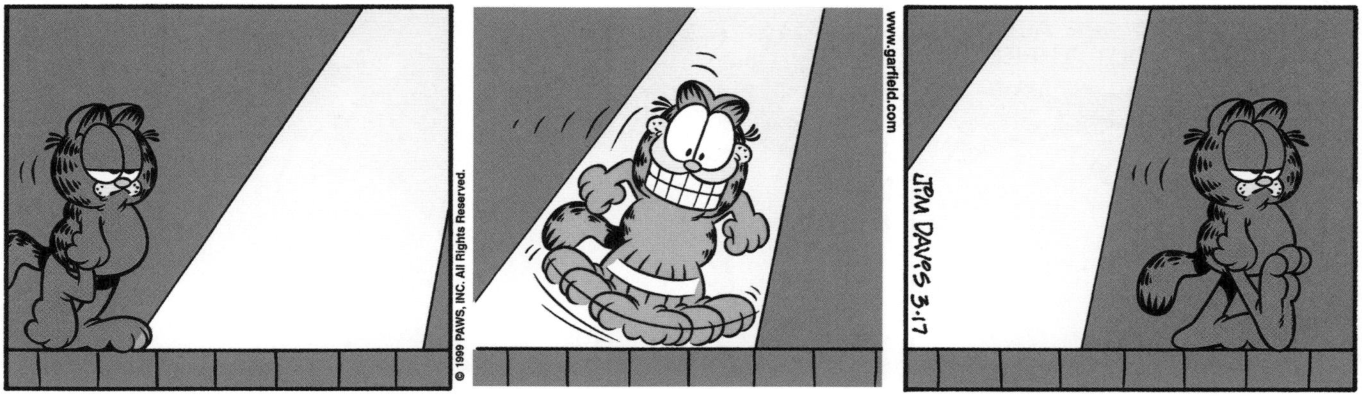
© 1999 PAWS, INC. All Rights Reserved.
www.garfield.com
JIM DAVIS 3-17

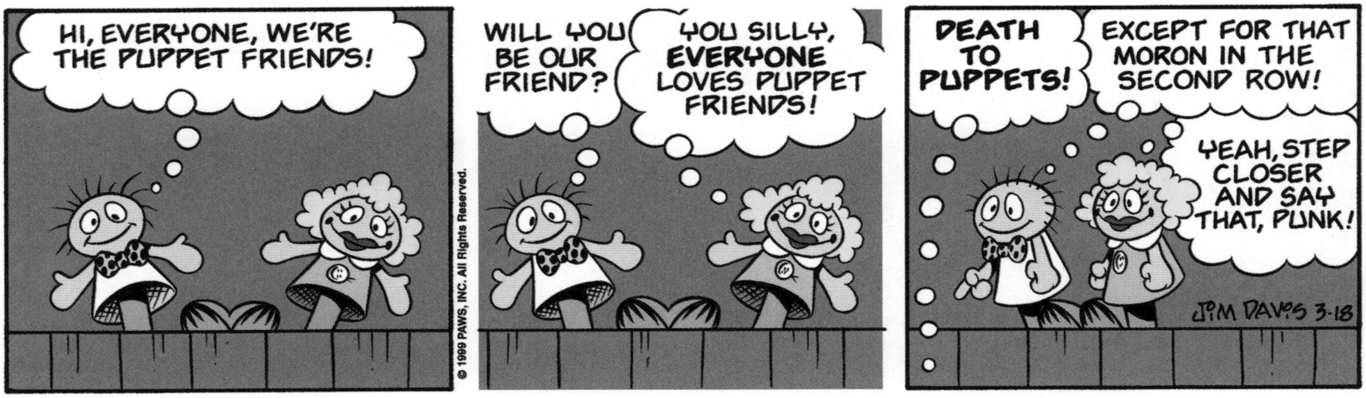
HI, EVERYONE, WE'RE THE PUPPET FRIENDS!
© 1999 PAWS, INC. All Rights Reserved.
WILL YOU BE OUR FRIEND?
YOU SILLY, EVERYONE LOVES PUPPET FRIENDS!
DEATH TO PUPPETS!
EXCEPT FOR THAT MORON IN THE SECOND ROW!
YEAH, STEP CLOSER AND SAY THAT, PUNK!
JIM DAVIS 3-18

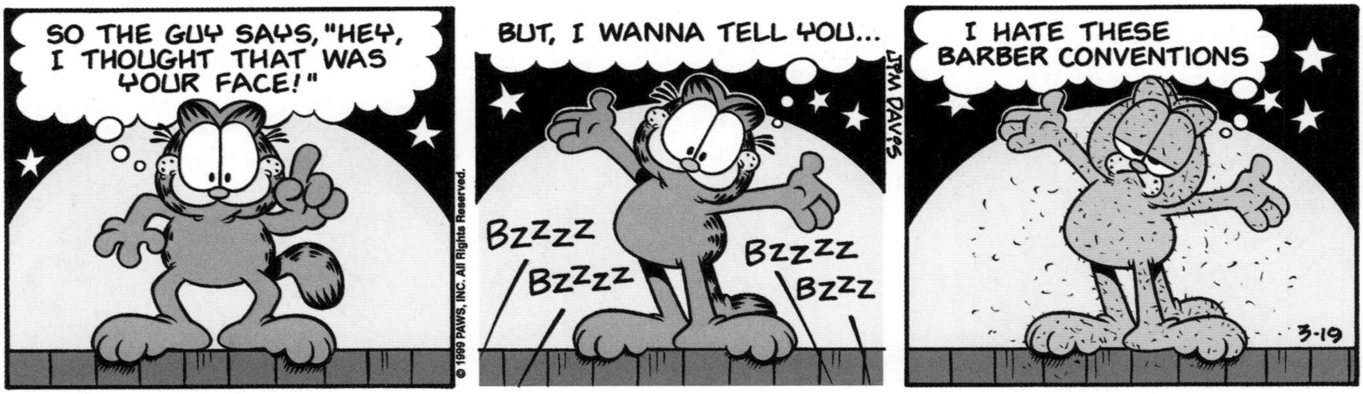
SO THE GUY SAYS, "HEY, I THOUGHT THAT WAS YOUR FACE!"
© 1999 PAWS, INC. All Rights Reserved.
BUT, I WANNA TELL YOU...
JIM DAVIS
BZZZZ
BZZZZ
BZZZZ
BZZZ
I HATE THESE BARBER CONVENTIONS
3-19

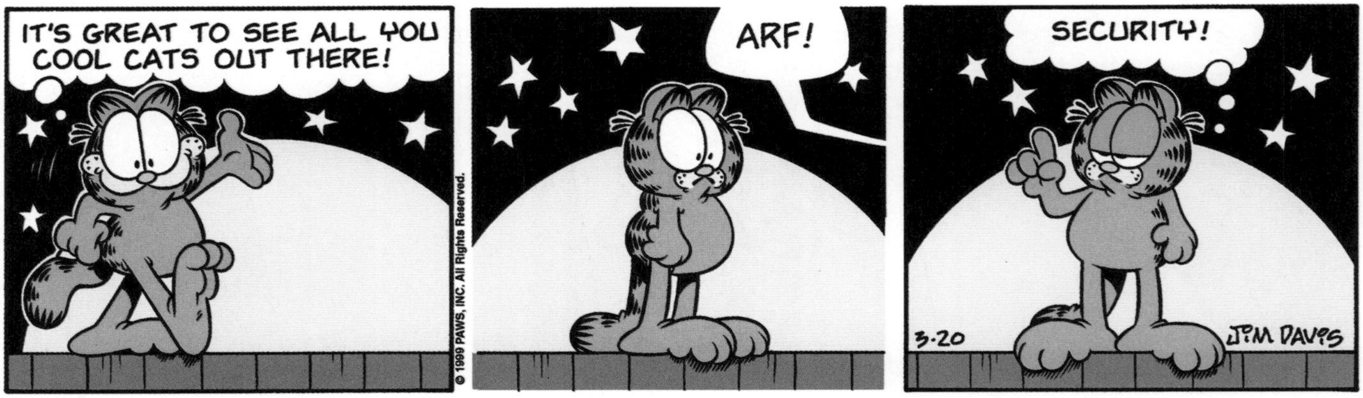
IT'S GREAT TO SEE ALL YOU COOL CATS OUT THERE!
© 1999 PAWS, INC. All Rights Reserved.
ARF!
SECURITY!
3-20
JIM DAVIS

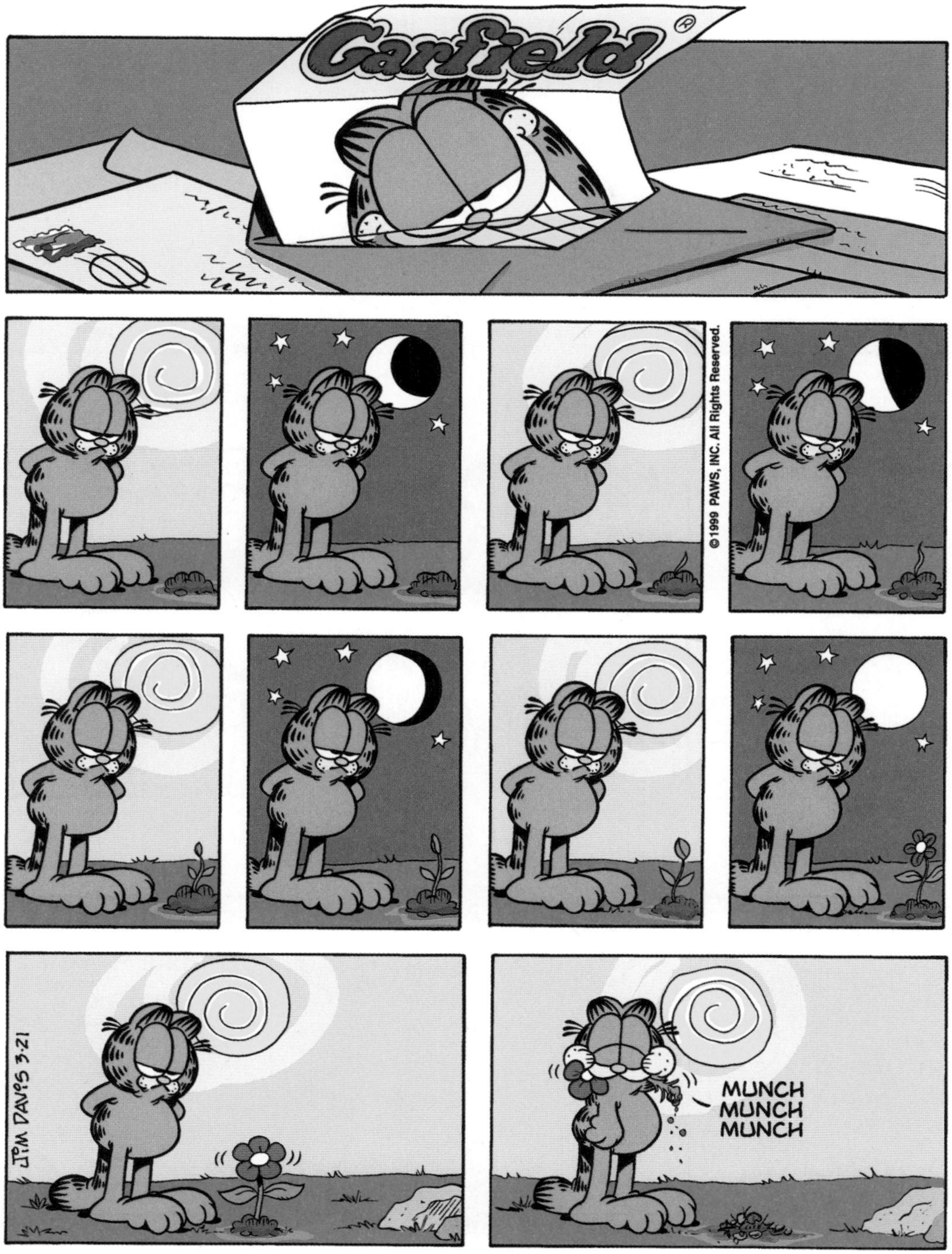
Garfield®
©1999 PAWS, INC. All Rights Reserved.
JIM DAVIS 3-21
MUNCH
MUNCH
MUNCH

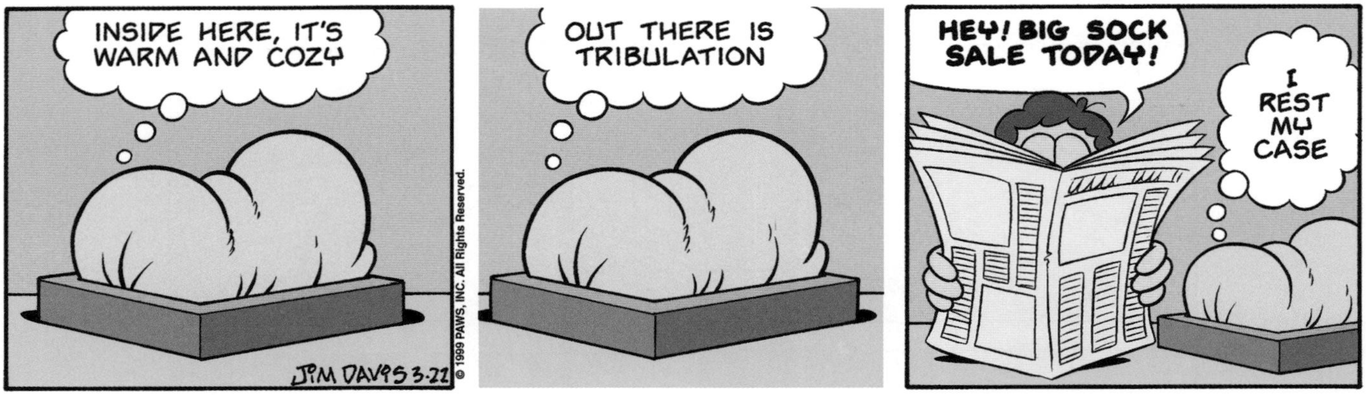
INSIDE HERE, IT'S WARM AND COZY
JIM DAVIS 3-22
© 1999 PAWS, INC. All Rights Reserved.
OUT THERE IS TRIBULATION
HEY! BIG SOCK SALE TODAY!
I REST MY CASE

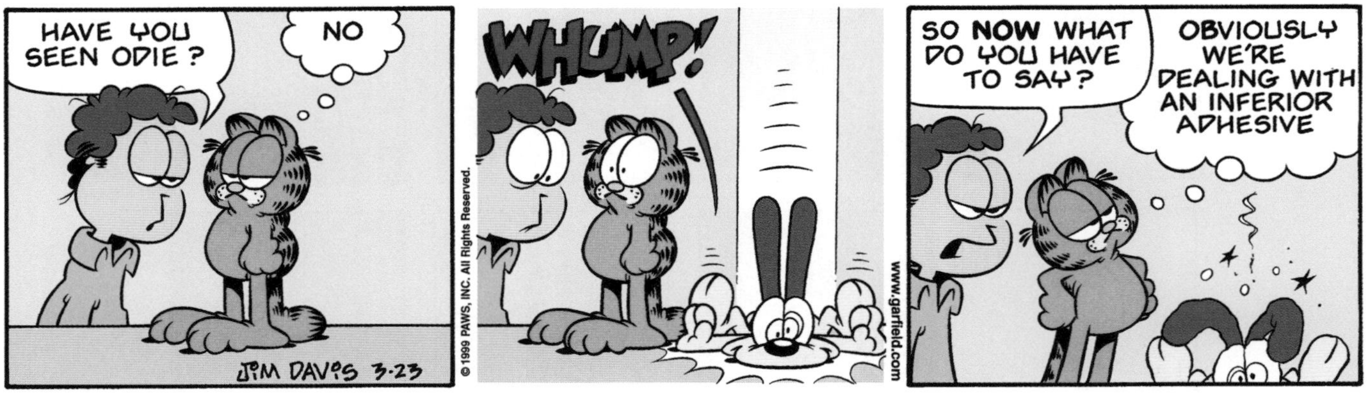
HAVE YOU SEEN ODIE ?
NO
JIM DAVIS 3-23
© 1999 PAWS, INC. All Rights Reserved.
WHUMP!
www.garfield.com
SO NOW WHAT DO YOU HAVE TO SAY ?
OBVIOUSLY WE'RE DEALING WITH AN INFERIOR ADHESIVE

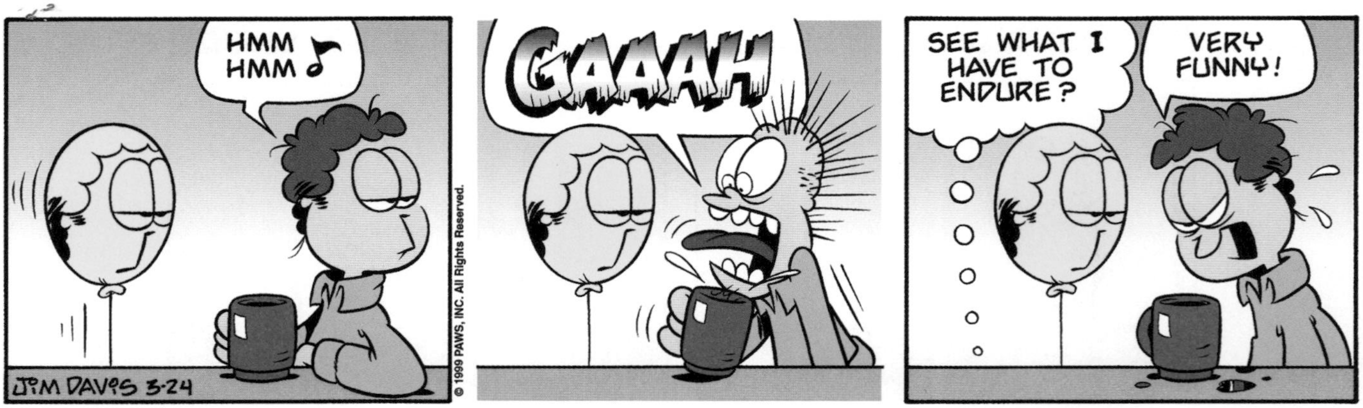
HMM HMM ♪
JIM DAVIS 3-24
© 1999 PAWS, INC. All Rights Reserved.
GAAAH
SEE WHAT I HAVE TO ENDURE ?
VERY FUNNY!

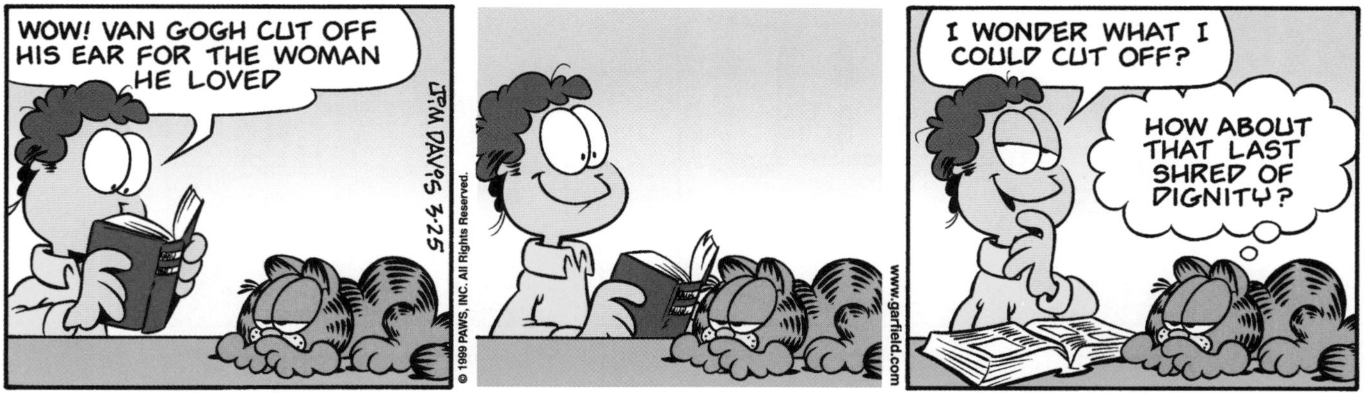
WOW! VAN GOGH CUT OFF HIS EAR FOR THE WOMAN HE LOVED
JIM DAVIS 3-25
© 1999 PAWS, INC. All Rights Reserved.
I WONDER WHAT I COULD CUT OFF?
HOW ABOUT THAT LAST SHRED OF DIGNITY?
www.garfield.com

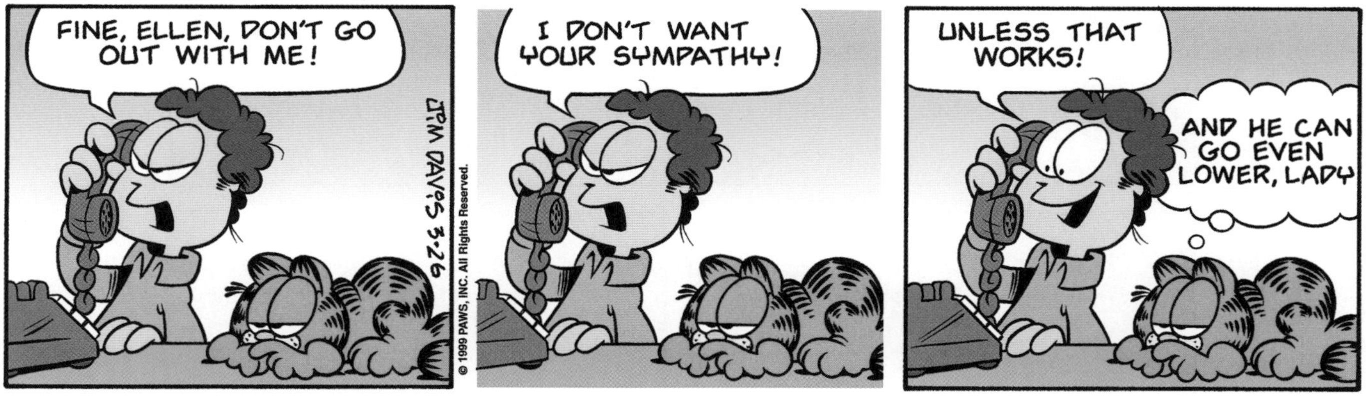
FINE, ELLEN, DON'T GO OUT WITH ME!
JIM DAVIS 3-26
© 1999 PAWS, INC. All Rights Reserved.
I DON'T WANT YOUR SYMPATHY!
UNLESS THAT WORKS!
AND HE CAN GO EVEN LOWER, LADY

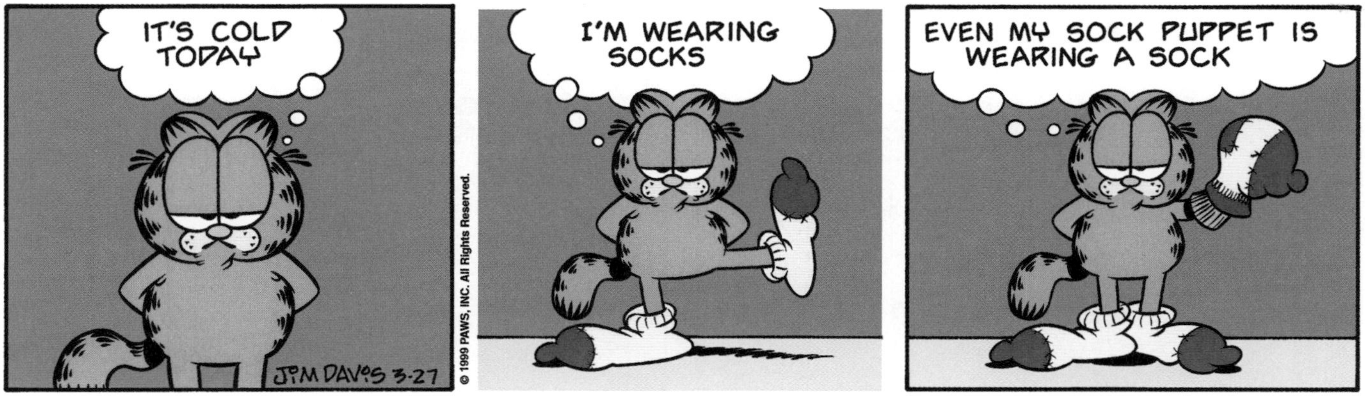
IT'S COLD TODAY
JIM DAVIS 3-27
© 1999 PAWS, INC. All Rights Reserved.
I'M WEARING SOCKS
EVEN MY SOCK PUPPET IS WEARING A SOCK

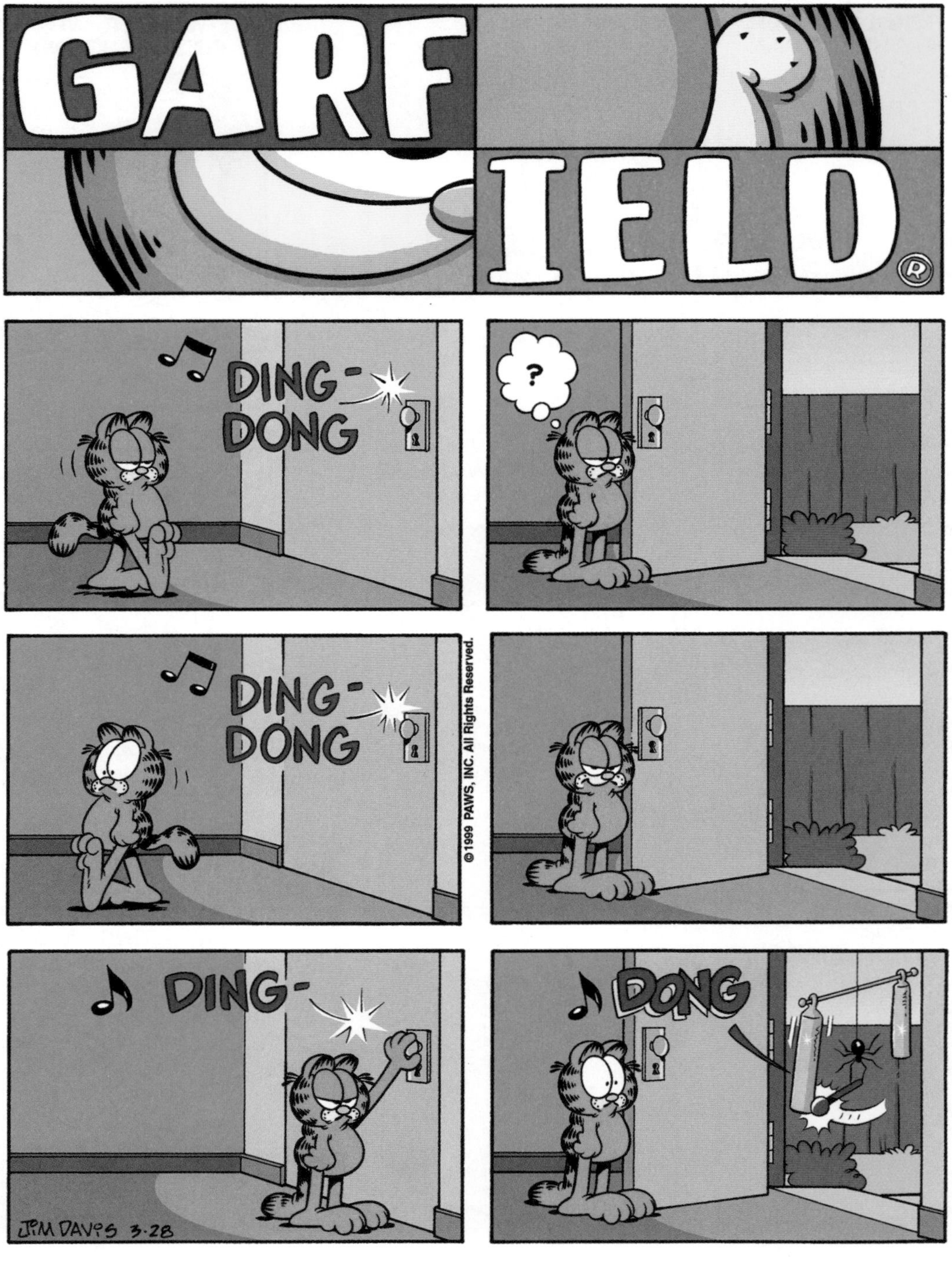
GARFIELD®
DING-DONG
?
DING-DONG
© 1999 PAWS, INC. All Rights Reserved.
DING-
DONG
JIM DAVIS 3·28

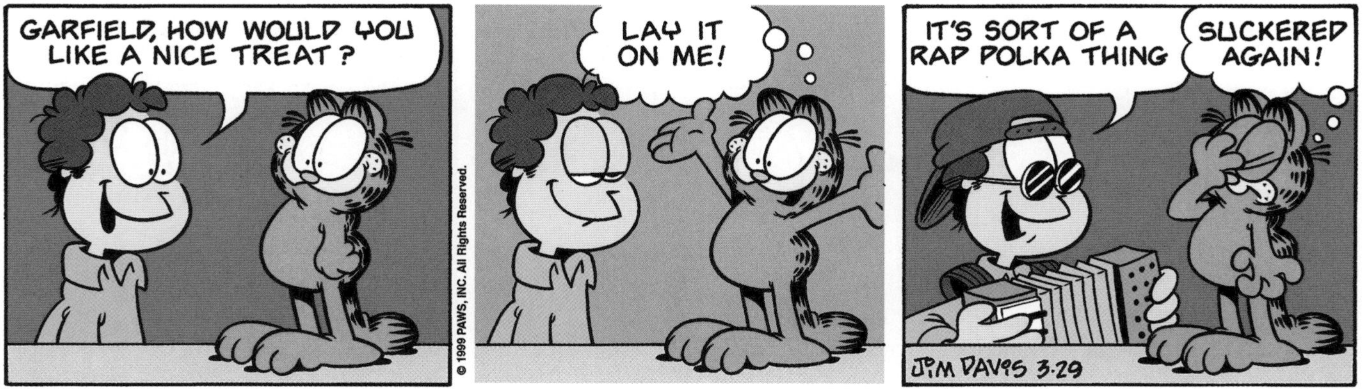
GARFIELD, HOW WOULD YOU LIKE A NICE TREAT?
LAY IT ON ME!
IT'S SORT OF A RAP POLKA THING
SUCKERED AGAIN!
JIM DAVIS 3-29

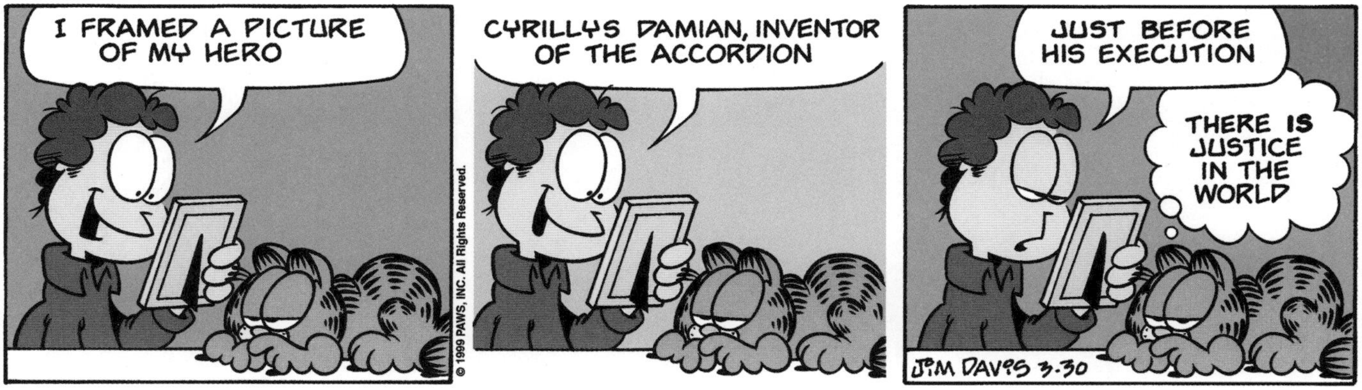
I FRAMED A PICTURE OF MY HERO
CYRILLYS DAMIAN, INVENTOR OF THE ACCORDION
JUST BEFORE HIS EXECUTION
THERE **IS** JUSTICE IN THE WORLD
JIM DAVIS 3-30

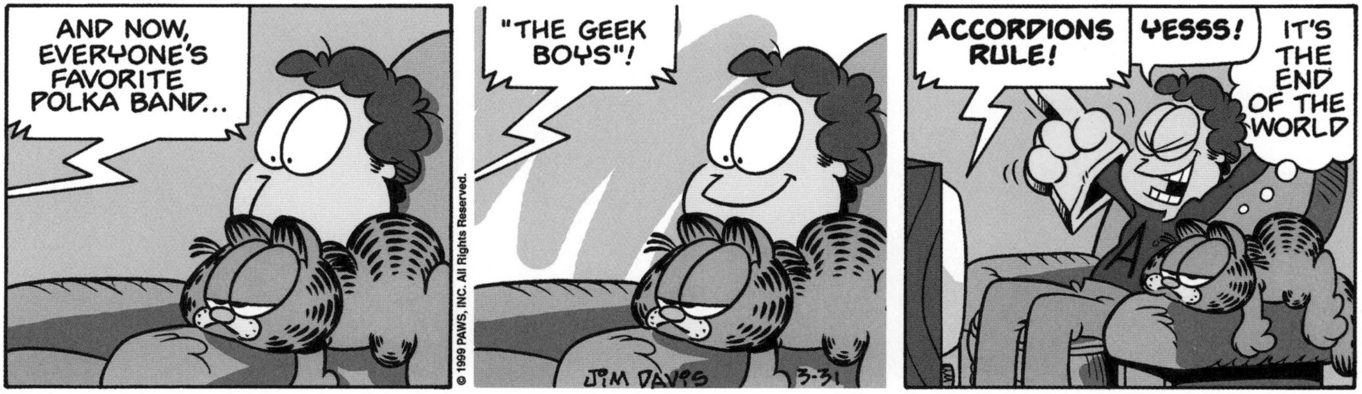
AND NOW, EVERYONE'S FAVORITE POLKA BAND...
"THE GEEK BOYS"!
JIM DAVIS 3-31
ACCORDIONS RULE!
YESSS!
IT'S THE END OF THE WORLD

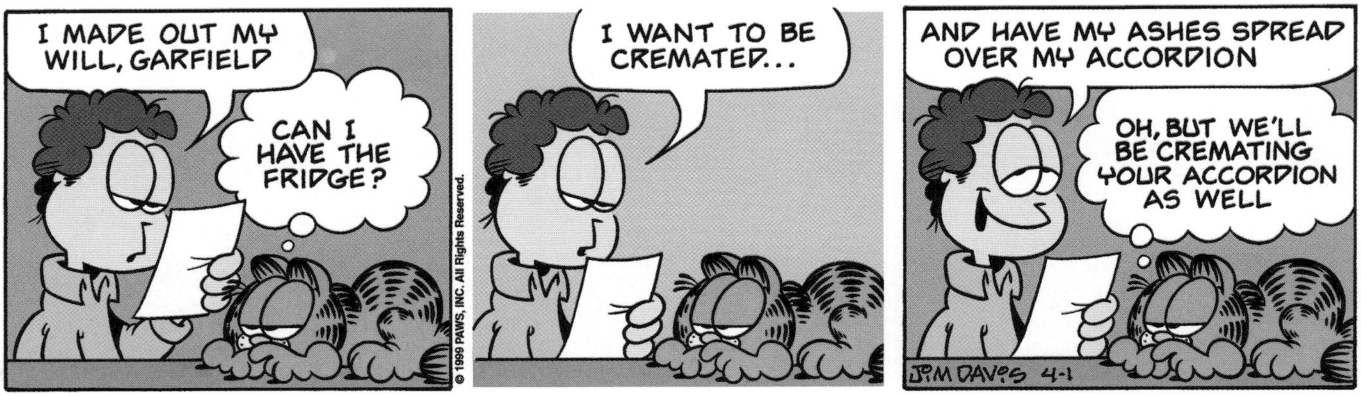
I MADE OUT MY WILL, GARFIELD
CAN I HAVE THE FRIDGE?
© 1999 PAWS, INC. All Rights Reserved.
I WANT TO BE CREMATED...
AND HAVE MY ASHES SPREAD OVER MY ACCORDION
OH, BUT WE'LL BE CREMATING YOUR ACCORDION AS WELL
JIM DAVIS 4-1

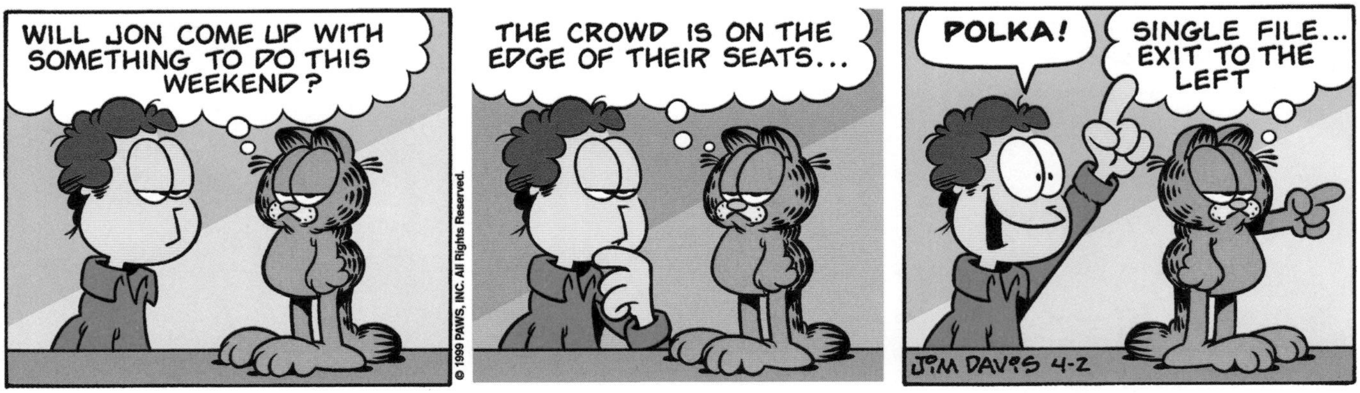
WILL JON COME UP WITH SOMETHING TO DO THIS WEEKEND?
© 1999 PAWS, INC. All Rights Reserved.
THE CROWD IS ON THE EDGE OF THEIR SEATS...
POLKA!
SINGLE FILE... EXIT TO THE LEFT
JIM DAVIS 4-2

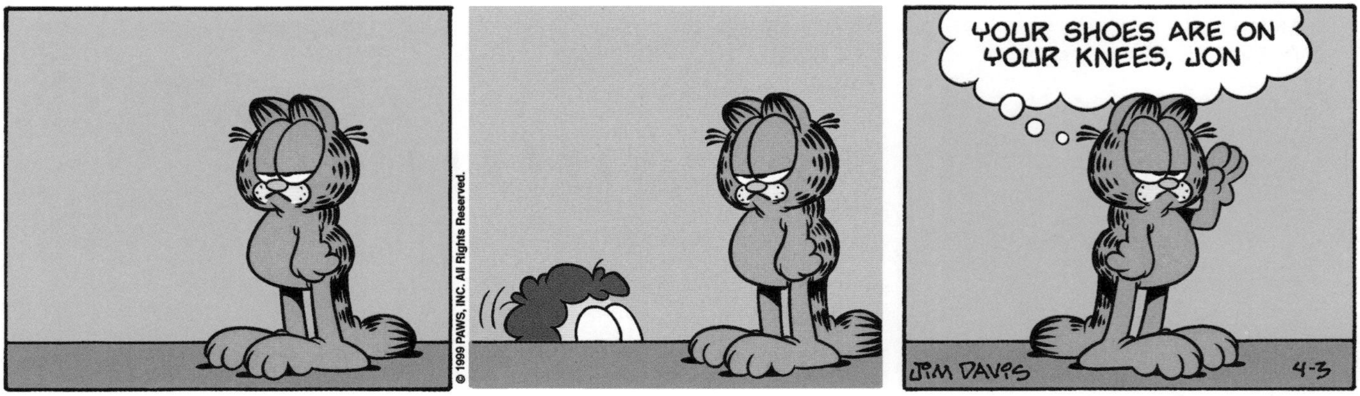
© 1999 PAWS, INC. All Rights Reserved.
YOUR SHOES ARE ON YOUR KNEES, JON
JIM DAVIS 4-3

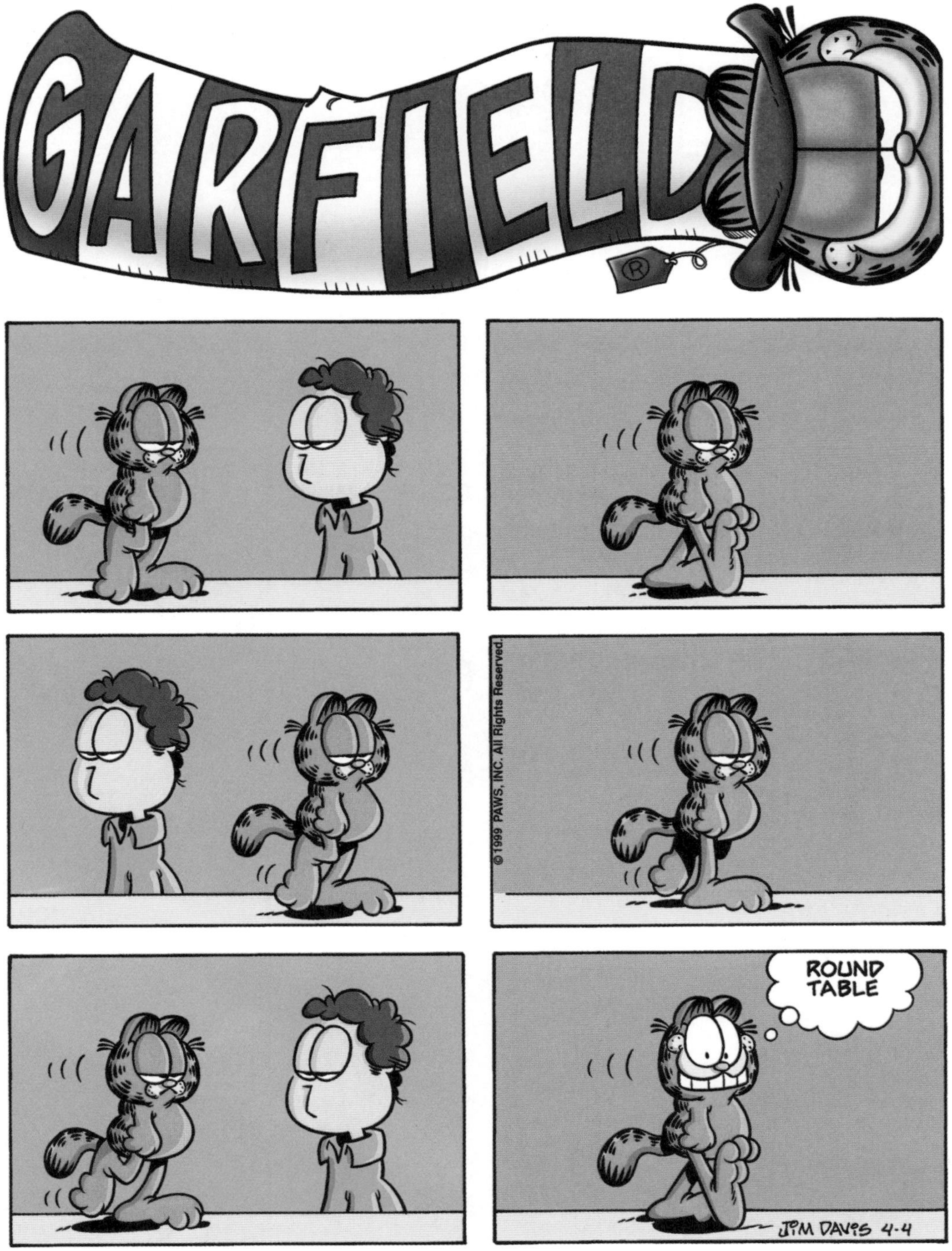
GARFIELD
ROUND TABLE
JIM DAVIS 4-4

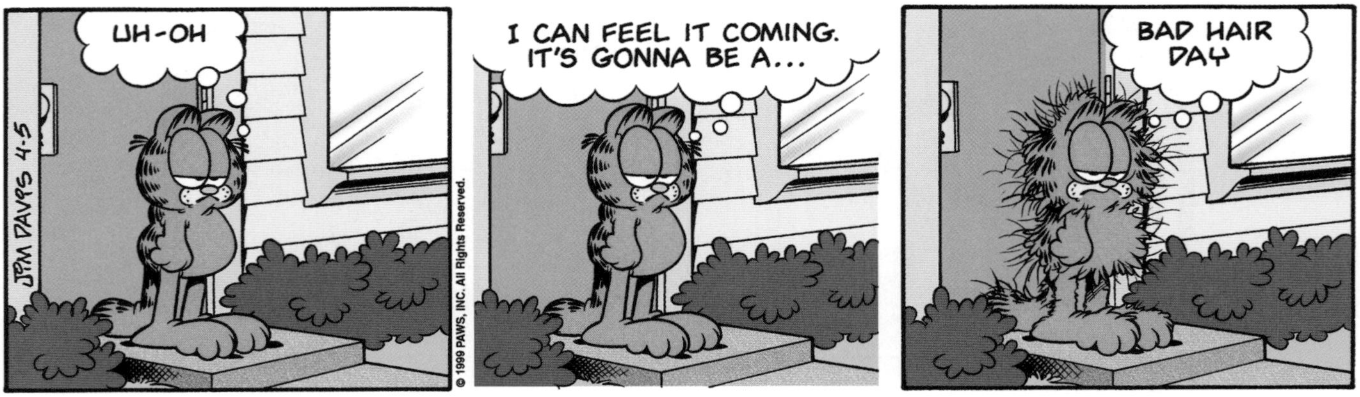
UH-OH
JIM DAVIS 4-5
I CAN FEEL IT COMING. IT'S GONNA BE A...
© 1999 PAWS, INC. All Rights Reserved.
BAD HAIR DAY

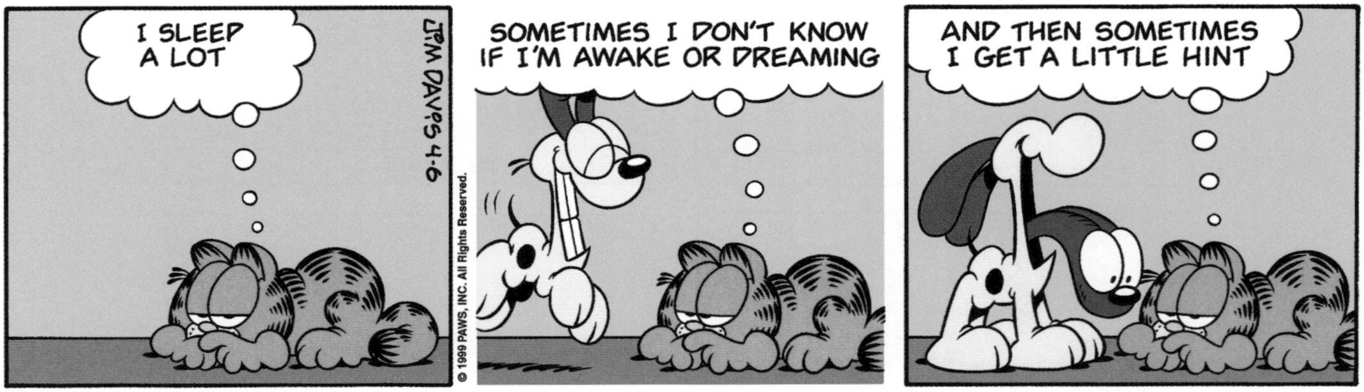
I SLEEP A LOT
JIM DAVIS 4-6
© 1999 PAWS, INC. All Rights Reserved.
SOMETIMES I DON'T KNOW IF I'M AWAKE OR DREAMING
AND THEN SOMETIMES I GET A LITTLE HINT

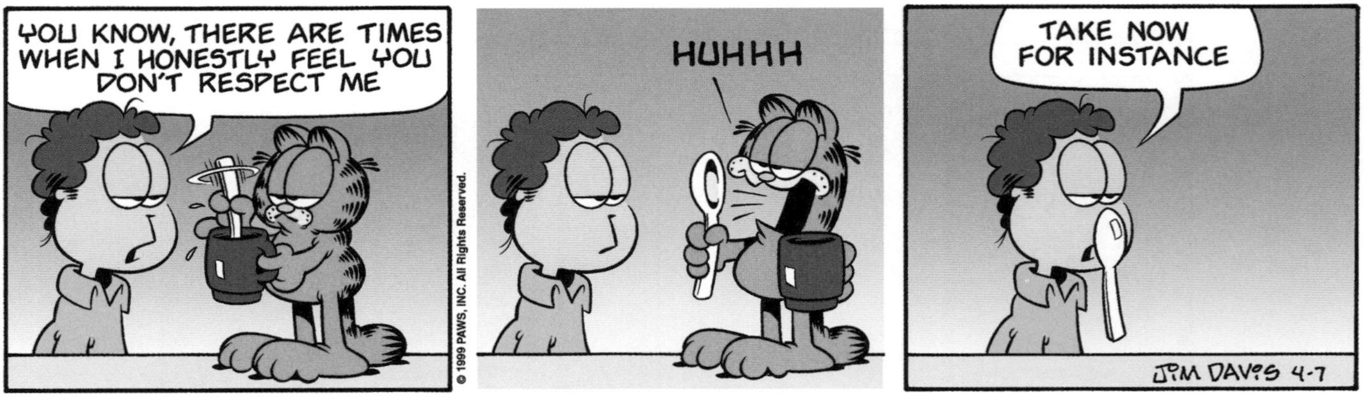
YOU KNOW, THERE ARE TIMES WHEN I HONESTLY FEEL YOU DON'T RESPECT ME
© 1999 PAWS, INC. All Rights Reserved.
HUHHH
TAKE NOW FOR INSTANCE
JIM DAVIS 4-7

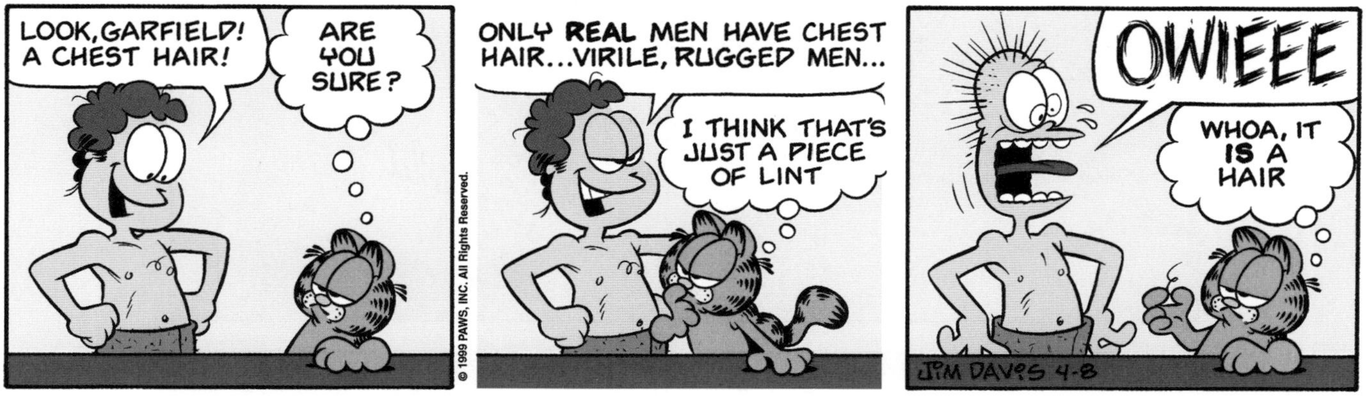
LOOK, GARFIELD! A CHEST HAIR!
ARE YOU SURE?
© 1999 PAWS, INC. All Rights Reserved.
ONLY REAL MEN HAVE CHEST HAIR...VIRILE, RUGGED MEN...
I THINK THAT'S JUST A PIECE OF LINT
OWIEEE
WHOA, IT IS A HAIR
JIM DAVIS 4-8

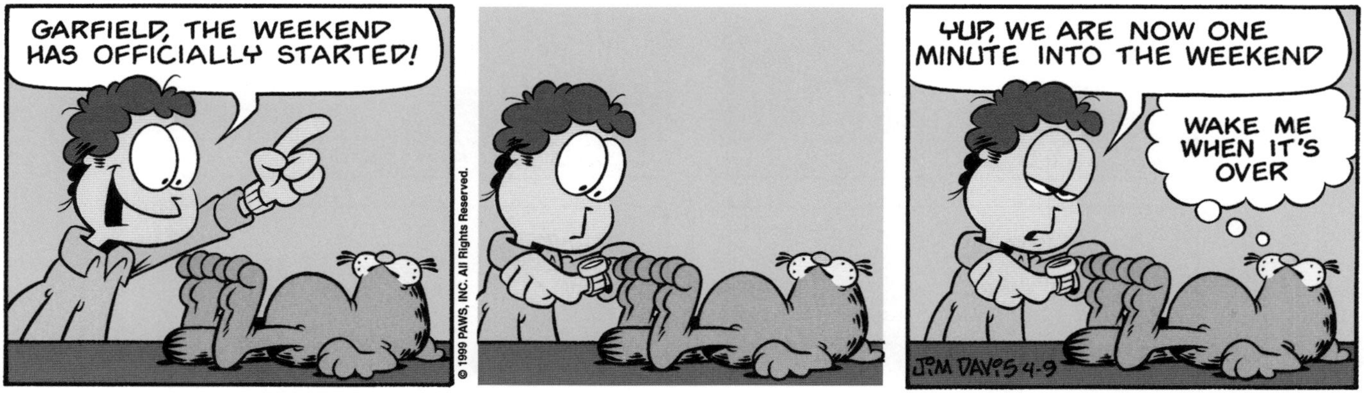
GARFIELD, THE WEEKEND HAS OFFICIALLY STARTED!
© 1999 PAWS, INC. All Rights Reserved.
YUP, WE ARE NOW ONE MINUTE INTO THE WEEKEND
WAKE ME WHEN IT'S OVER
JIM DAVIS 4-9

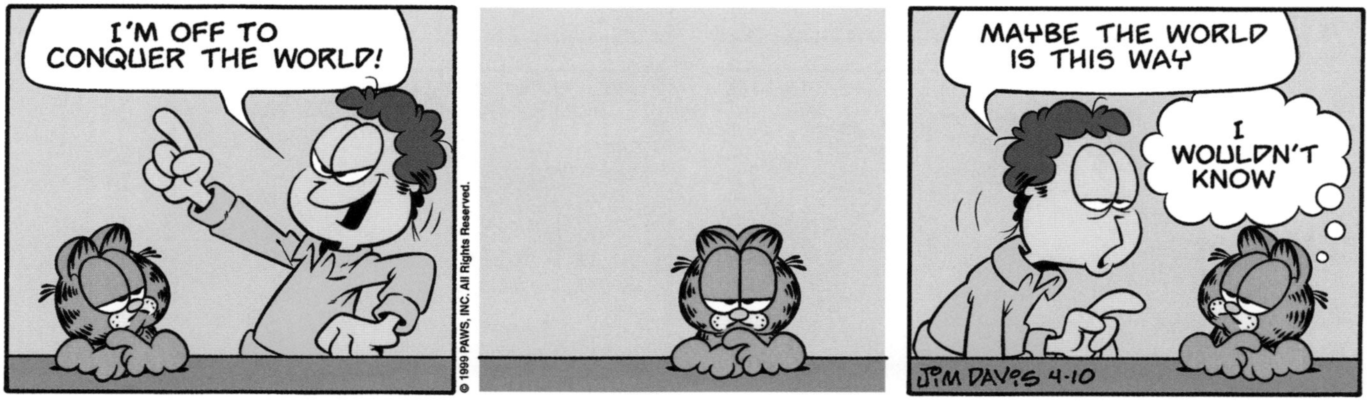
I'M OFF TO CONQUER THE WORLD!
© 1999 PAWS, INC. All Rights Reserved.
MAYBE THE WORLD IS THIS WAY
I WOULDN'T KNOW
JIM DAVIS 4-10

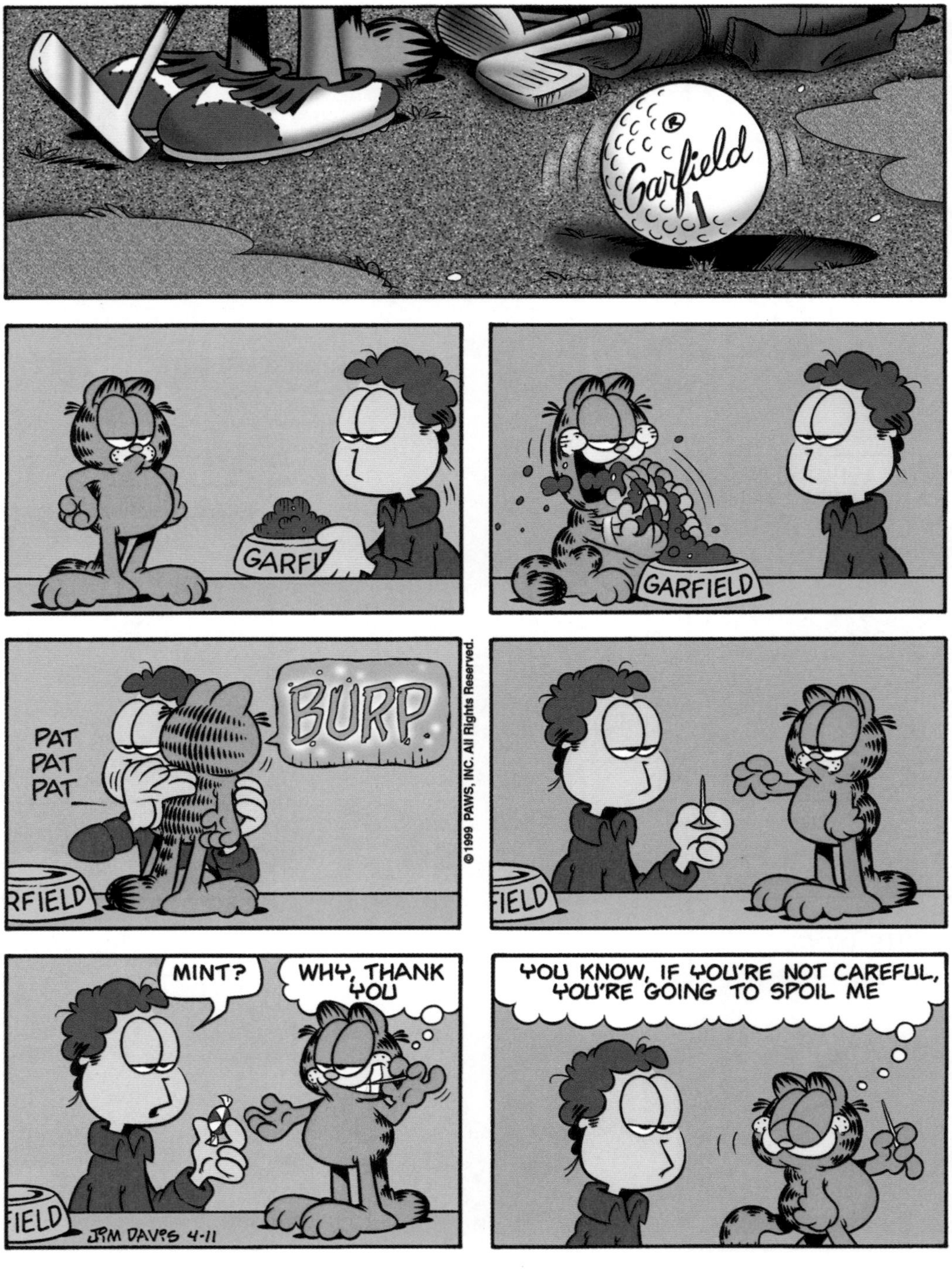
Garfield
GARFI
GARFIELD
PAT
PAT
PAT
BURP
©1999 PAWS, INC. All Rights Reserved.
RFIELD
IELD
MINT?
WHY, THANK YOU
IELD
JIM DAVIS 4-11
YOU KNOW, IF YOU'RE NOT CAREFUL, YOU'RE GOING TO SPOIL ME

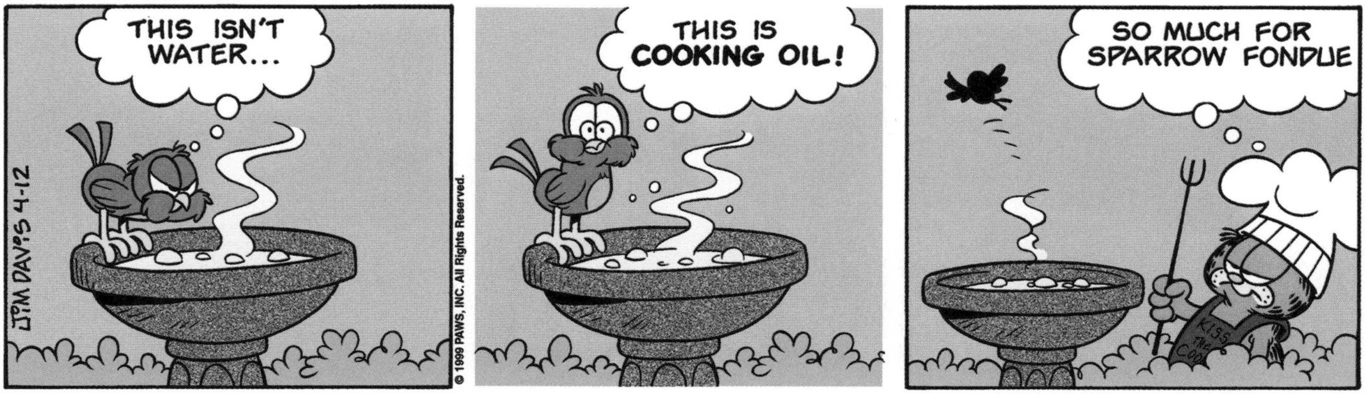
THIS ISN'T WATER...
JIM DAVIS 4-12
© 1999 PAWS, INC. All Rights Reserved.
THIS IS **COOKING OIL!**
SO MUCH FOR SPARROW FONDUE

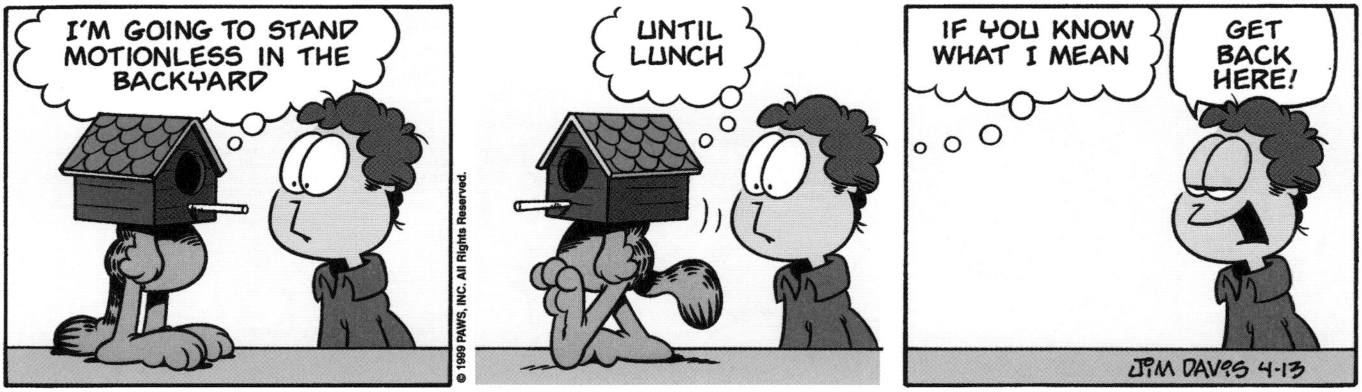
I'M GOING TO STAND MOTIONLESS IN THE BACKYARD
© 1999 PAWS, INC. All Rights Reserved.
UNTIL LUNCH
IF YOU KNOW WHAT I MEAN
GET BACK HERE!
JIM DAVIS 4-13

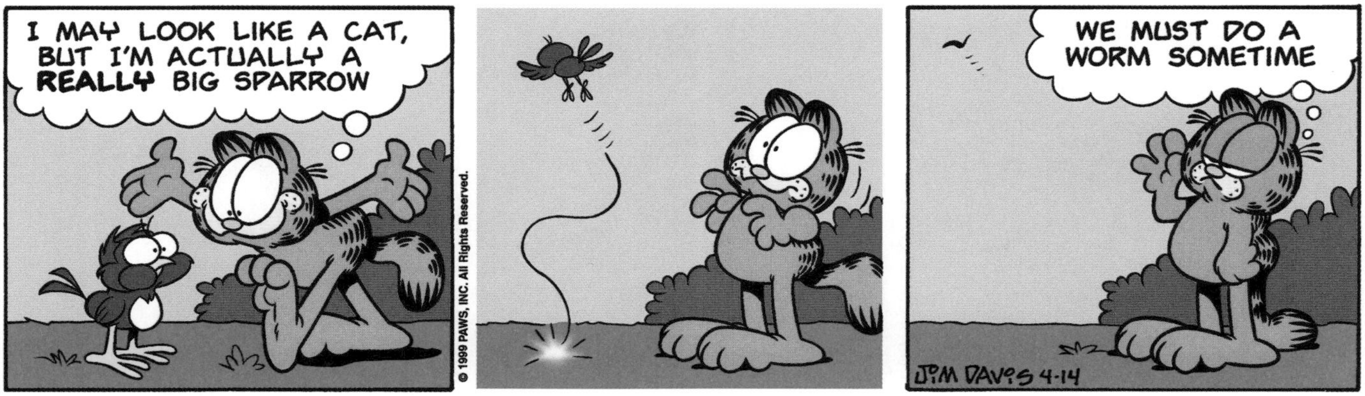
I MAY LOOK LIKE A CAT, BUT I'M ACTUALLY A **REALLY** BIG SPARROW
© 1999 PAWS, INC. All Rights Reserved.
WE MUST DO A WORM SOMETIME
JIM DAVIS 4-14

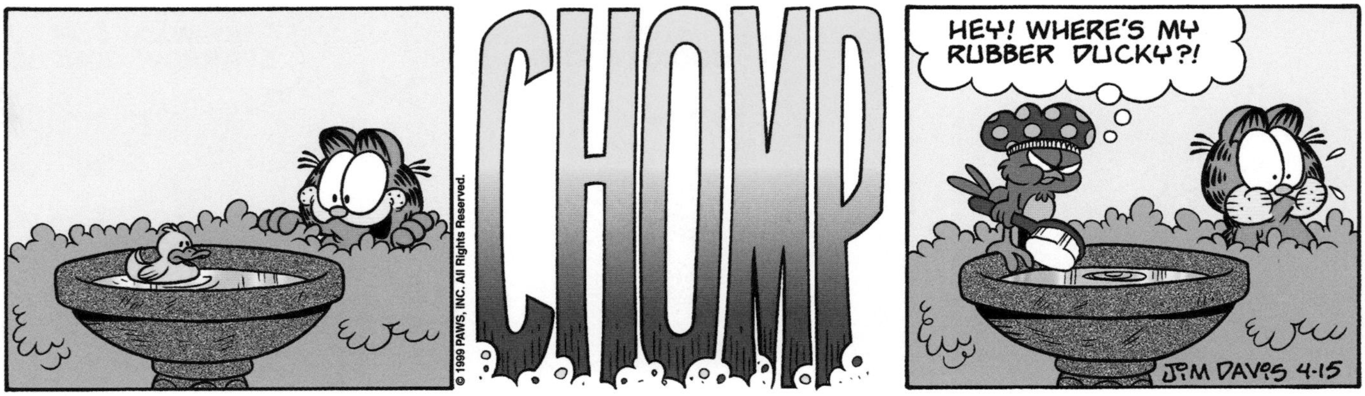
© 1999 PAWS, INC. All Rights Reserved.
CHOMP
HEY! WHERE'S MY RUBBER DUCKY?!
JIM DAVIS 4-15

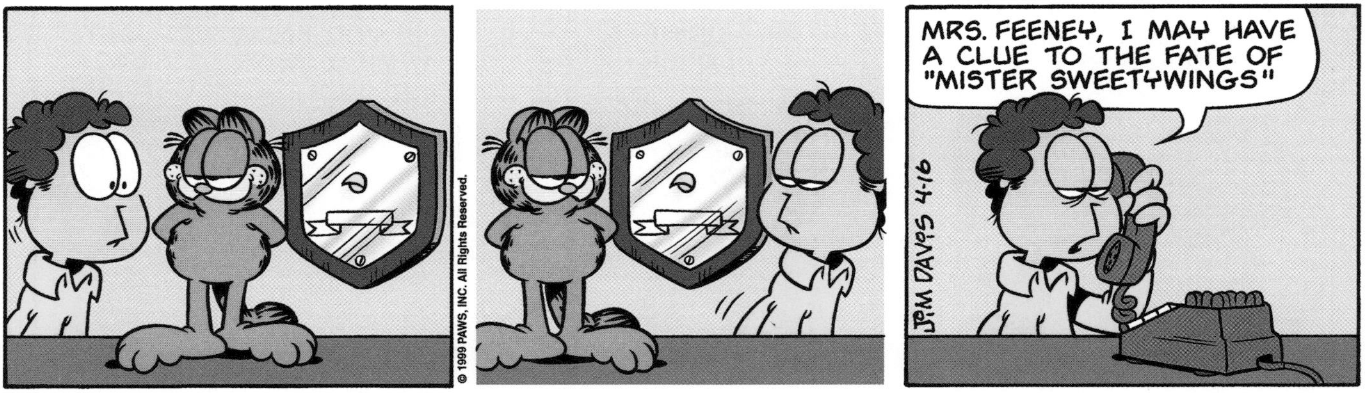
© 1999 PAWS, INC. All Rights Reserved.
MRS. FEENEY, I MAY HAVE A CLUE TO THE FATE OF "MISTER SWEETYWINGS"
JIM DAVIS 4-16

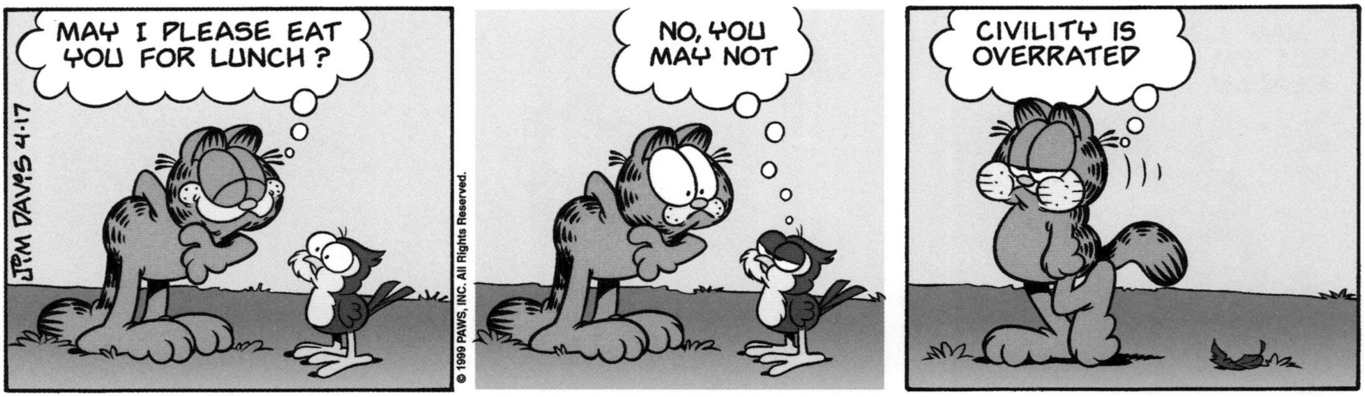
MAY I PLEASE EAT YOU FOR LUNCH?
JIM DAVIS 4-17
© 1999 PAWS, INC. All Rights Reserved.
NO, YOU MAY NOT
CIVILITY IS OVERRATED

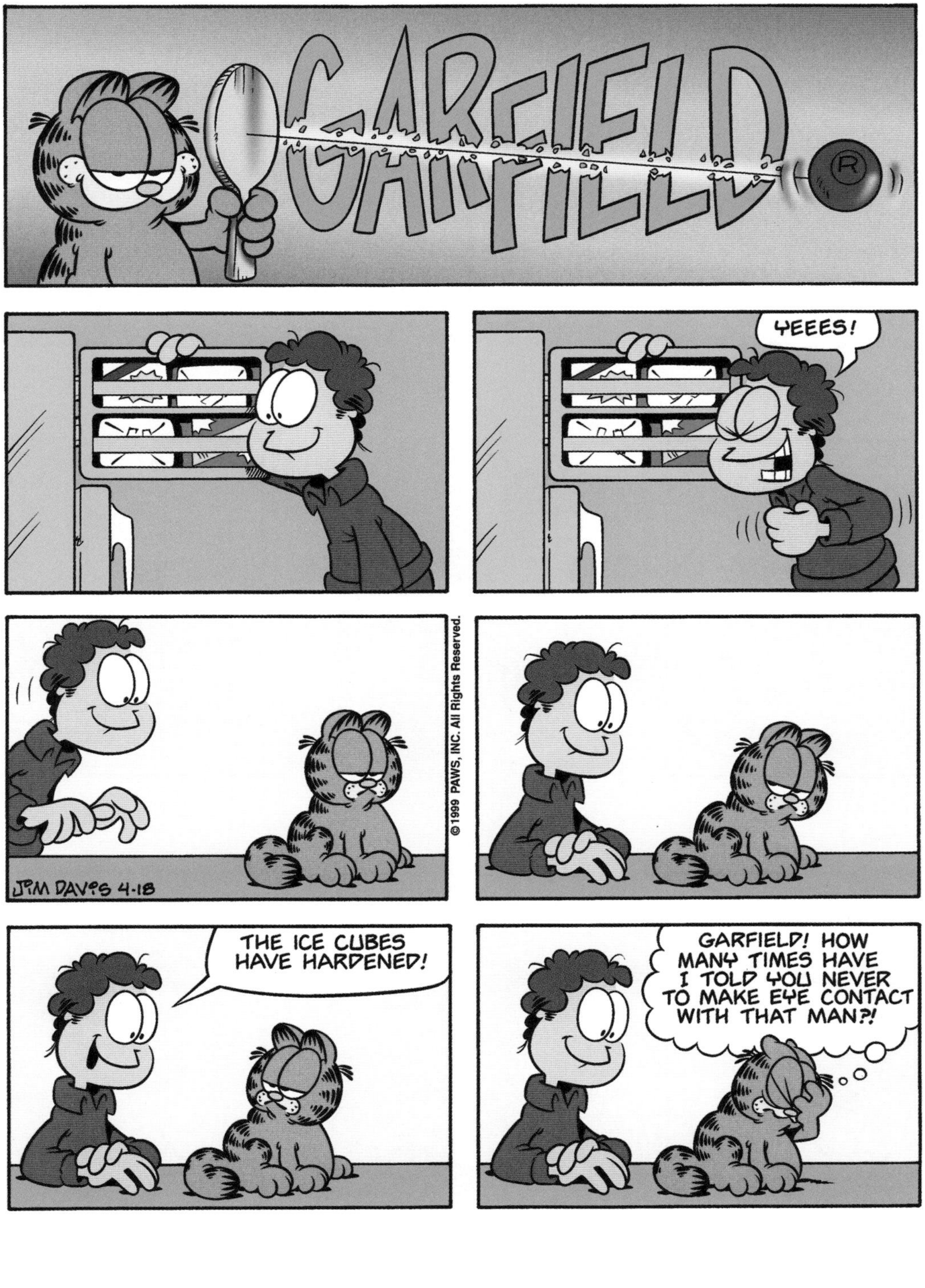
GARFIELD®
YEEES!
©1999 PAWS, INC. All Rights Reserved.
JIM DAVIS 4-18
THE ICE CUBES HAVE HARDENED!
GARFIELD! HOW MANY TIMES HAVE I TOLD YOU NEVER TO MAKE EYE CONTACT WITH THAT MAN?!

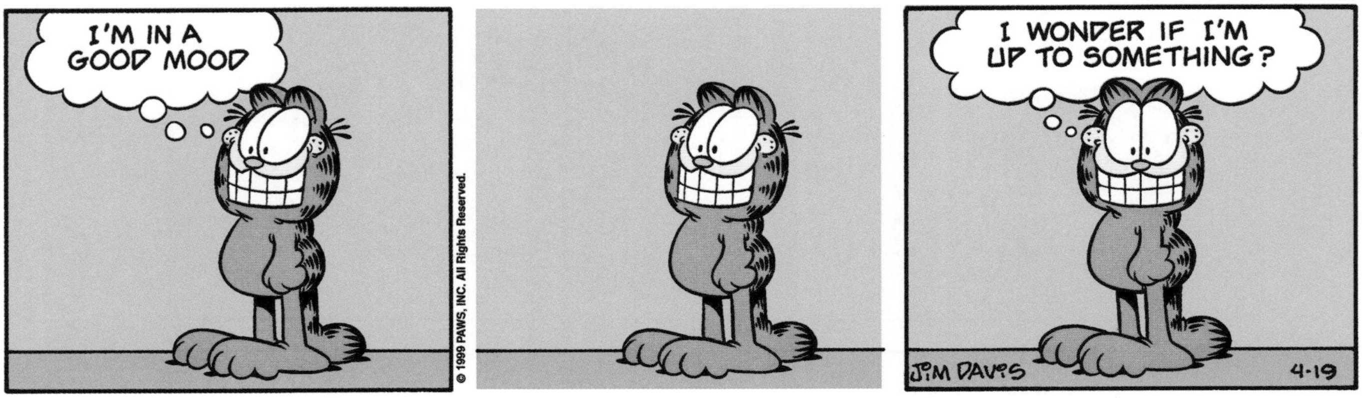
I'M IN A GOOD MOOD
I WONDER IF I'M UP TO SOMETHING?
JIM DAVIS
4-19

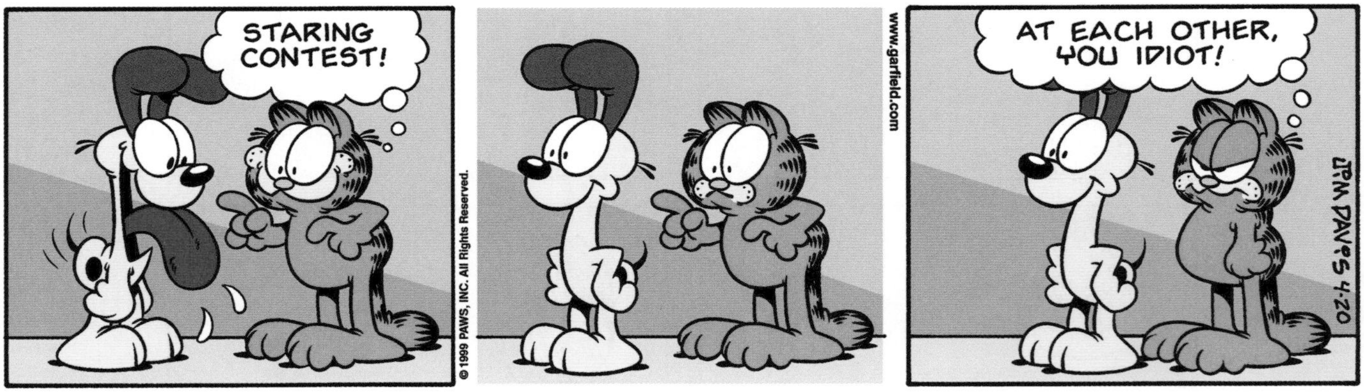
STARING CONTEST!
AT EACH OTHER, YOU IDIOT!
JIM DAVIS 4-20

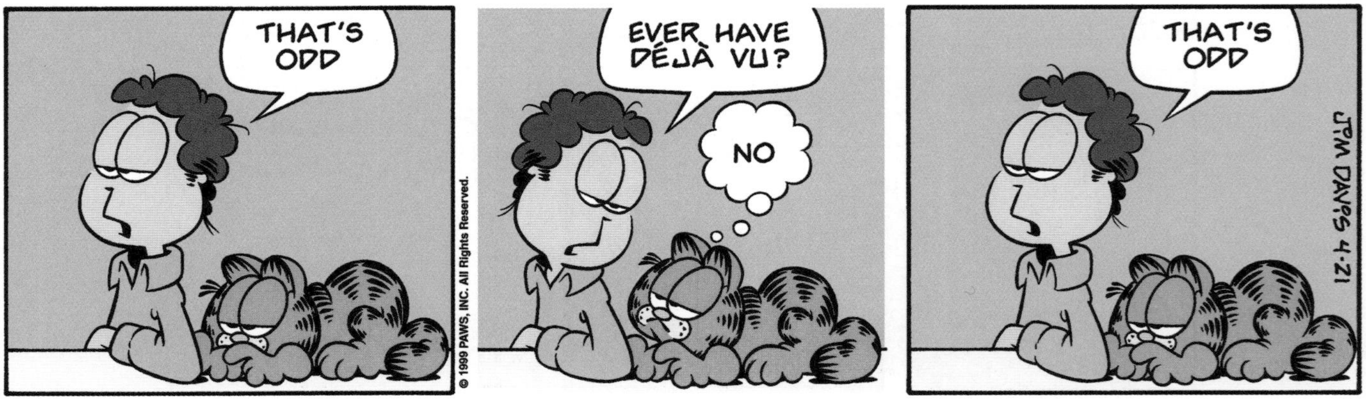
THAT'S ODD
EVER HAVE DÉJÀ VU?
NO
THAT'S ODD
JIM DAVIS 4-21

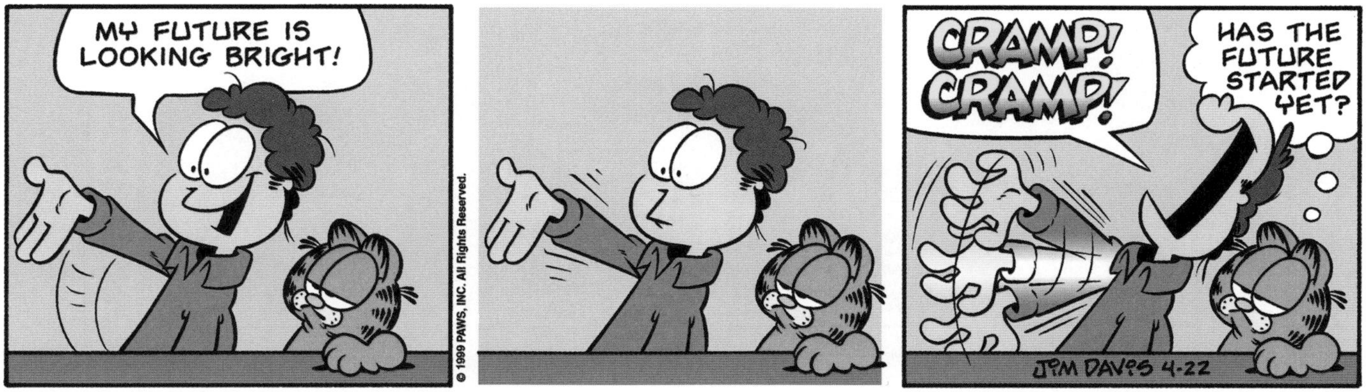
MY FUTURE IS LOOKING BRIGHT!
CRAMP! CRAMP!
HAS THE FUTURE STARTED YET?
JIM DAVIS 4-22

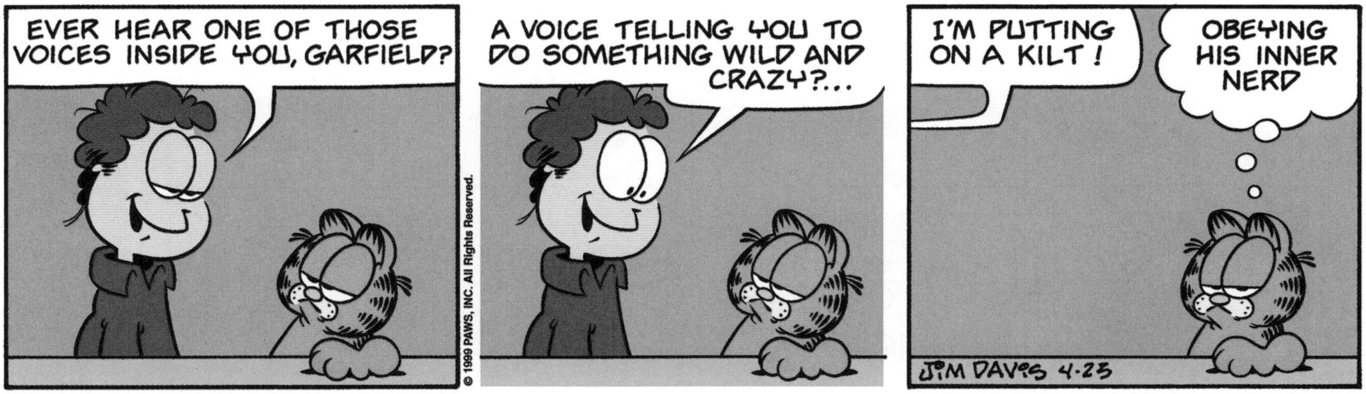
EVER HEAR ONE OF THOSE VOICES INSIDE YOU, GARFIELD?
A VOICE TELLING YOU TO DO SOMETHING WILD AND CRAZY?...
I'M PUTTING ON A KILT!
OBEYING HIS INNER NERD
JIM DAVIS 4-23

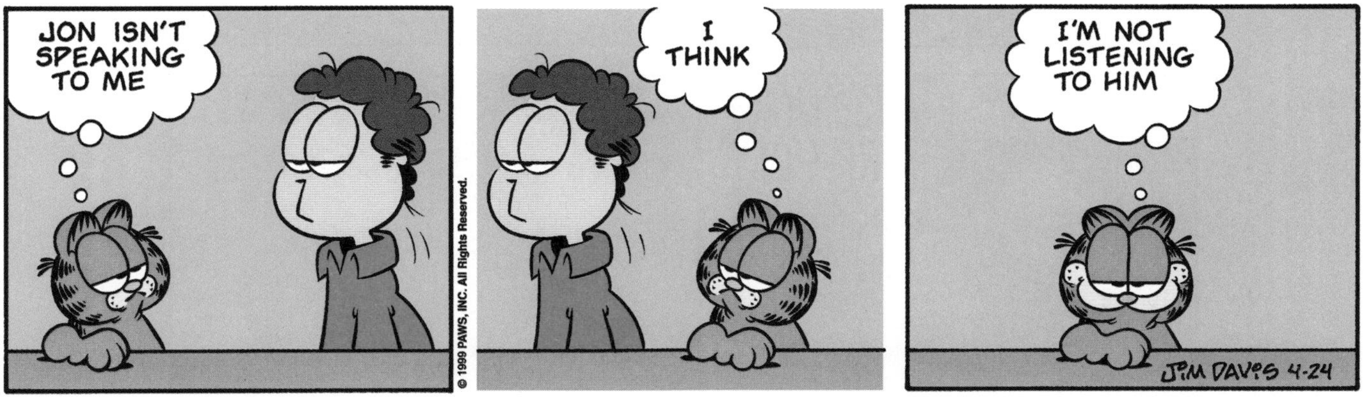
JON ISN'T SPEAKING TO ME
I THINK
I'M NOT LISTENING TO HIM
JIM DAVIS 4-24

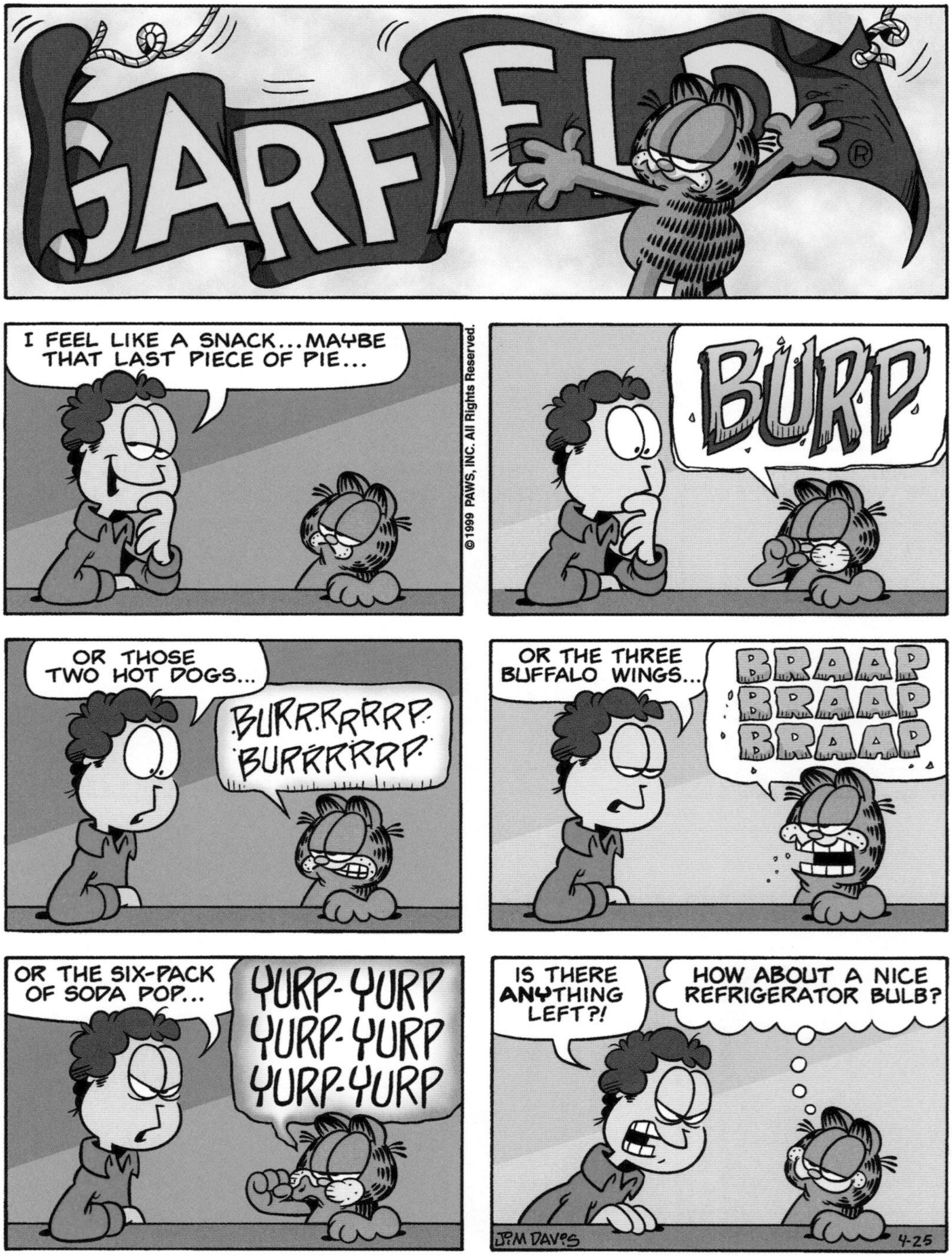
GARFIELD®
I FEEL LIKE A SNACK... MAYBE THAT LAST PIECE OF PIE...
BURP
OR THOSE TWO HOT DOGS...
BURRRRRRP BURRRRRRP
OR THE THREE BUFFALO WINGS...
BRAAP BRAAP BRAAP
OR THE SIX-PACK OF SODA POP...
YURP-YURP YURP-YURP YURP-YURP
IS THERE **ANY**THING LEFT?!
HOW ABOUT A NICE REFRIGERATOR BULB?
JIM DAVIS
4-25

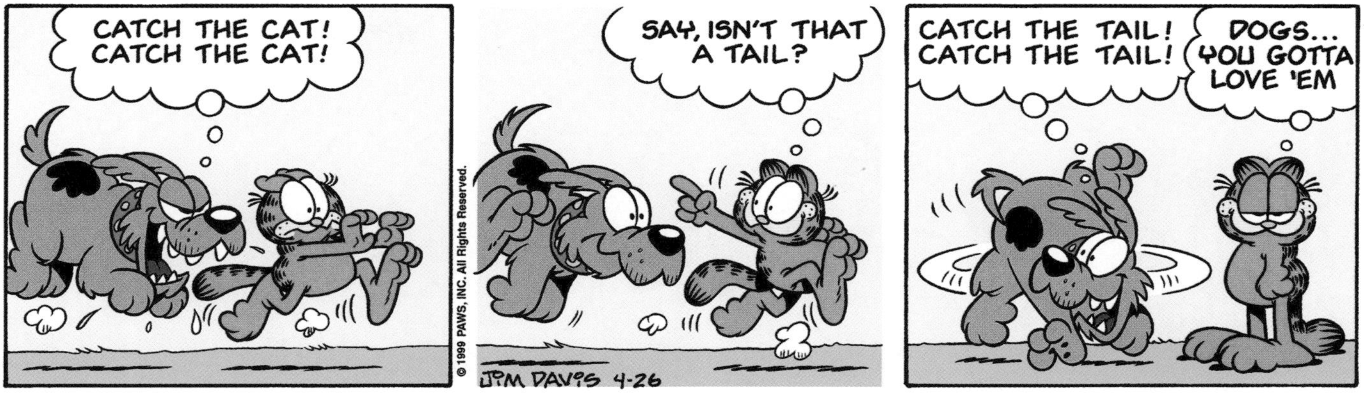
CATCH THE CAT! CATCH THE CAT!
SAY, ISN'T THAT A TAIL?
© 1999 PAWS, INC. All Rights Reserved.
JIM DAVIS 4-26
CATCH THE TAIL! CATCH THE TAIL!
DOGS... YOU GOTTA LOVE 'EM

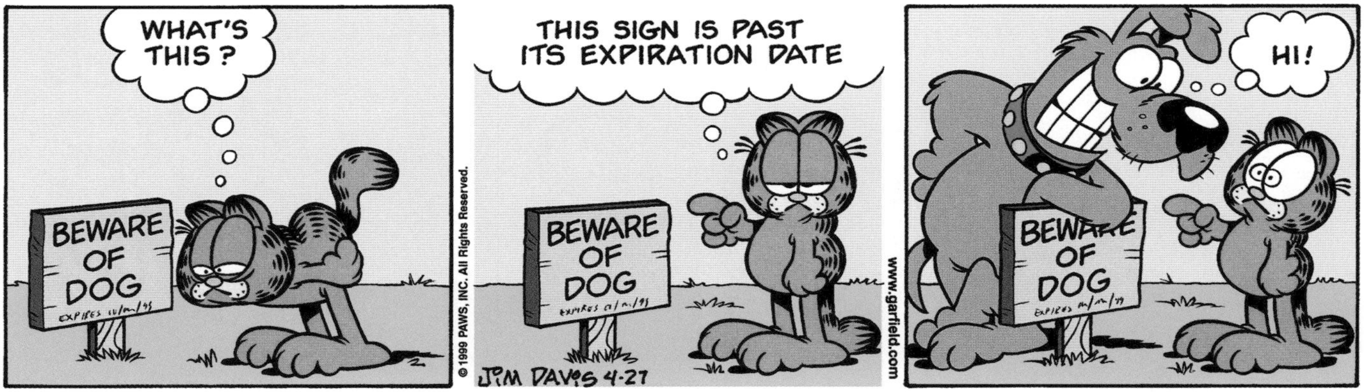
WHAT'S THIS?
BEWARE OF DOG
© 1999 PAWS, INC. All Rights Reserved.
THIS SIGN IS PAST ITS EXPIRATION DATE
BEWARE OF DOG
JIM DAVIS 4-27
www.garfield.com
HI!
BEWARE OF DOG

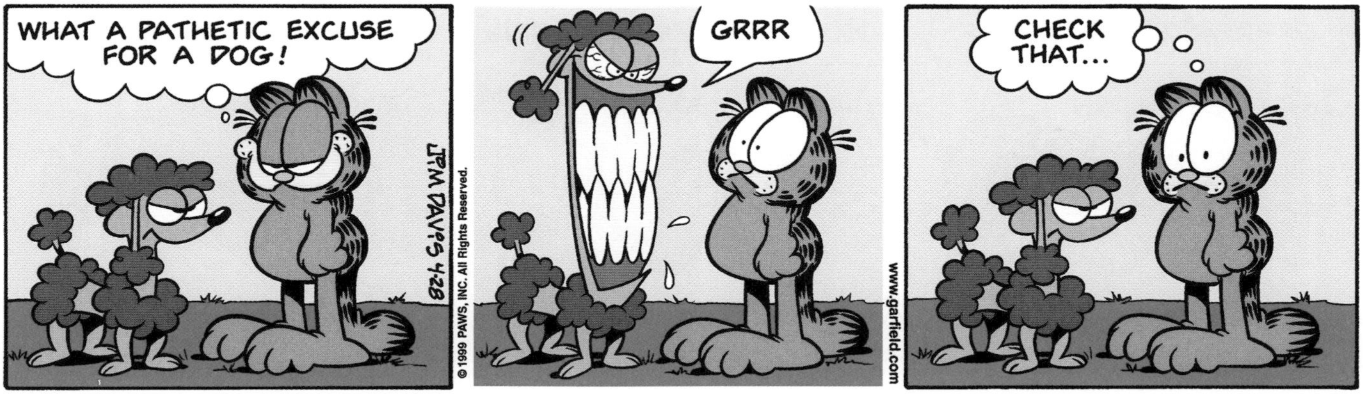
WHAT A PATHETIC EXCUSE FOR A DOG!
JIM DAVIS 4-28
© 1999 PAWS, INC. All Rights Reserved.
GRRR
www.garfield.com
CHECK THAT...

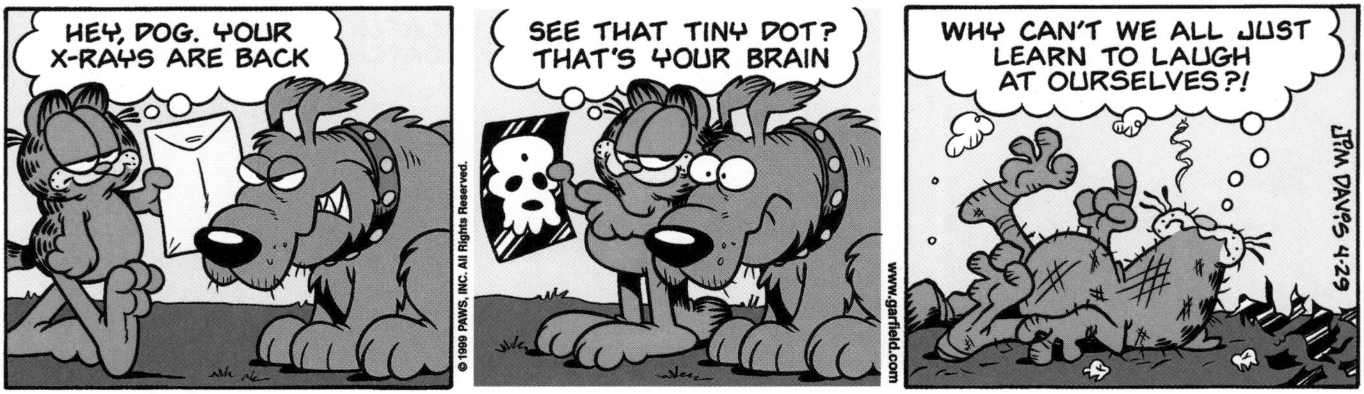
HEY, DOG. YOUR X-RAYS ARE BACK
SEE THAT TINY DOT? THAT'S YOUR BRAIN
WHY CAN'T WE ALL JUST LEARN TO LAUGH AT OURSELVES?!
JIM DAVIS 4-29
© 1999 PAWS, INC. All Rights Reserved.
www.garfield.com

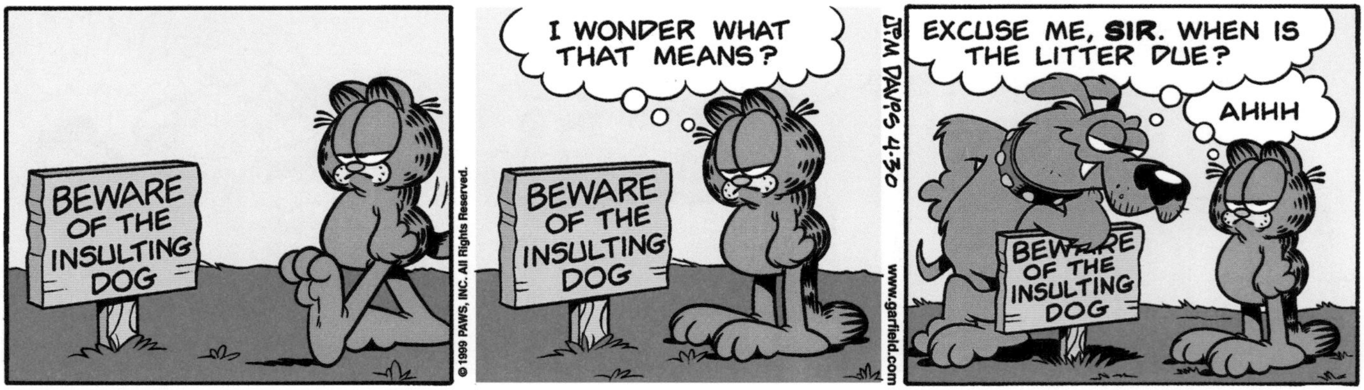
BEWARE OF THE INSULTING DOG
I WONDER WHAT THAT MEANS?
EXCUSE ME, **SIR**. WHEN IS THE LITTER DUE?
AHHH
JIM DAVIS 4-30
© 1999 PAWS, INC. All Rights Reserved.
www.garfield.com

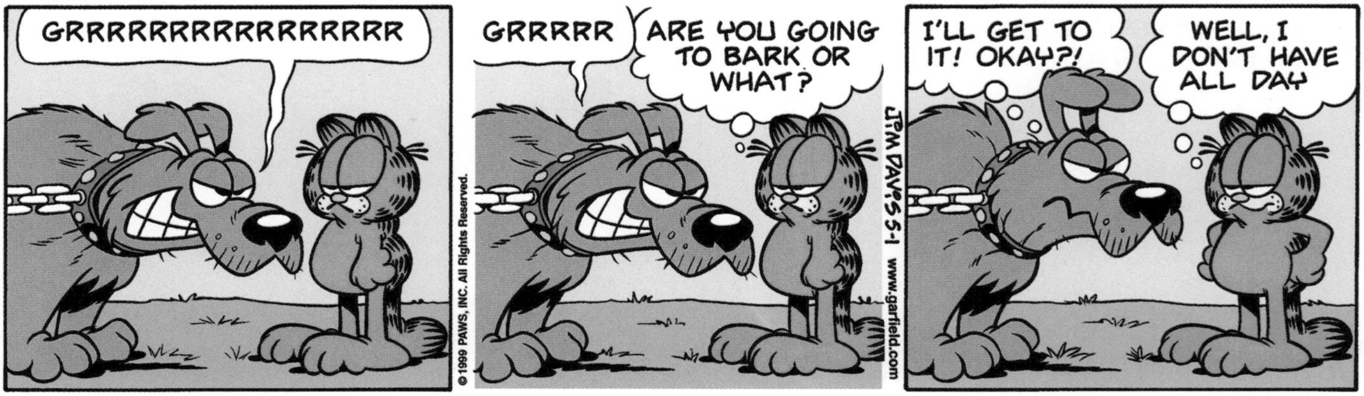
GRRRRRRRRRRRRRRRR
GRRRRR
ARE YOU GOING TO BARK OR WHAT?
I'LL GET TO IT! OKAY?!
WELL, I DON'T HAVE ALL DAY
JIM DAVIS 5-1
© 1999 PAWS, INC. All Rights Reserved.
www.garfield.com

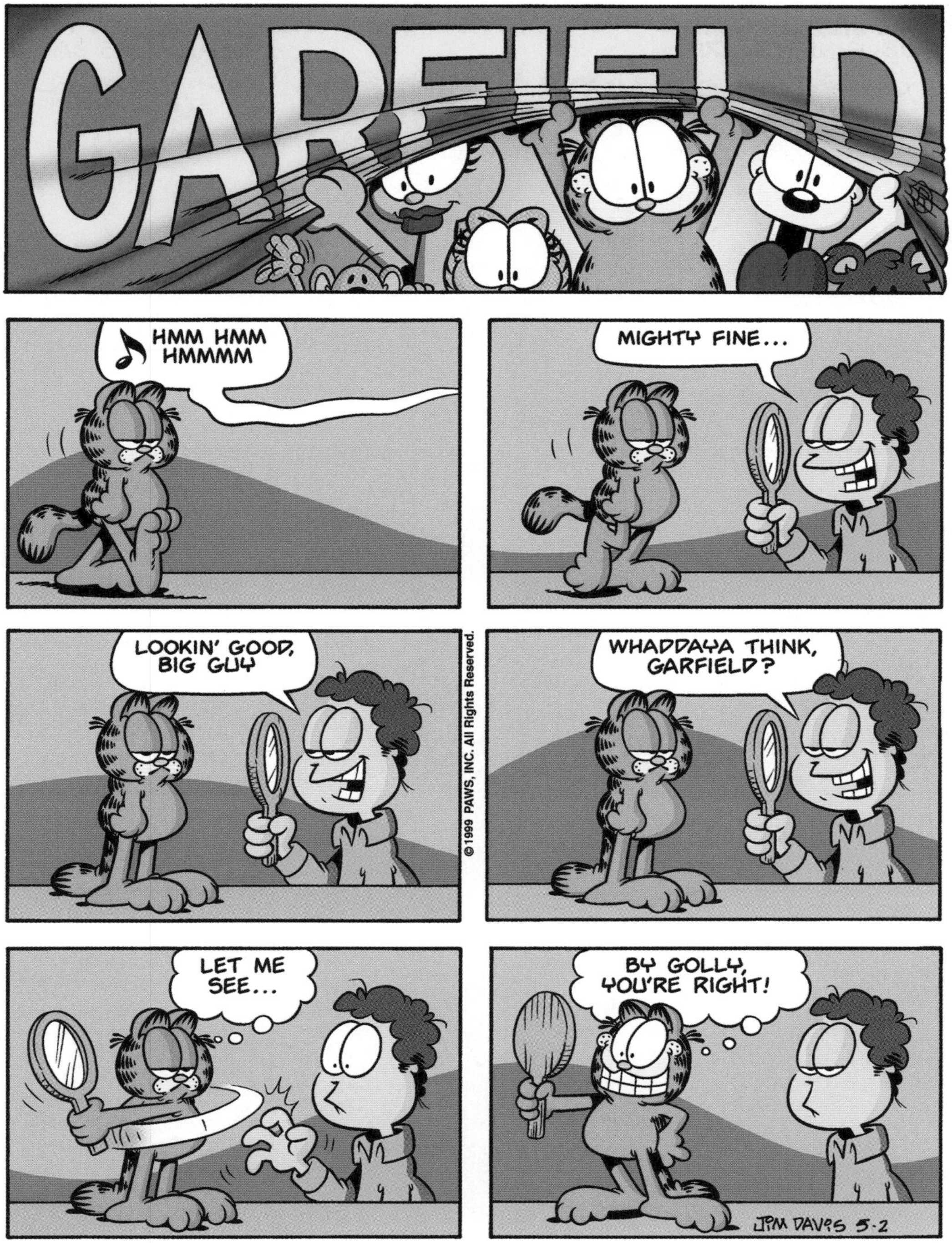
GARFIELD
HMM HMM HMMMM
MIGHTY FINE...
LOOKIN' GOOD, BIG GUY
WHADDAYA THINK, GARFIELD?
LET ME SEE...
BY GOLLY, YOU'RE RIGHT!
JIM DAVIS 5-2

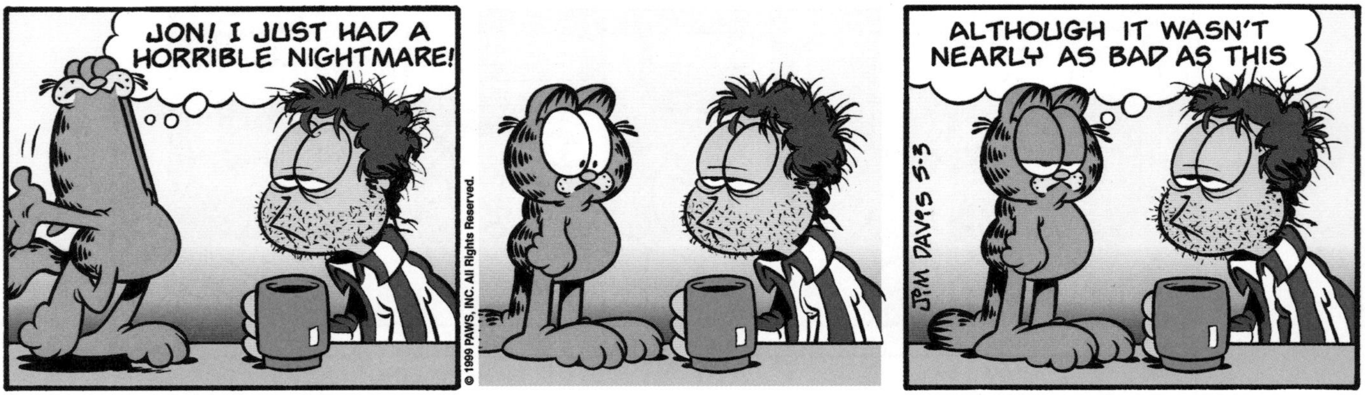
JON! I JUST HAD A HORRIBLE NIGHTMARE!
© 1999 PAWS, INC. All Rights Reserved.
ALTHOUGH IT WASN'T NEARLY AS BAD AS THIS
JIM DAVIS 5-3

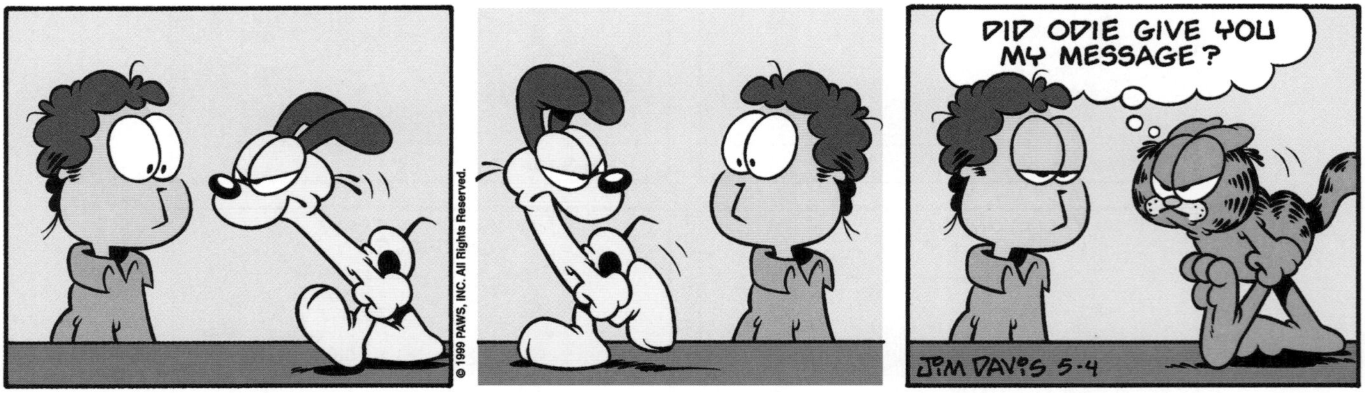
© 1999 PAWS, INC. All Rights Reserved.
DID ODIE GIVE YOU MY MESSAGE?
JIM DAVIS 5-4

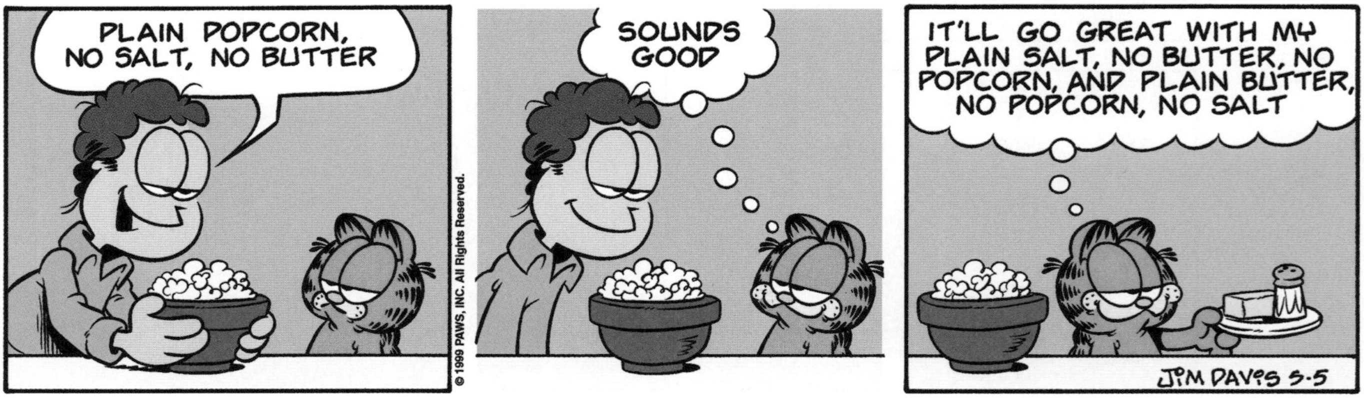
PLAIN POPCORN, NO SALT, NO BUTTER
© 1999 PAWS, INC. All Rights Reserved.
SOUNDS GOOD
IT'LL GO GREAT WITH MY PLAIN SALT, NO BUTTER, NO POPCORN, AND PLAIN BUTTER, NO POPCORN, NO SALT
JIM DAVIS 5-5

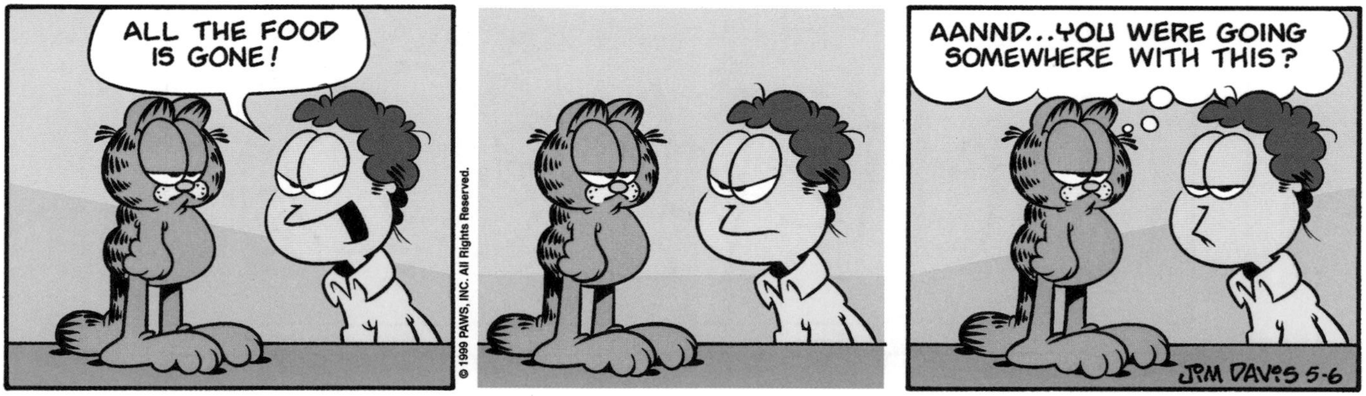
ALL THE FOOD IS GONE!
AANND...YOU WERE GOING SOMEWHERE WITH THIS?
JIM DAVIS 5-6

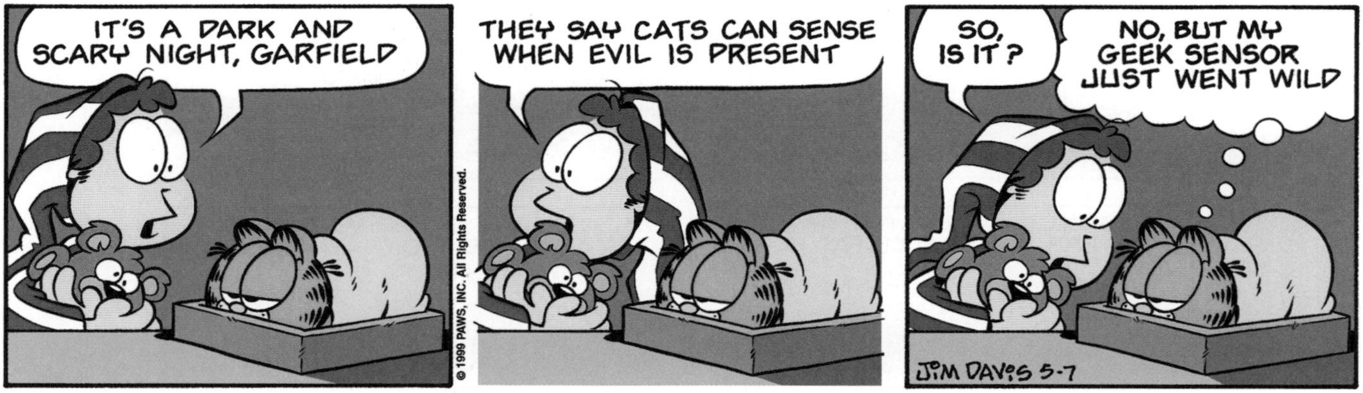
IT'S A DARK AND SCARY NIGHT, GARFIELD
THEY SAY CATS CAN SENSE WHEN EVIL IS PRESENT
SO, IS IT?
NO, BUT MY GEEK SENSOR JUST WENT WILD
JIM DAVIS 5-7

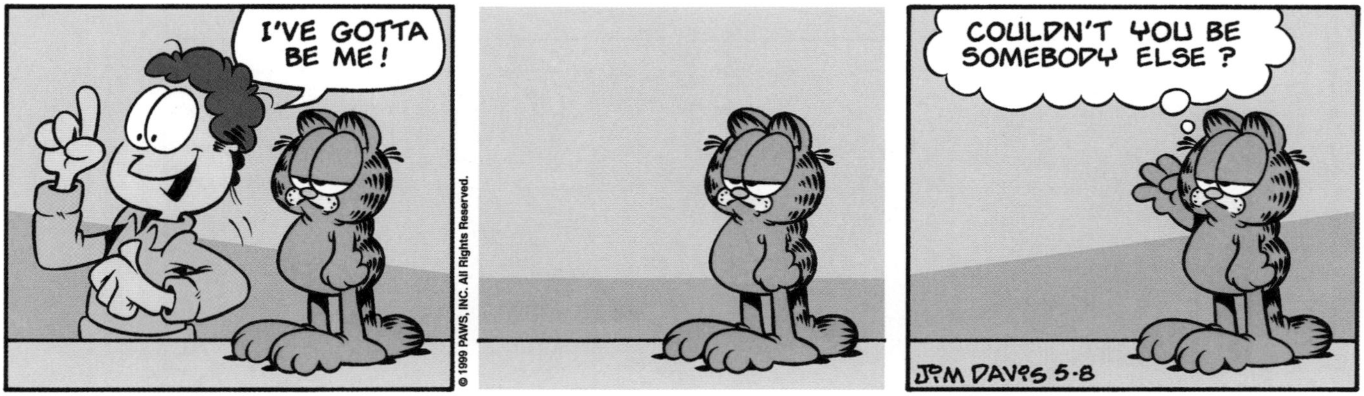
I'VE GOTTA BE ME!
COULDN'T YOU BE SOMEBODY ELSE?
JIM DAVIS 5-8

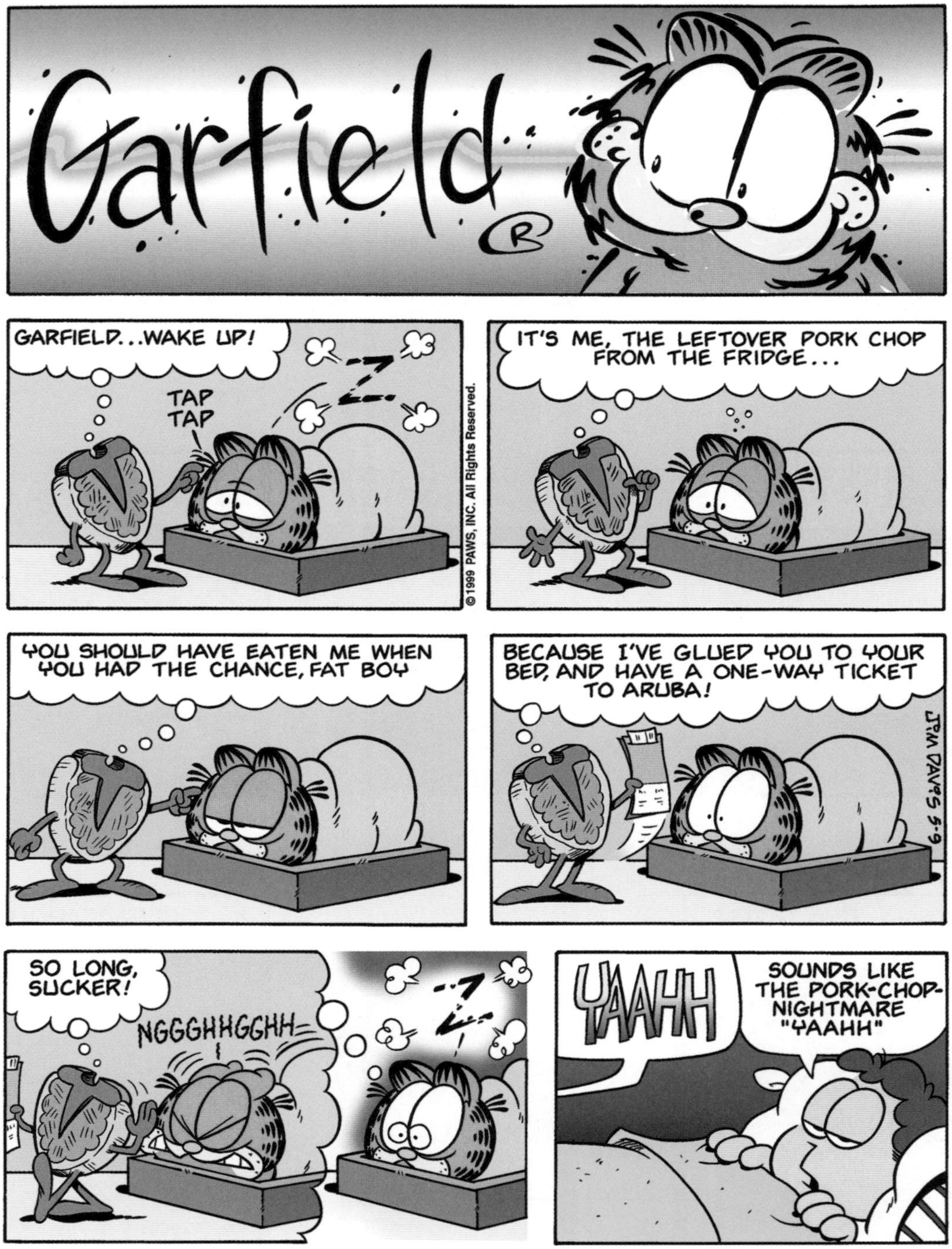
Garfield®
GARFIELD...WAKE UP!
TAP TAP
©1999 PAWS, INC. All Rights Reserved.
IT'S ME, THE LEFTOVER PORK CHOP FROM THE FRIDGE...
YOU SHOULD HAVE EATEN ME WHEN YOU HAD THE CHANCE, FAT BOY
BECAUSE I'VE GLUED YOU TO YOUR BED, AND HAVE A ONE-WAY TICKET TO ARUBA!
JIM DAVIS 5-9
SO LONG, SUCKER!
NGGGHHGGHH!
YAAHH
SOUNDS LIKE THE PORK-CHOP-NIGHTMARE "YAAHH"

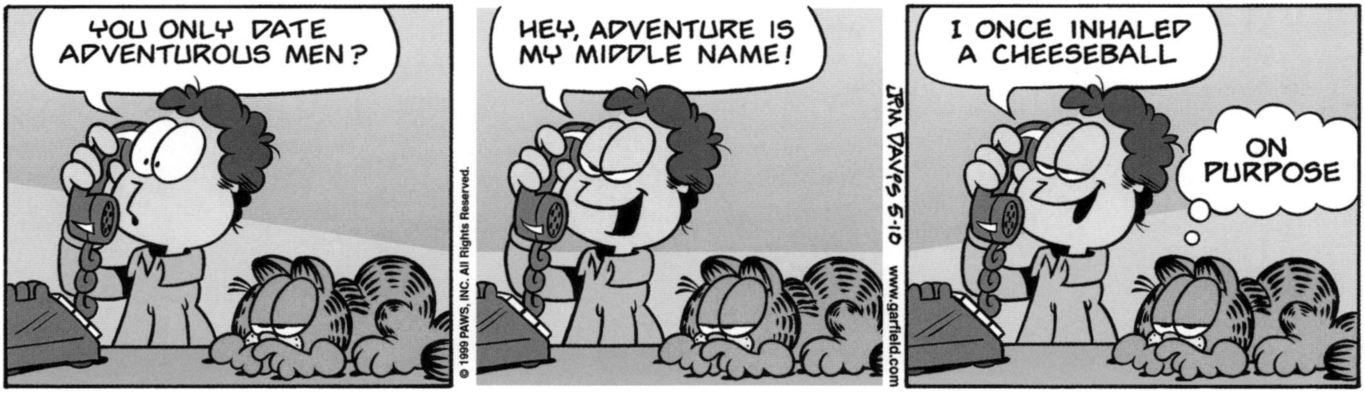
YOU ONLY DATE ADVENTUROUS MEN?
HEY, ADVENTURE IS MY MIDDLE NAME!
I ONCE INHALED A CHEESEBALL
ON PURPOSE
© 1999 PAWS, INC. All Rights Reserved.
JIM DAVIS 5-10
www.garfield.com

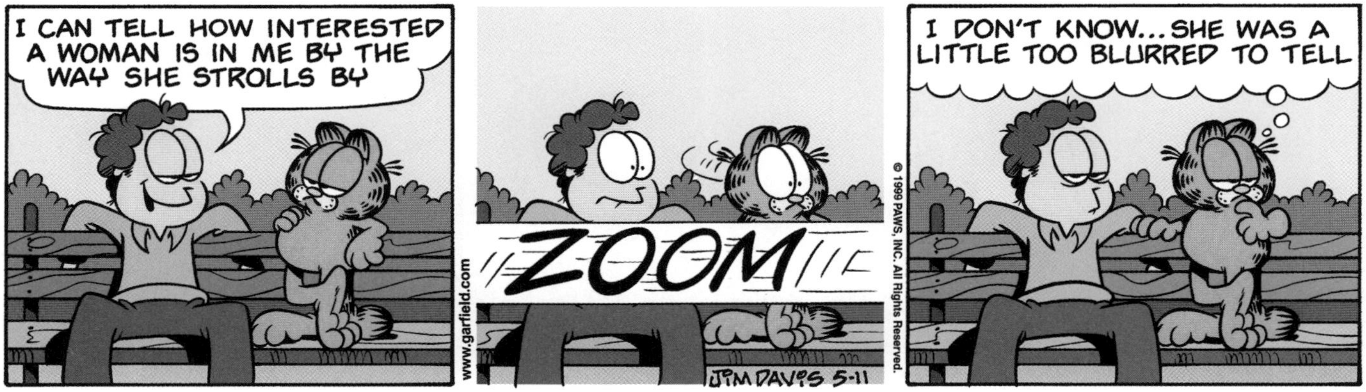
I CAN TELL HOW INTERESTED A WOMAN IS IN ME BY THE WAY SHE STROLLS BY
ZOOM
I DON'T KNOW... SHE WAS A LITTLE TOO BLURRED TO TELL
www.garfield.com
JIM DAVIS 5-11
© 1999 PAWS, INC. All Rights Reserved.

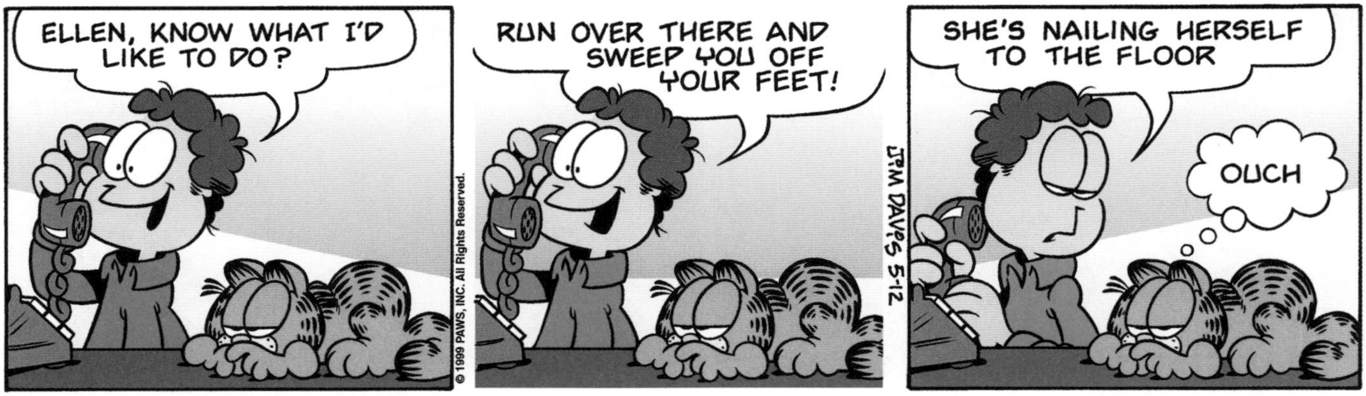
ELLEN, KNOW WHAT I'D LIKE TO DO?
RUN OVER THERE AND SWEEP YOU OFF YOUR FEET!
SHE'S NAILING HERSELF TO THE FLOOR
OUCH
© 1999 PAWS, INC. All Rights Reserved.
JIM DAVIS 5-12

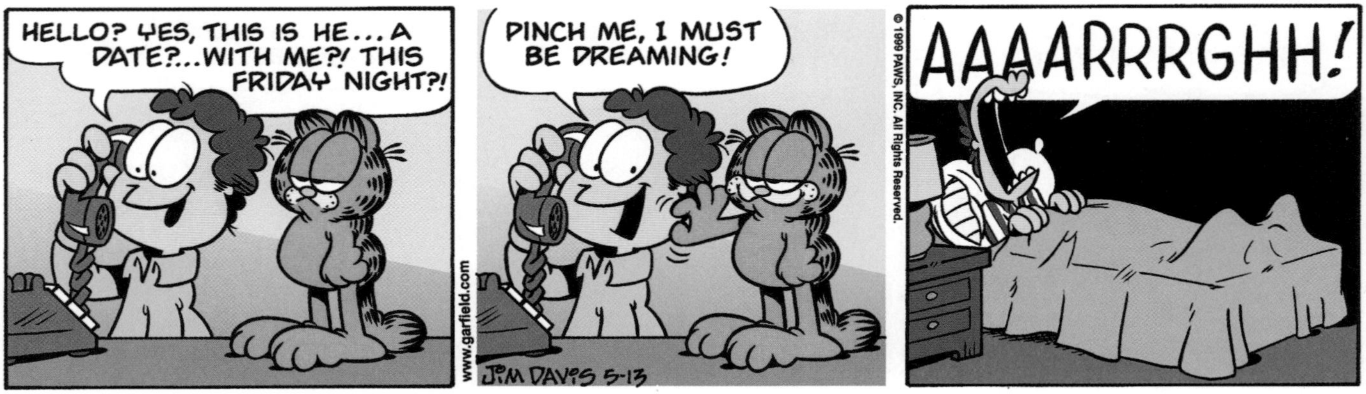
HELLO? YES, THIS IS HE... A DATE?...WITH ME?! THIS FRIDAY NIGHT?!
PINCH ME, I MUST BE DREAMING!
AAAARRRGHH!
JIM DAVIS 5-13
www.garfield.com
© 1999 PAWS, INC. All Rights Reserved.

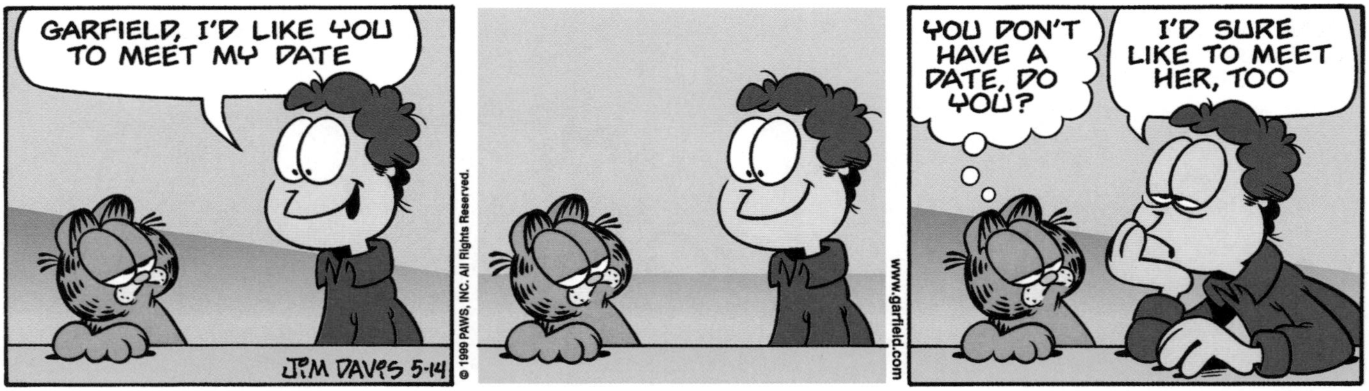
GARFIELD, I'D LIKE YOU TO MEET MY DATE
YOU DON'T HAVE A DATE, DO YOU?
I'D SURE LIKE TO MEET HER, TOO
JIM DAVIS 5-14
© 1999 PAWS, INC. All Rights Reserved.
www.garfield.com

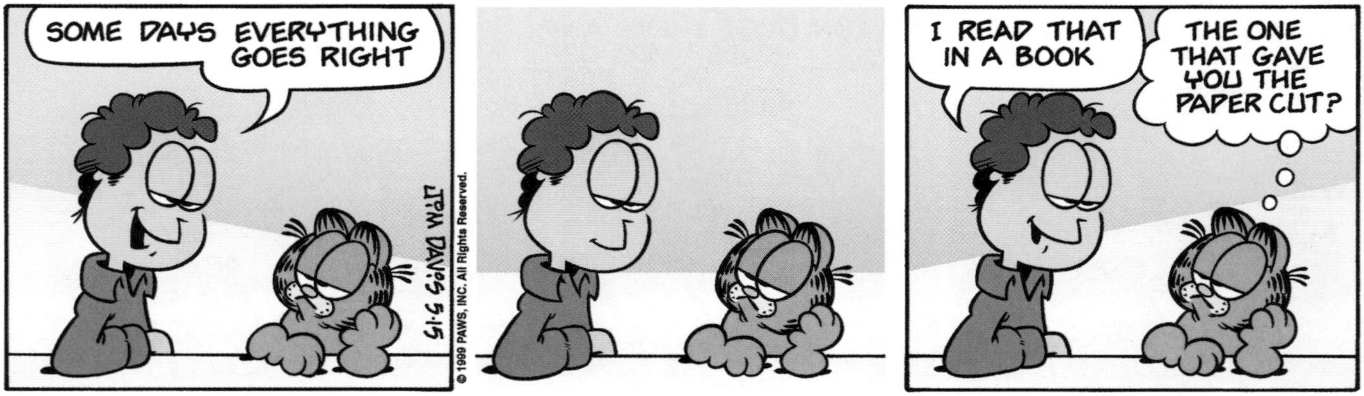
SOME DAYS EVERYTHING GOES RIGHT
I READ THAT IN A BOOK
THE ONE THAT GAVE YOU THE PAPER CUT?
JIM DAVIS 5-15
© 1999 PAWS, INC. All Rights Reserved.

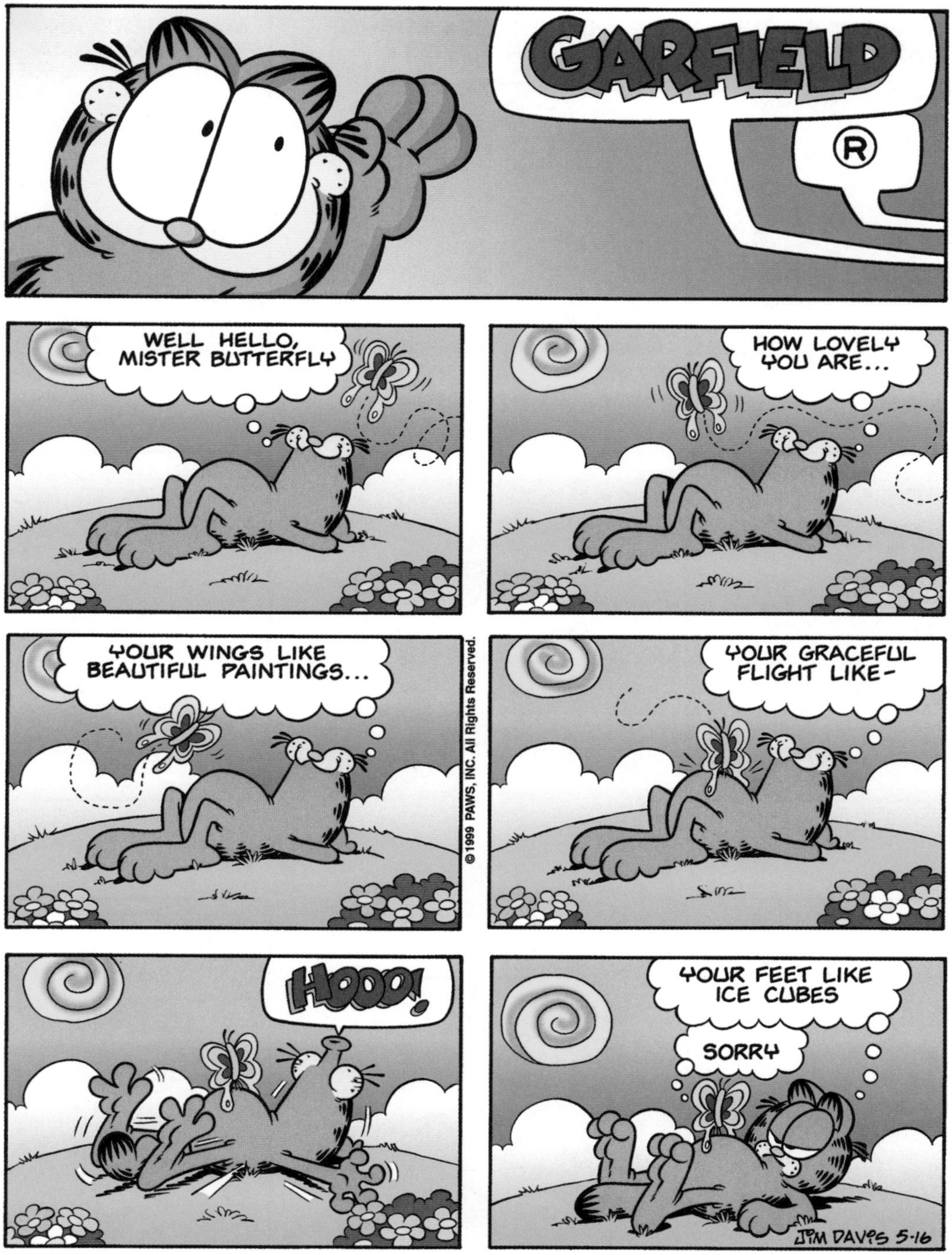
GARFIELD®
WELL HELLO, MISTER BUTTERFLY
HOW LOVELY YOU ARE...
YOUR WINGS LIKE BEAUTIFUL PAINTINGS...
© 1999 PAWS, INC. All Rights Reserved.
YOUR GRACEFUL FLIGHT LIKE-
HOOO!
YOUR FEET LIKE ICE CUBES
SORRY
JIM DAVIS 5-16

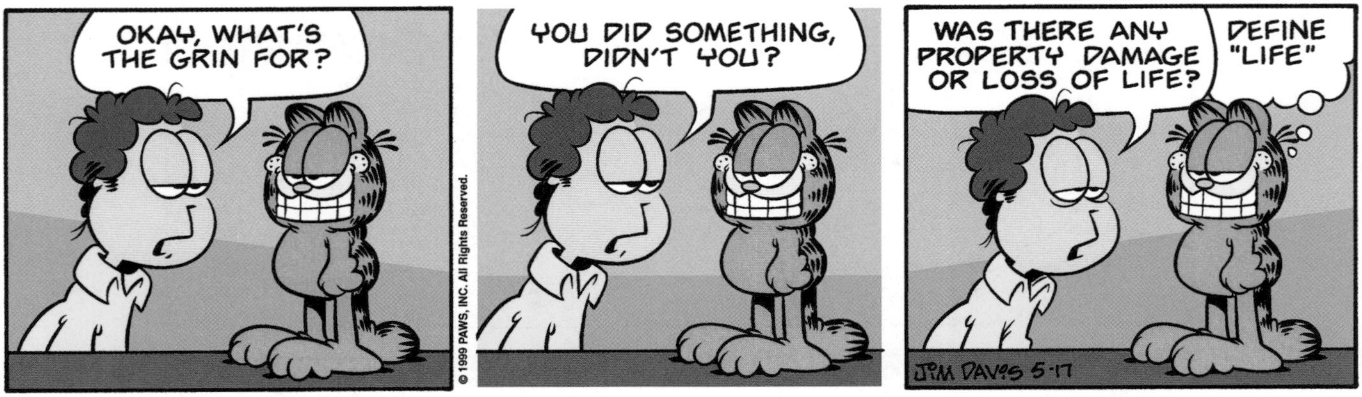
OKAY, WHAT'S THE GRIN FOR?
YOU DID SOMETHING, DIDN'T YOU?
WAS THERE ANY PROPERTY DAMAGE OR LOSS OF LIFE?
DEFINE "LIFE"
JIM DAVIS 5-17
© 1999 PAWS, INC. All Rights Reserved.

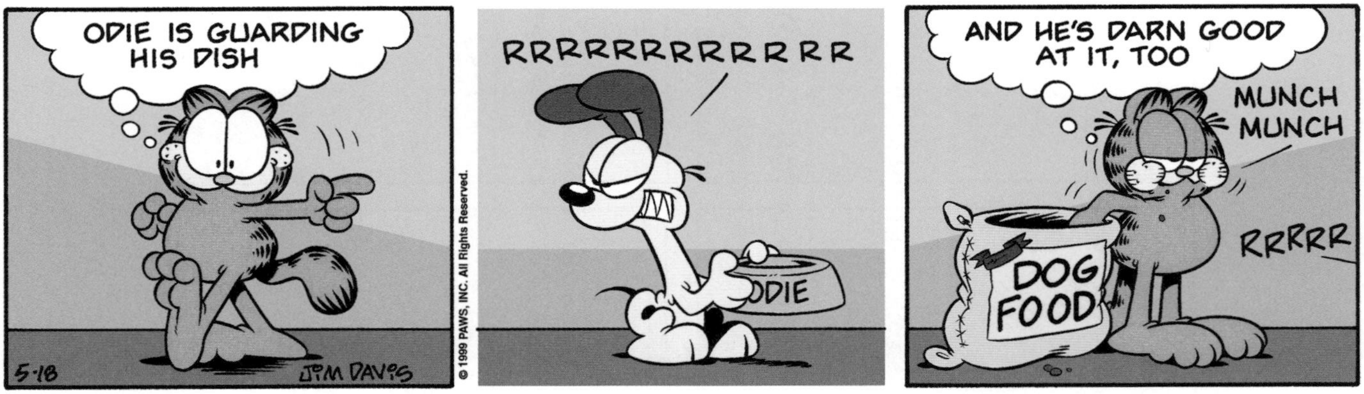
ODIE IS GUARDING HIS DISH
5-18
JIM DAVIS
RRRRRRRRRRRRR
ODIE
AND HE'S DARN GOOD AT IT, TOO
MUNCH MUNCH
DOG FOOD
RRRRR
© 1999 PAWS, INC. All Rights Reserved.

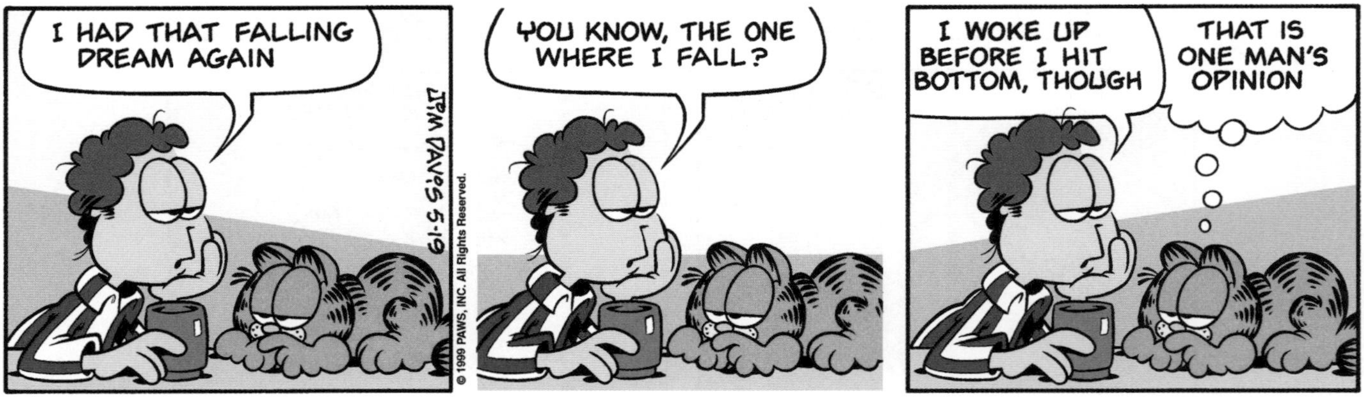
I HAD THAT FALLING DREAM AGAIN
JIM DAVIS 5-19
YOU KNOW, THE ONE WHERE I FALL?
I WOKE UP BEFORE I HIT BOTTOM, THOUGH
THAT IS ONE MAN'S OPINION
© 1999 PAWS, INC. All Rights Reserved.

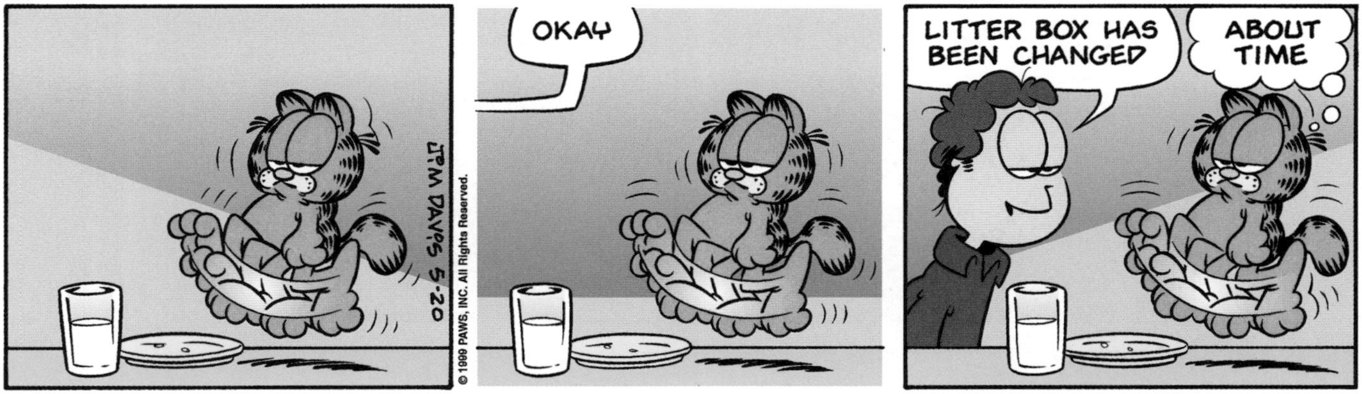
JIM DAVIS 5-20
© 1999 PAWS, INC. All Rights Reserved.
OKAY
LITTER BOX HAS BEEN CHANGED
ABOUT TIME

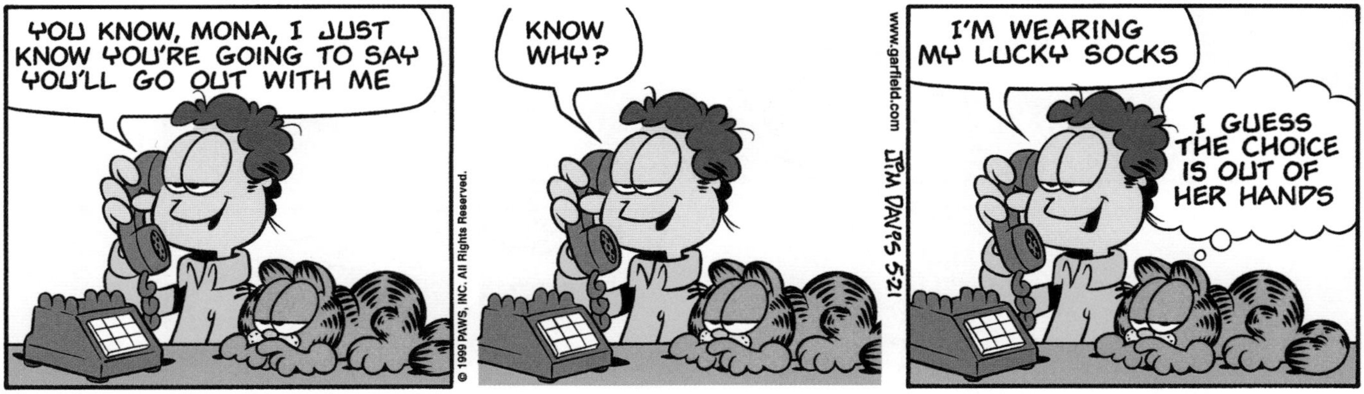
YOU KNOW, MONA, I JUST KNOW YOU'RE GOING TO SAY YOU'LL GO OUT WITH ME
© 1999 PAWS, INC. All Rights Reserved.
KNOW WHY?
www.garfield.com
JIM DAVIS 5-21
I'M WEARING MY LUCKY SOCKS
I GUESS THE CHOICE IS OUT OF HER HANDS

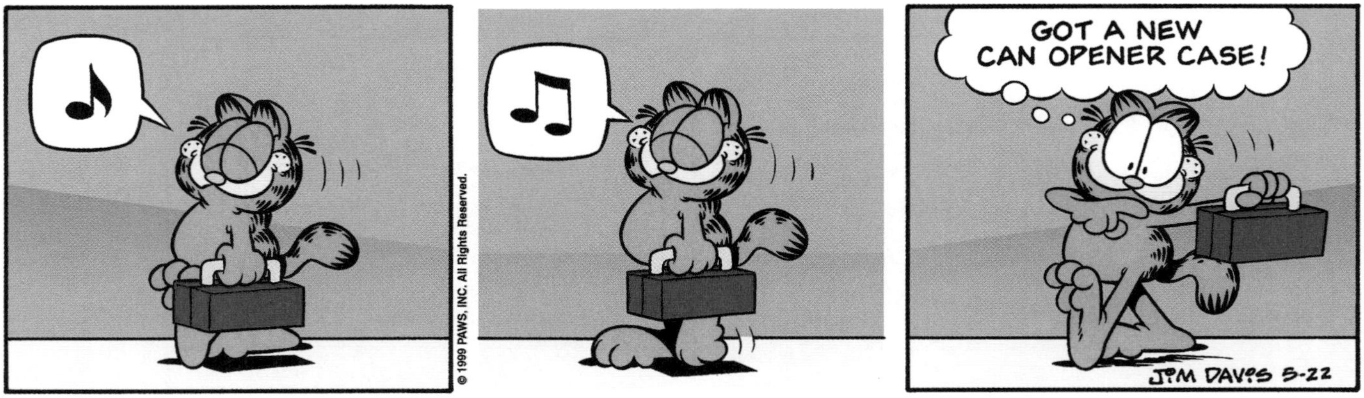
© 1999 PAWS, INC. All Rights Reserved.
GOT A NEW CAN OPENER CASE!
JIM DAVIS 5-22

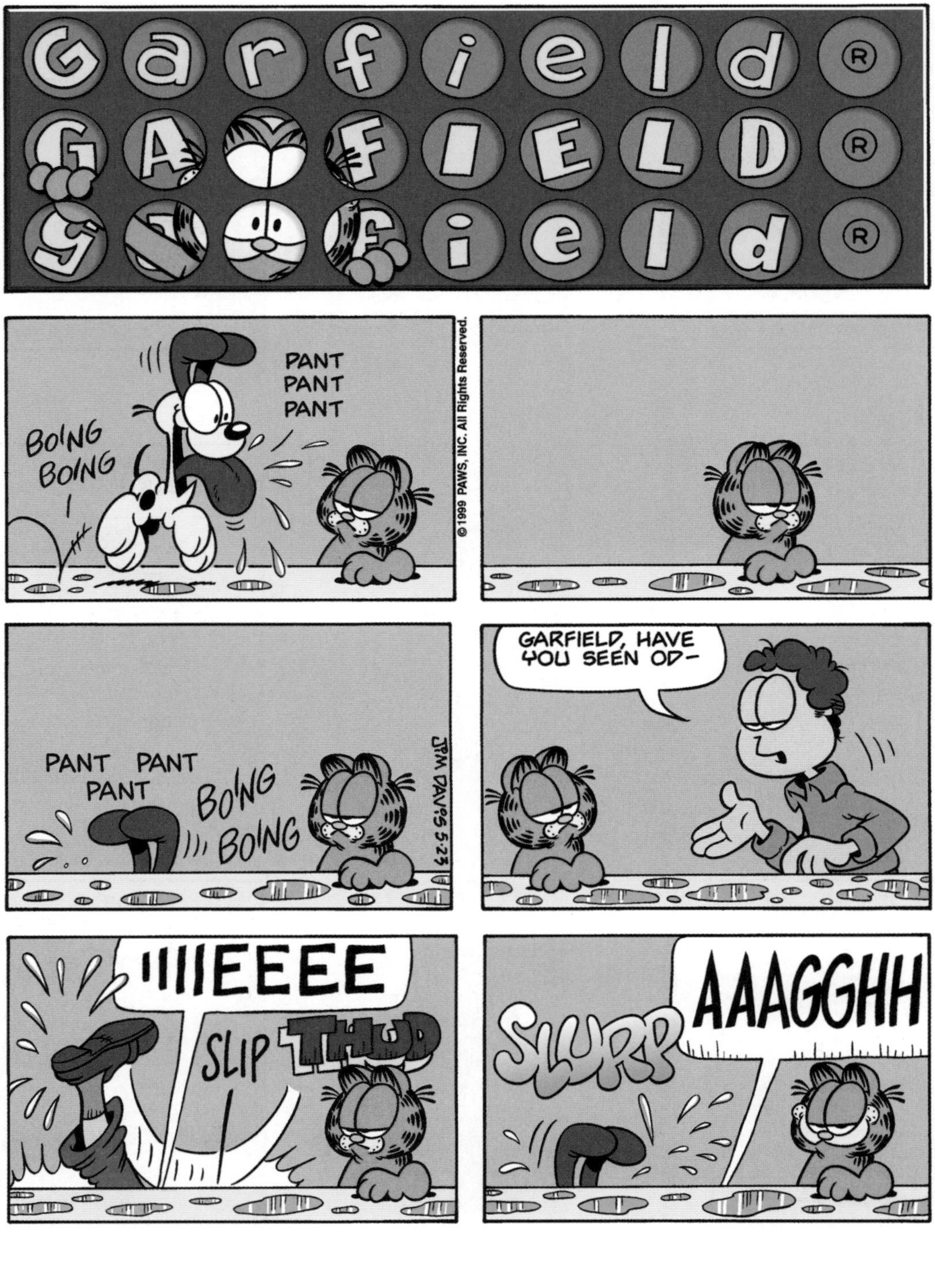

Garfield®
GARFIELD®
garfield®
PANT PANT PANT
BOING BOING
© 1999 PAWS, INC. All Rights Reserved.
PANT PANT PANT
BOING BOING
JPM DAVPS 5-23
GARFIELD, HAVE YOU SEEN OD-
'IIIEEEE
SLIP
THUD
SLURP
AAAGGHH

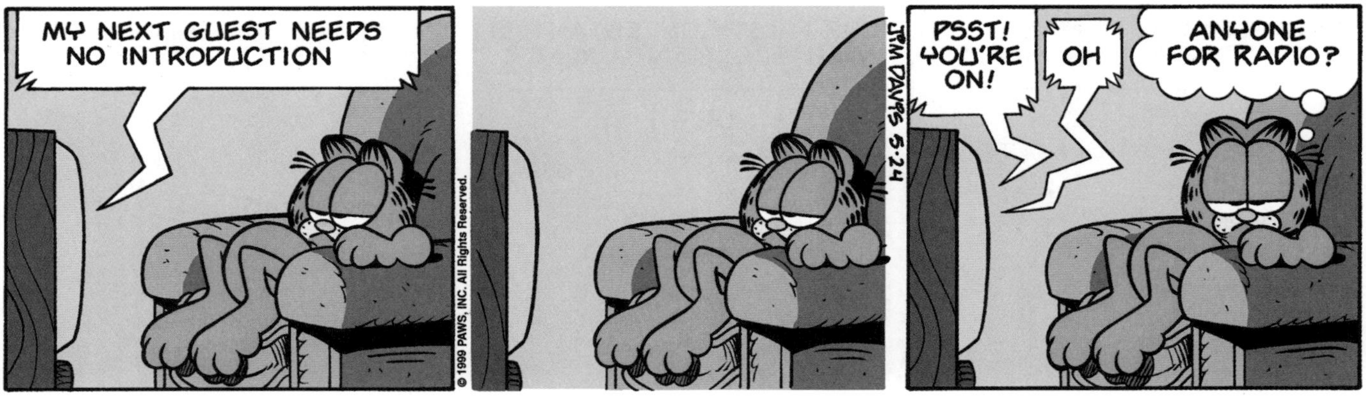
MY NEXT GUEST NEEDS NO INTRODUCTION
© 1999 PAWS, INC. All Rights Reserved.
JIM DAVIS 5-24
PSST! YOU'RE ON!
OH
ANYONE FOR RADIO?

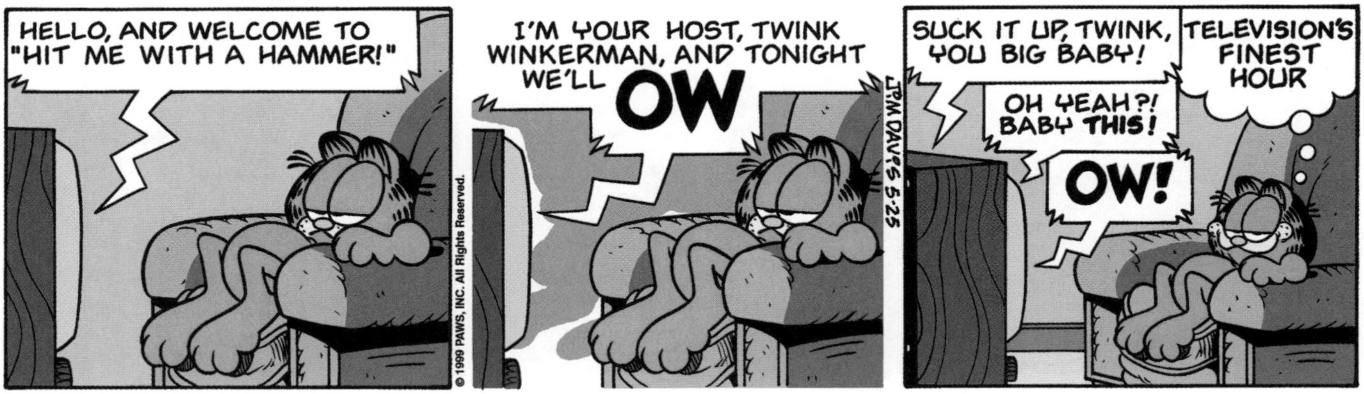
HELLO, AND WELCOME TO "HIT ME WITH A HAMMER!"
© 1999 PAWS, INC. All Rights Reserved.
I'M YOUR HOST, TWINK WINKERMAN, AND TONIGHT WE'LL
OW
JIM DAVIS 5-25
SUCK IT UP, TWINK, YOU BIG BABY!
OH YEAH?! BABY THIS!
OW!
TELEVISION'S FINEST HOUR

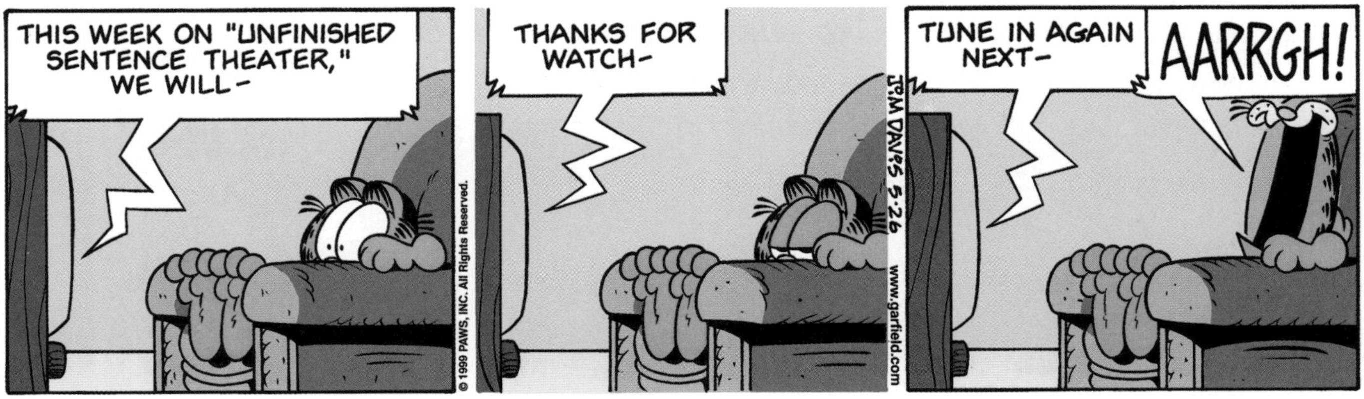
THIS WEEK ON "UNFINISHED SENTENCE THEATER," WE WILL-
© 1999 PAWS, INC. All Rights Reserved.
THANKS FOR WATCH-
JIM DAVIS 5-26
www.garfield.com
TUNE IN AGAIN NEXT-
AARRGH!

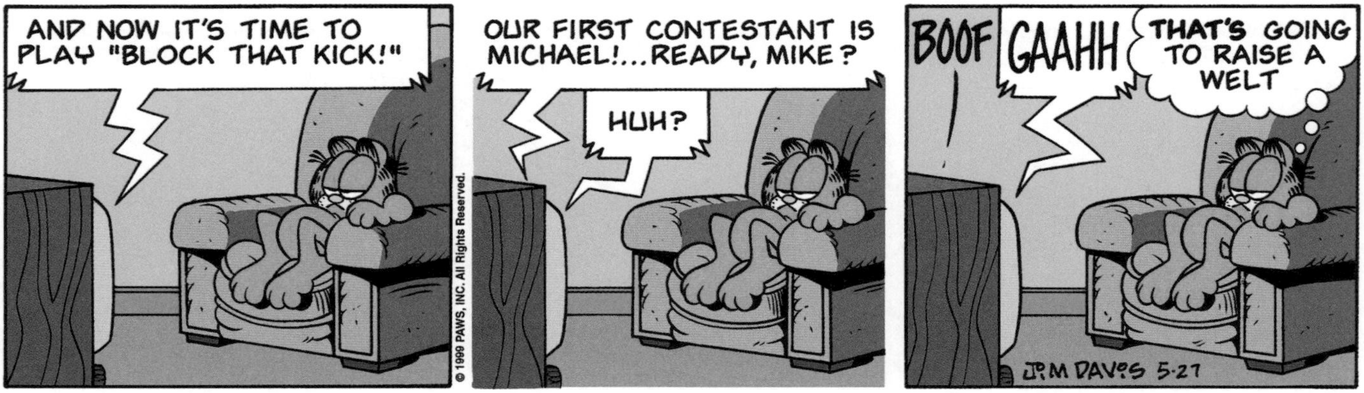
AND NOW IT'S TIME TO PLAY "BLOCK THAT KICK!"
OUR FIRST CONTESTANT IS MICHAEL!...READY, MIKE?
HUH?
BOOF
GAAHH
THAT'S GOING TO RAISE A WELT
© 1999 PAWS, INC. All Rights Reserved.
JIM DAVIS 5-27

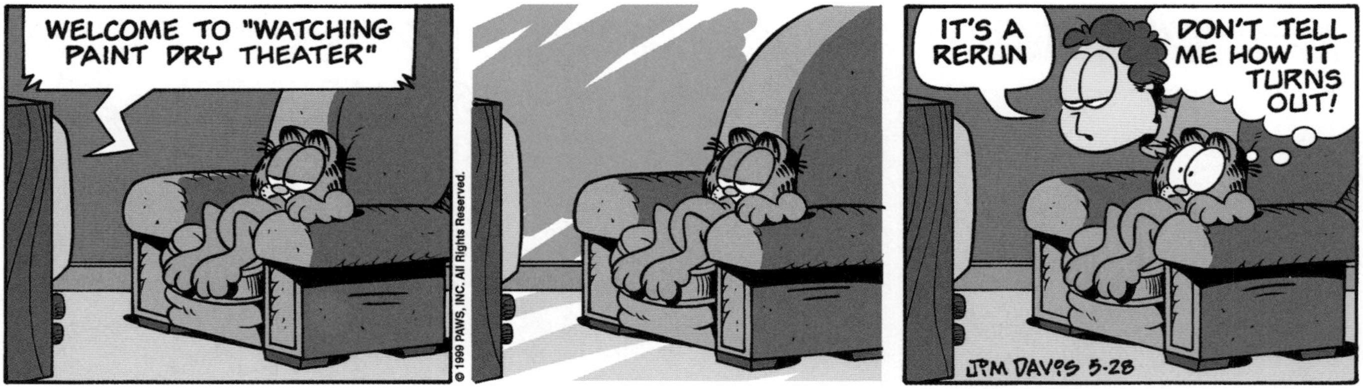
WELCOME TO "WATCHING PAINT DRY THEATER"
IT'S A RERUN
DON'T TELL ME HOW IT TURNS OUT!
© 1999 PAWS, INC. All Rights Reserved.
JIM DAVIS 5-28

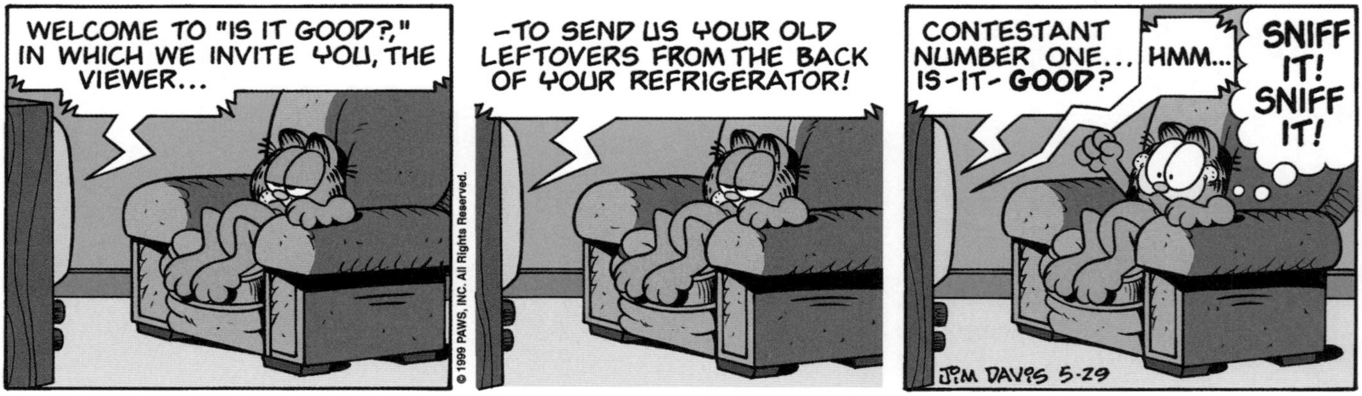
WELCOME TO "IS IT GOOD?," IN WHICH WE INVITE YOU, THE VIEWER...
-TO SEND US YOUR OLD LEFTOVERS FROM THE BACK OF YOUR REFRIGERATOR!
CONTESTANT NUMBER ONE... IS-IT-**GOOD**?
HMM...
SNIFF IT! SNIFF IT!
© 1999 PAWS, INC. All Rights Reserved.
JIM DAVIS 5-29

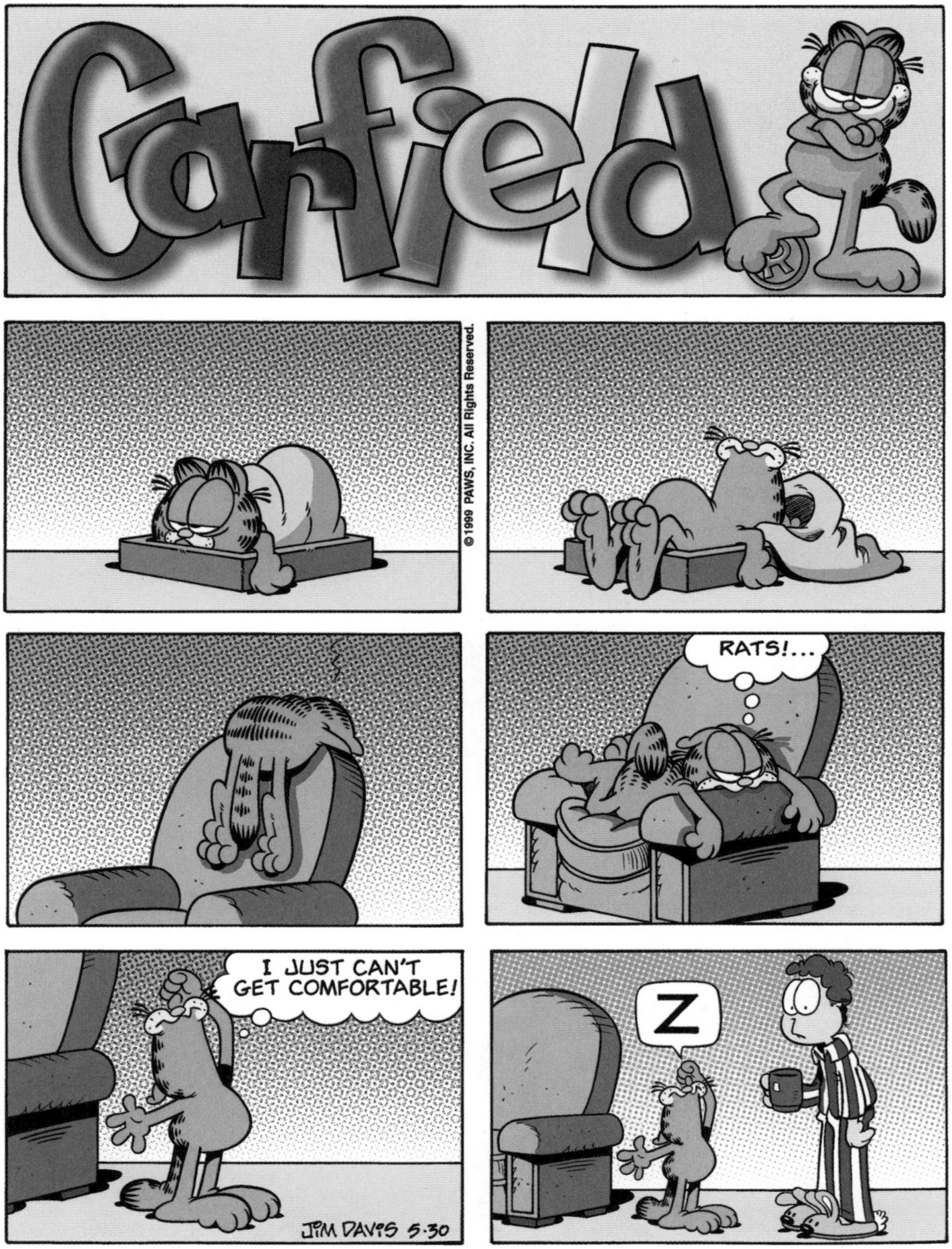
Garfield
©1999 PAWS, INC. All Rights Reserved.
RATS!...
I JUST CAN'T GET COMFORTABLE!
JIM DAVIS 5-30
Z

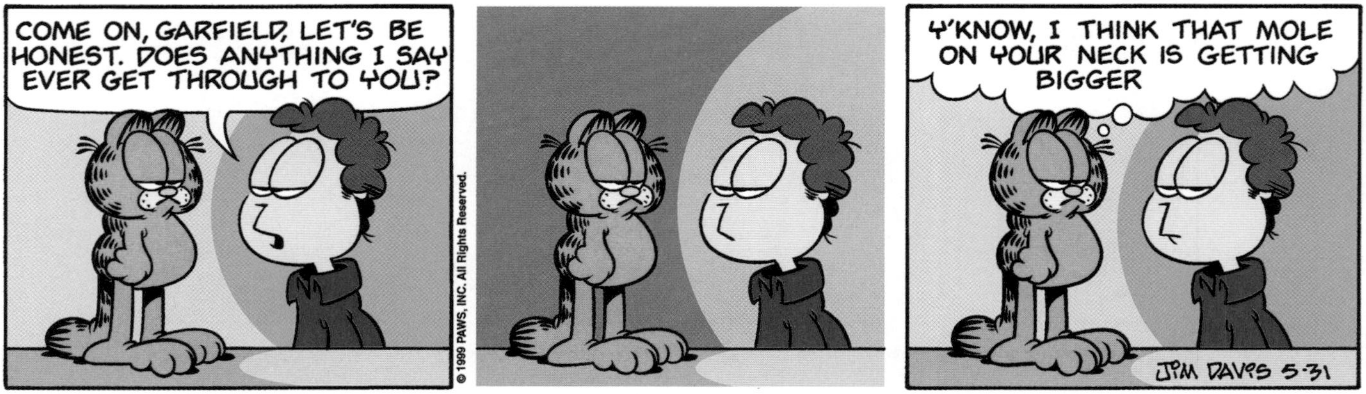
COME ON, GARFIELD, LET'S BE HONEST. DOES ANYTHING I SAY EVER GET THROUGH TO YOU?
© 1999 PAWS, INC. All Rights Reserved.
Y'KNOW, I THINK THAT MOLE ON YOUR NECK IS GETTING BIGGER
JIM DAVIS 5-31

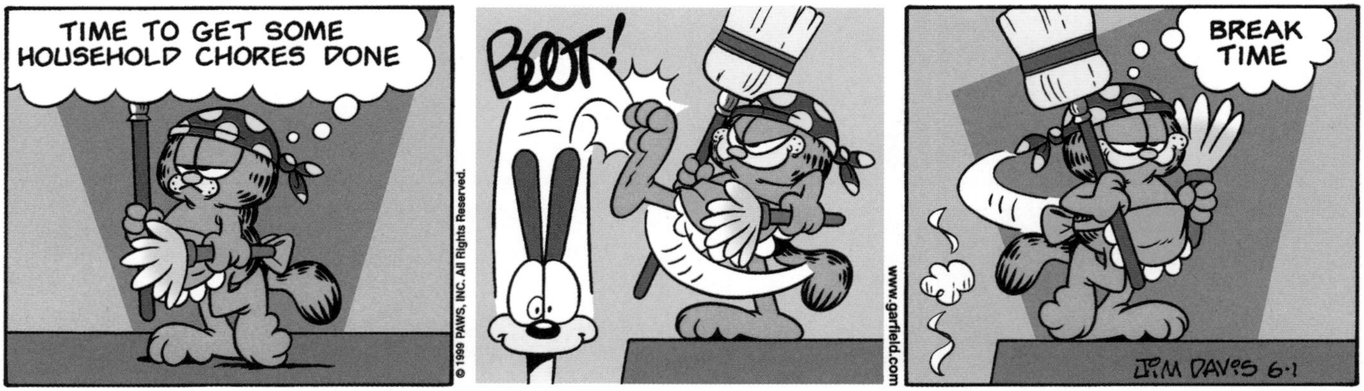
TIME TO GET SOME HOUSEHOLD CHORES DONE
© 1999 PAWS, INC. All Rights Reserved.
BOOT!
www.garfield.com
BREAK TIME
JIM DAVIS 6-1

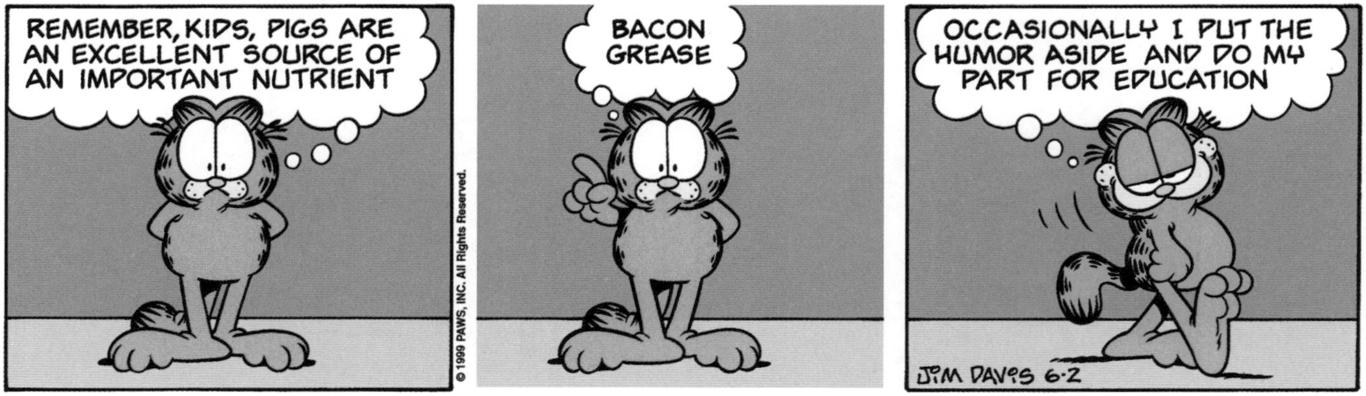
REMEMBER, KIDS, PIGS ARE AN EXCELLENT SOURCE OF AN IMPORTANT NUTRIENT
© 1999 PAWS, INC. All Rights Reserved.
BACON GREASE
OCCASIONALLY I PUT THE HUMOR ASIDE AND DO MY PART FOR EDUCATION
JIM DAVIS 6-2

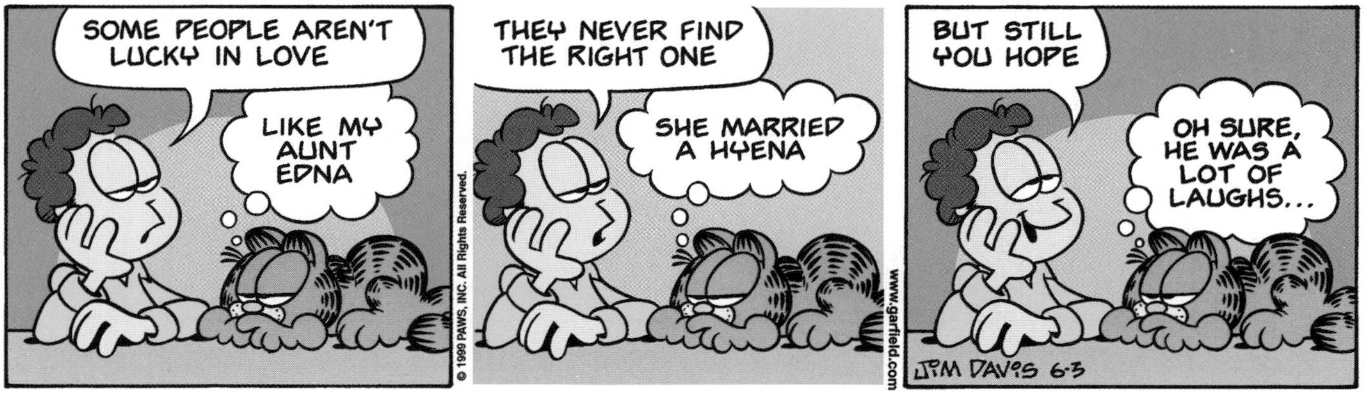
SOME PEOPLE AREN'T LUCKY IN LOVE
LIKE MY AUNT EDNA
THEY NEVER FIND THE RIGHT ONE
SHE MARRIED A HYENA
BUT STILL YOU HOPE
OH SURE, HE WAS A LOT OF LAUGHS...
© 1999 PAWS, INC. All Rights Reserved.
www.garfield.com
JIM DAVIS 6-3

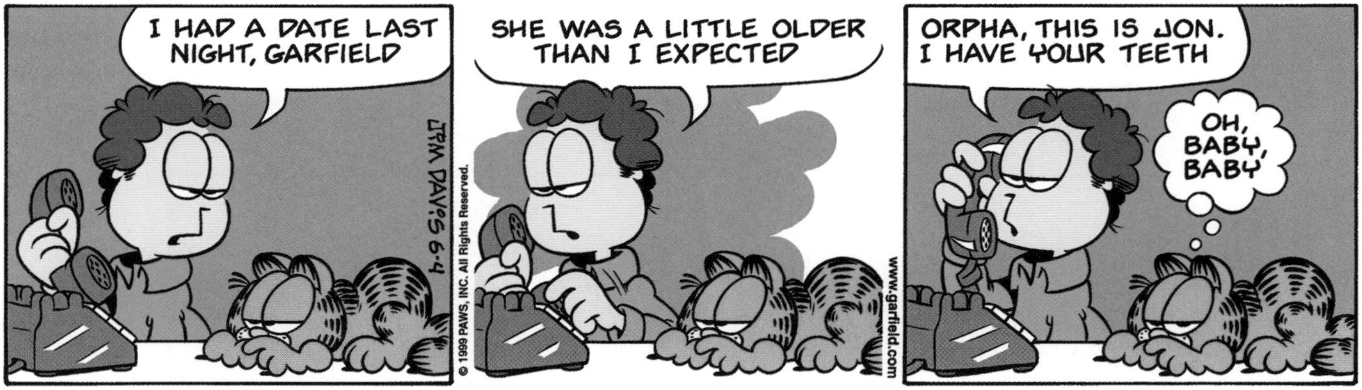
I HAD A DATE LAST NIGHT, GARFIELD
JIM DAVIS 6-4
SHE WAS A LITTLE OLDER THAN I EXPECTED
© 1999 PAWS, INC. All Rights Reserved.
ORPHA, THIS IS JON. I HAVE YOUR TEETH
OH, BABY, BABY
www.garfield.com

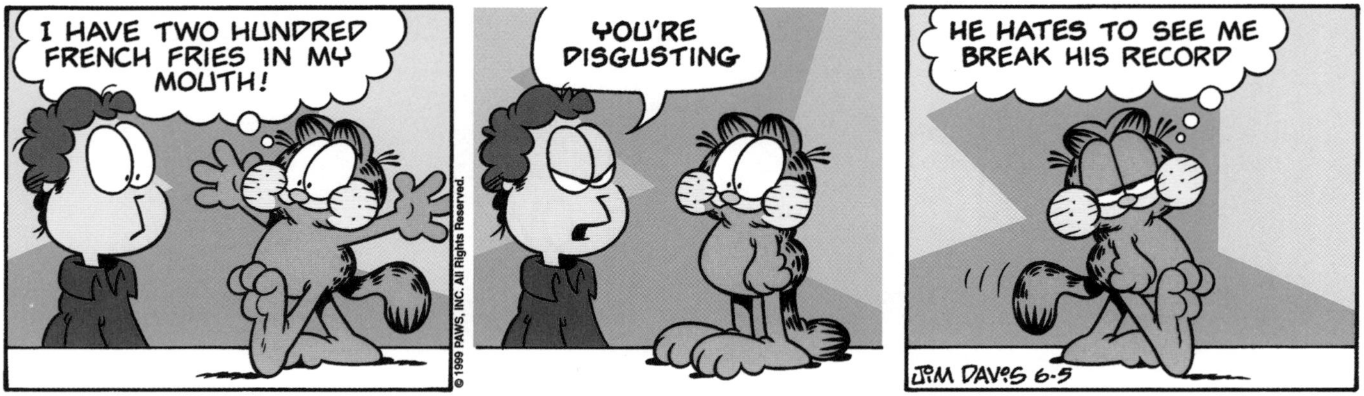
I HAVE TWO HUNDRED FRENCH FRIES IN MY MOUTH!
© 1999 PAWS, INC. All Rights Reserved.
YOU'RE DISGUSTING
HE HATES TO SEE ME BREAK HIS RECORD
JIM DAVIS 6-5

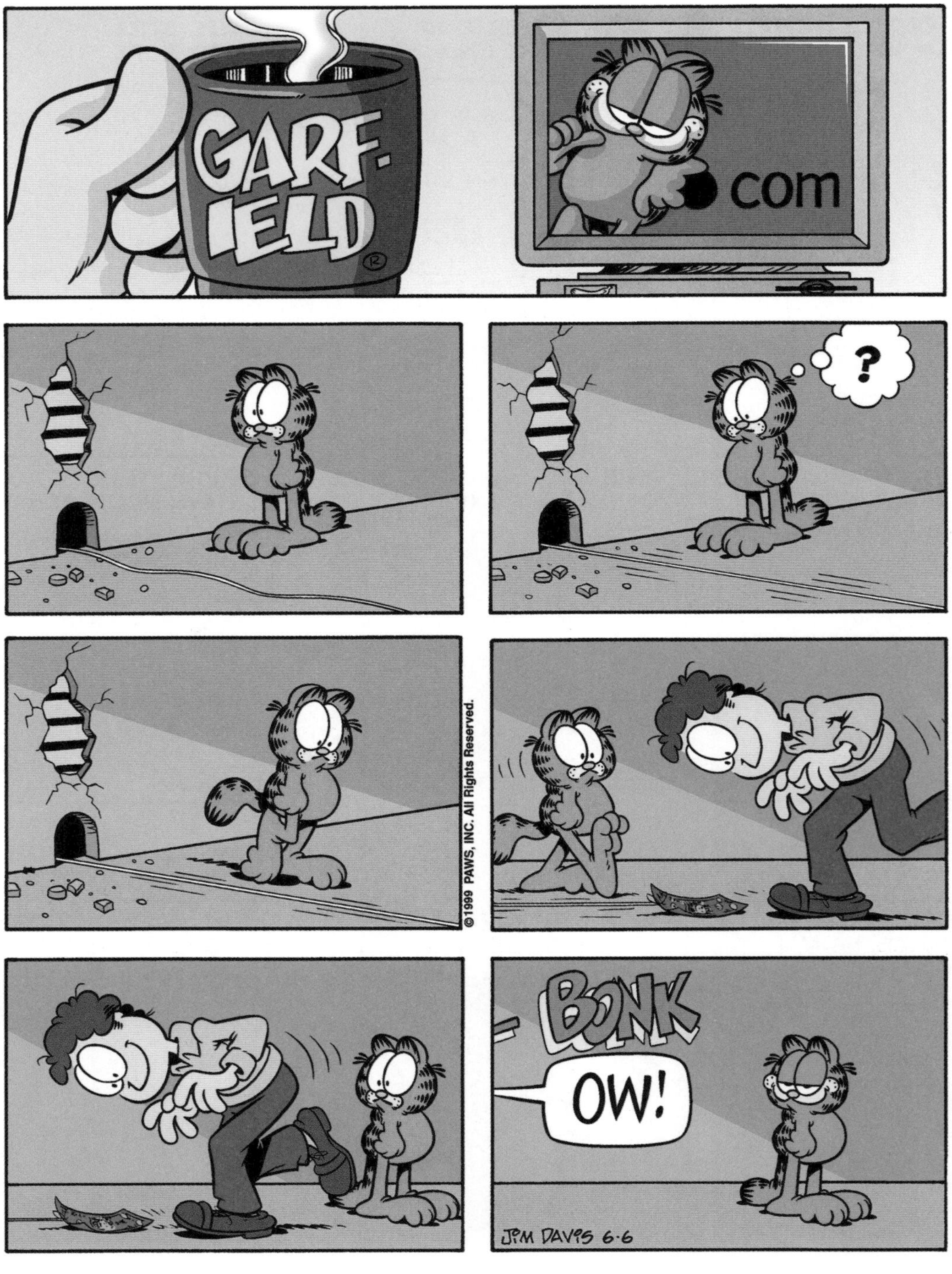
GARF.
IELD
● com
?
BONK
OW!
JIM DAVIS 6-6

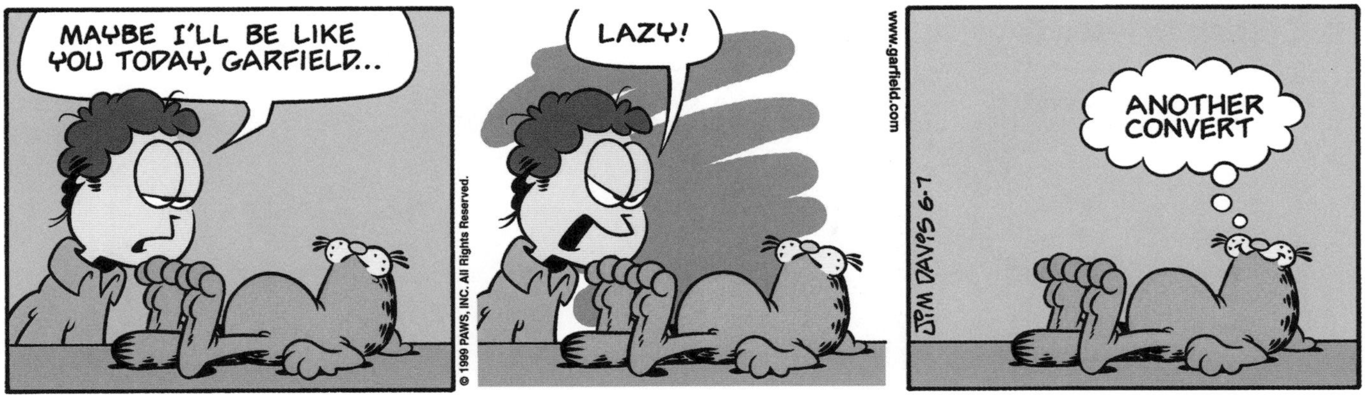
MAYBE I'LL BE LIKE YOU TODAY, GARFIELD...
LAZY!
ANOTHER CONVERT
© 1999 PAWS, INC. All Rights Reserved.
www.garfield.com
JIM DAVIS 6-7

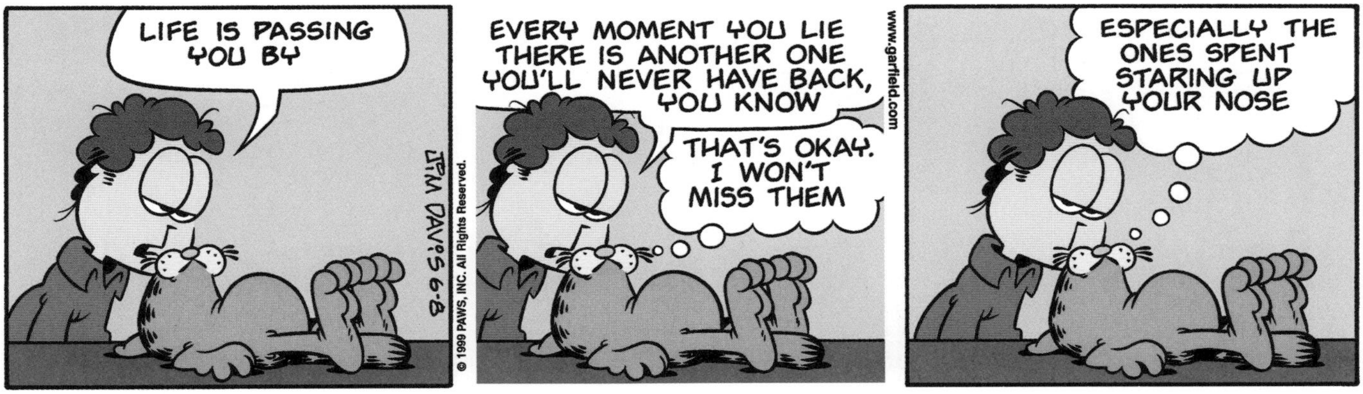
LIFE IS PASSING YOU BY
EVERY MOMENT YOU LIE THERE IS ANOTHER ONE YOU'LL NEVER HAVE BACK, YOU KNOW
THAT'S OKAY. I WON'T MISS THEM
ESPECIALLY THE ONES SPENT STARING UP YOUR NOSE
JIM DAVIS 6-8
© 1999 PAWS, INC. All Rights Reserved.
www.garfield.com

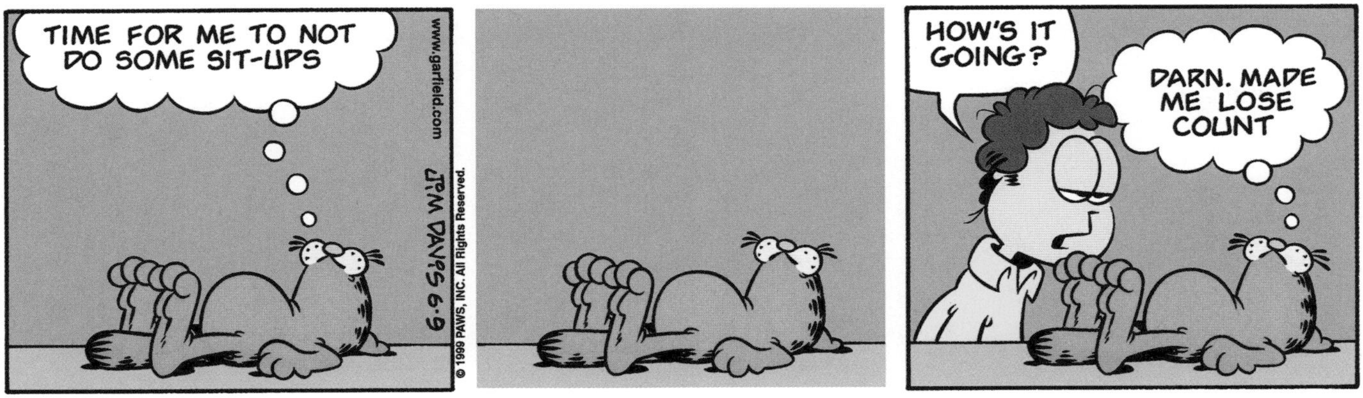
TIME FOR ME TO NOT DO SOME SIT-UPS
HOW'S IT GOING?
DARN. MADE ME LOSE COUNT
www.garfield.com
JIM DAVIS 6-9
© 1999 PAWS, INC. All Rights Reserved.

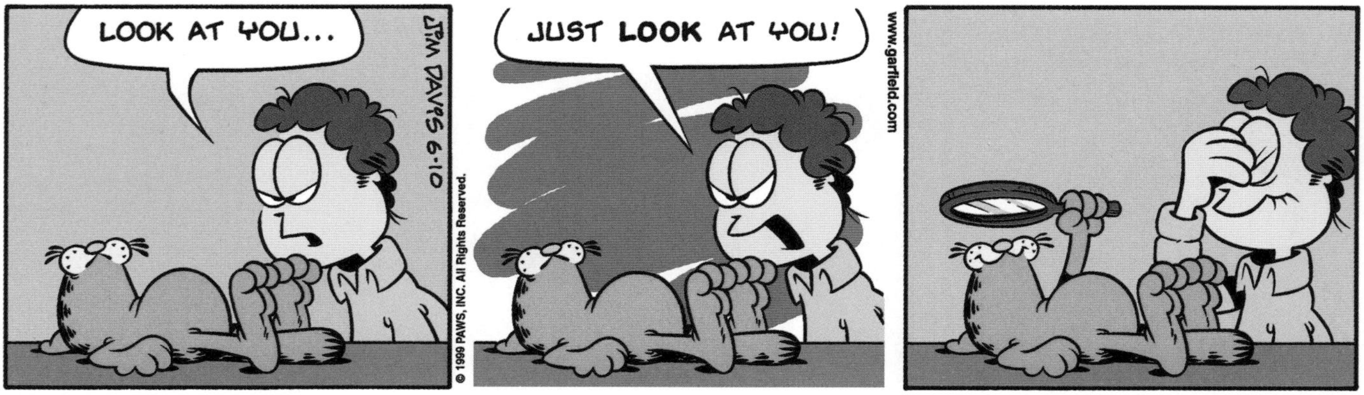
LOOK AT YOU...
JIM DAVIS 6-10
© 1999 PAWS, INC. All Rights Reserved.
JUST LOOK AT YOU!
www.garfield.com

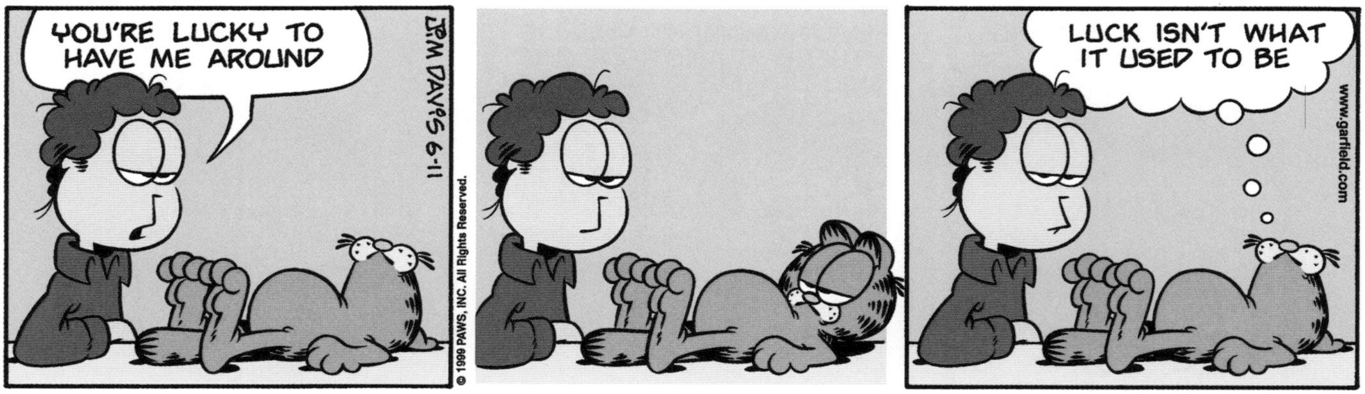
YOU'RE LUCKY TO HAVE ME AROUND
JIM DAVIS 6-11
© 1999 PAWS, INC. All Rights Reserved.
LUCK ISN'T WHAT IT USED TO BE
www.garfield.com

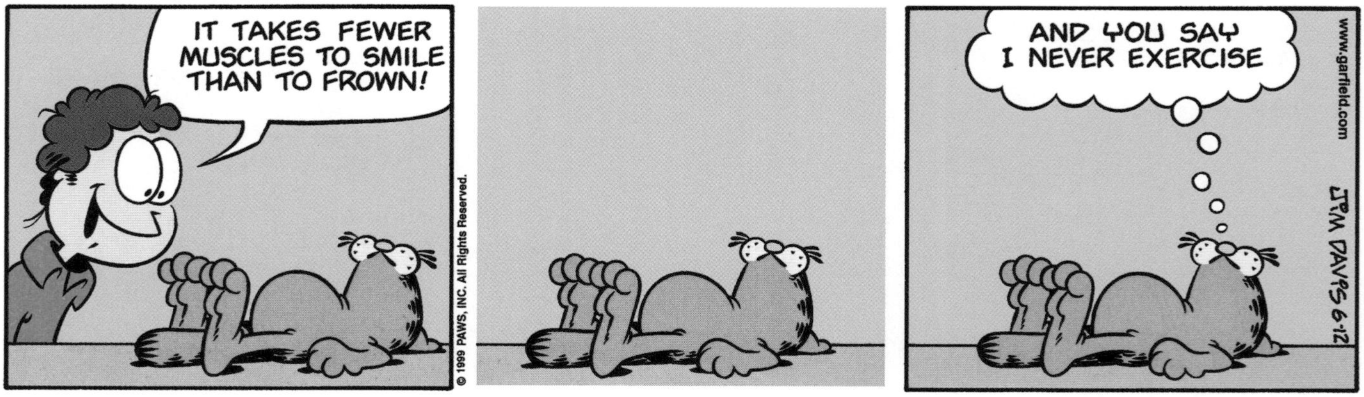
IT TAKES FEWER MUSCLES TO SMILE THAN TO FROWN!
© 1999 PAWS, INC. All Rights Reserved.
AND YOU SAY I NEVER EXERCISE
www.garfield.com
JIM DAVIS 6-12

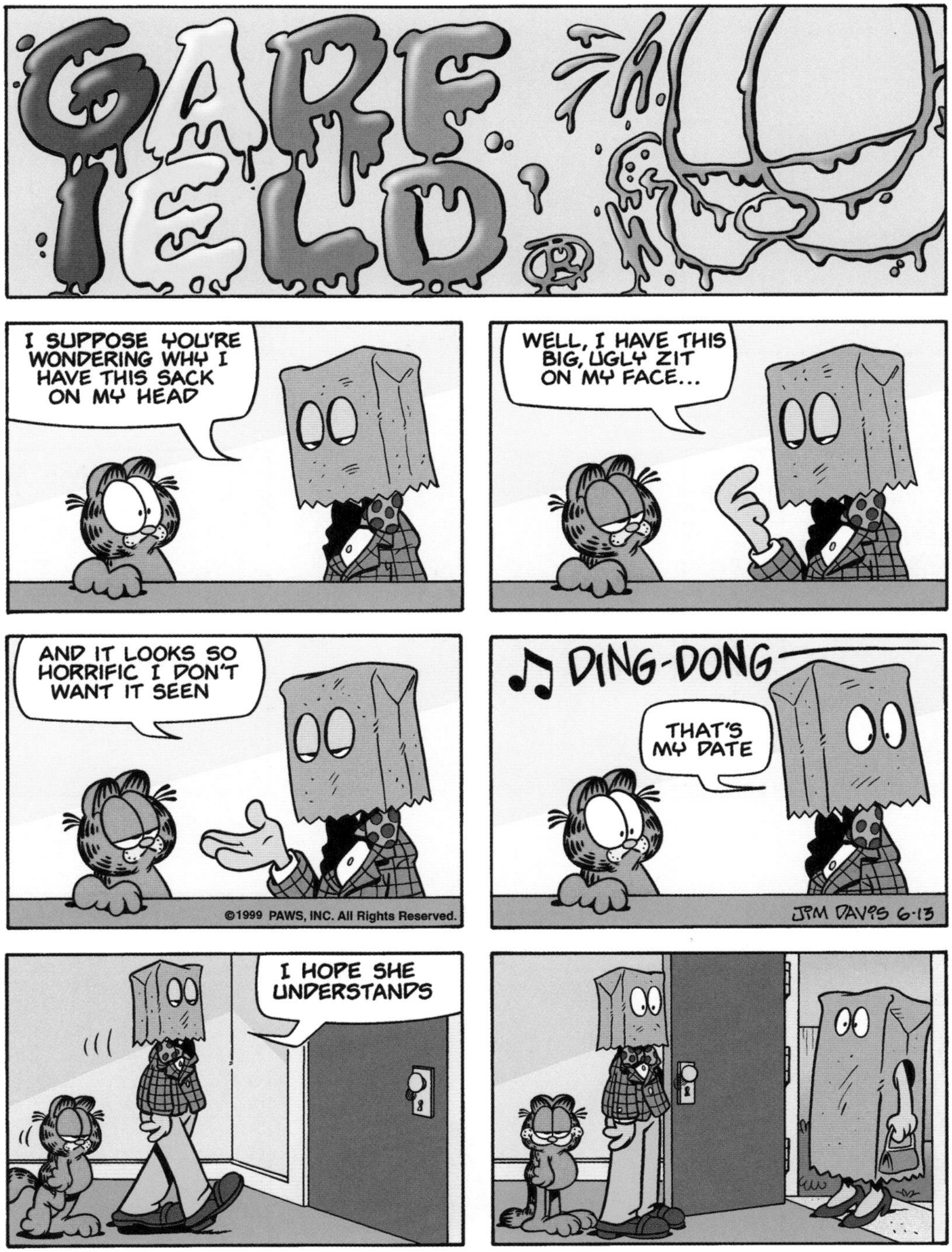
GARFIELD®
I SUPPOSE YOU'RE WONDERING WHY I HAVE THIS SACK ON MY HEAD
WELL, I HAVE THIS BIG, UGLY ZIT ON MY FACE...
AND IT LOOKS SO HORRIFIC I DON'T WANT IT SEEN
©1999 PAWS, INC. All Rights Reserved.
♫ DING-DONG
THAT'S MY DATE
JIM DAVIS 6-13
I HOPE SHE UNDERSTANDS

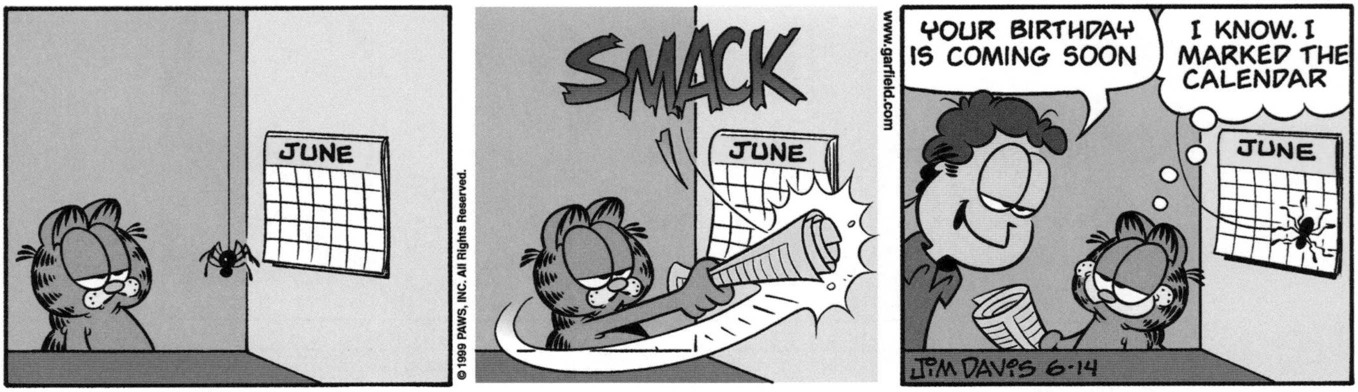
JUNE
SMACK
JUNE
© 1999 PAWS, INC. All Rights Reserved.
www.garfield.com
YOUR BIRTHDAY IS COMING SOON
I KNOW. I MARKED THE CALENDAR
JUNE
JIM DAVIS 6-14

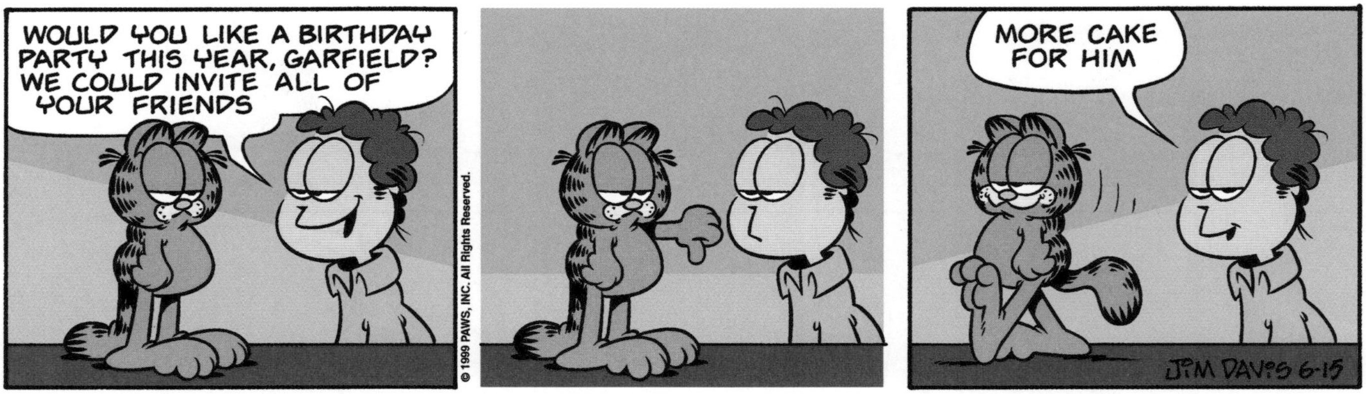
WOULD YOU LIKE A BIRTHDAY PARTY THIS YEAR, GARFIELD? WE COULD INVITE ALL OF YOUR FRIENDS
© 1999 PAWS, INC. All Rights Reserved.
MORE CAKE FOR HIM
JIM DAVIS 6-15

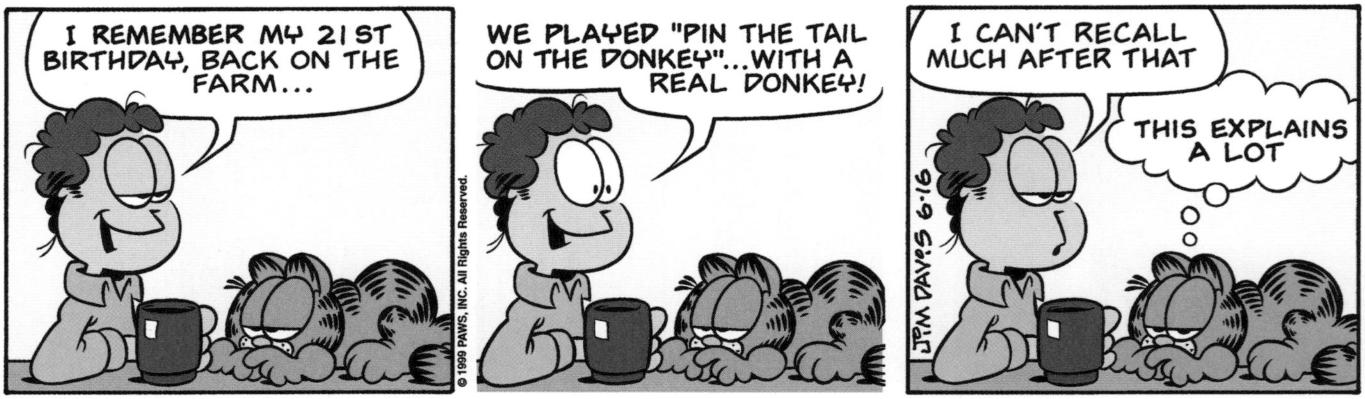
I REMEMBER MY 21ST BIRTHDAY, BACK ON THE FARM...
© 1999 PAWS, INC. All Rights Reserved.
WE PLAYED "PIN THE TAIL ON THE DONKEY"...WITH A REAL DONKEY!
JIM DAVIS 6-16
I CAN'T RECALL MUCH AFTER THAT
THIS EXPLAINS A LOT

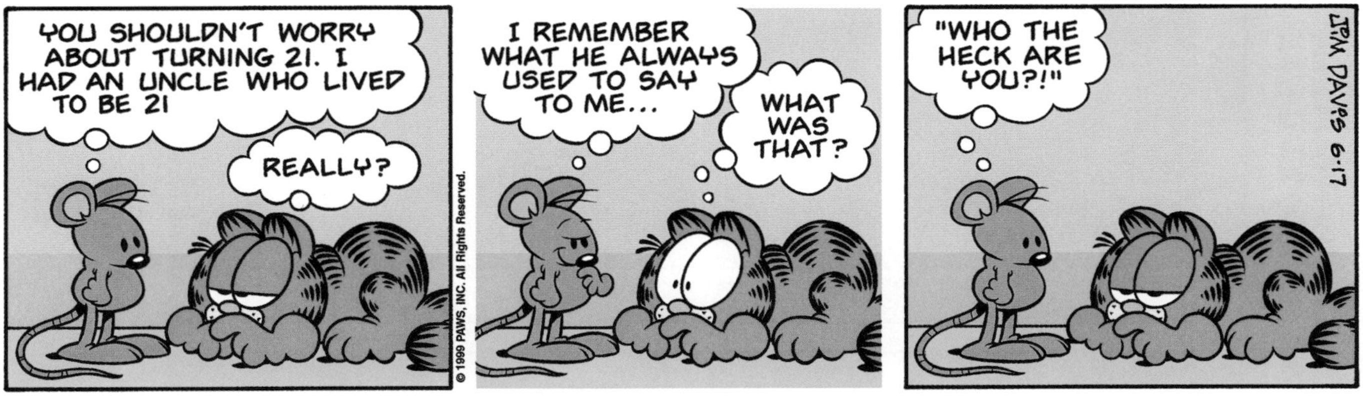
YOU SHOULDN'T WORRY ABOUT TURNING 21. I HAD AN UNCLE WHO LIVED TO BE 21
REALLY?
I REMEMBER WHAT HE ALWAYS USED TO SAY TO ME...
WHAT WAS THAT?
"WHO THE HECK ARE YOU?!"
JIM DAVIS 6-17

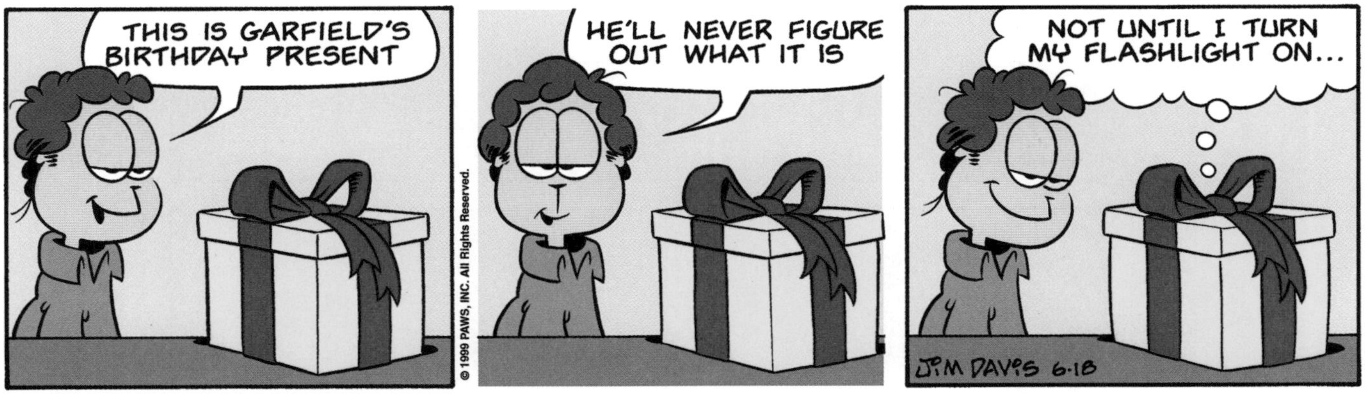
THIS IS GARFIELD'S BIRTHDAY PRESENT
HE'LL NEVER FIGURE OUT WHAT IT IS
NOT UNTIL I TURN MY FLASHLIGHT ON...
JIM DAVIS 6-18

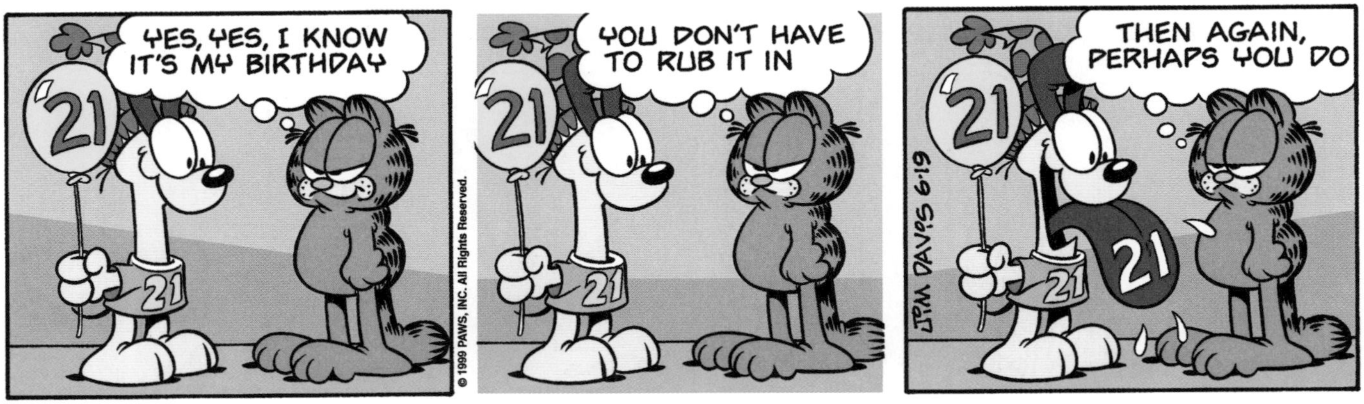
YES, YES, I KNOW IT'S MY BIRTHDAY
YOU DON'T HAVE TO RUB IT IN
THEN AGAIN, PERHAPS YOU DO
JIM DAVIS 6-19

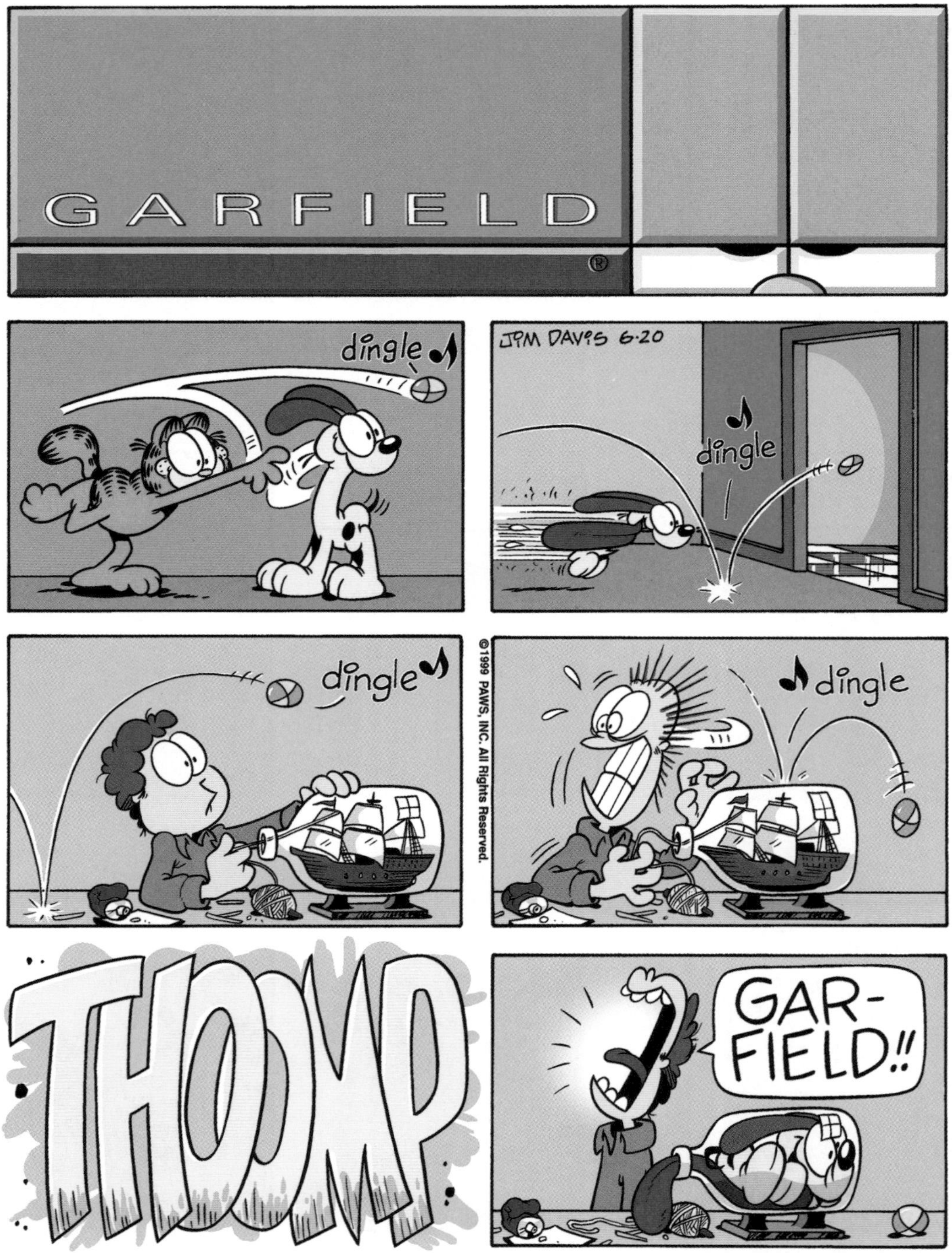
GARFIELD
dingle
JIM DAVIS 6-20
dingle
dingle
©1999 PAWS, INC. All Rights Reserved.
dingle
THOMP
GAR-
FIELD!!

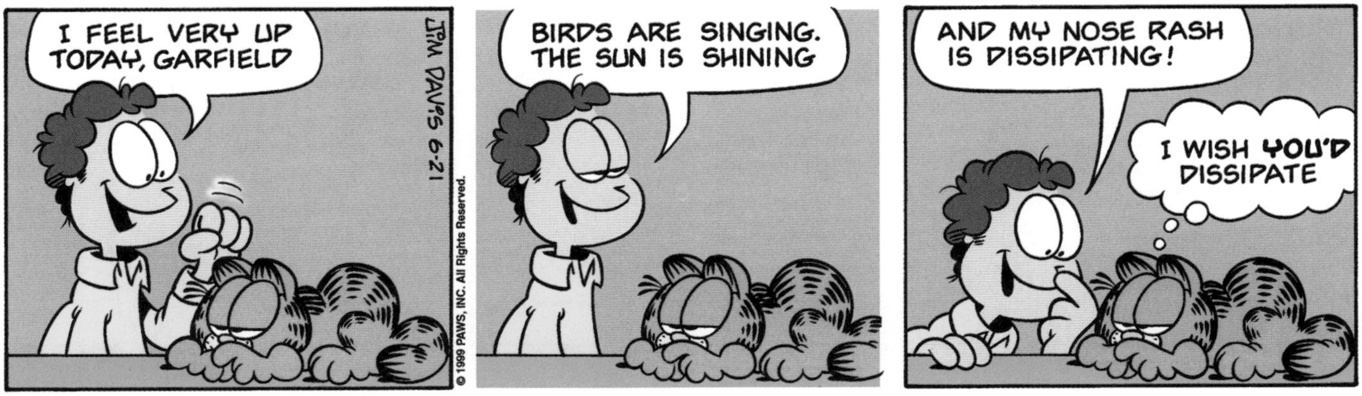
I FEEL VERY UP TODAY, GARFIELD
JIM DAVIS 6-21
© 1999 PAWS, INC. All Rights Reserved.
BIRDS ARE SINGING. THE SUN IS SHINING
AND MY NOSE RASH IS DISSIPATING!
I WISH **YOU'D** DISSIPATE

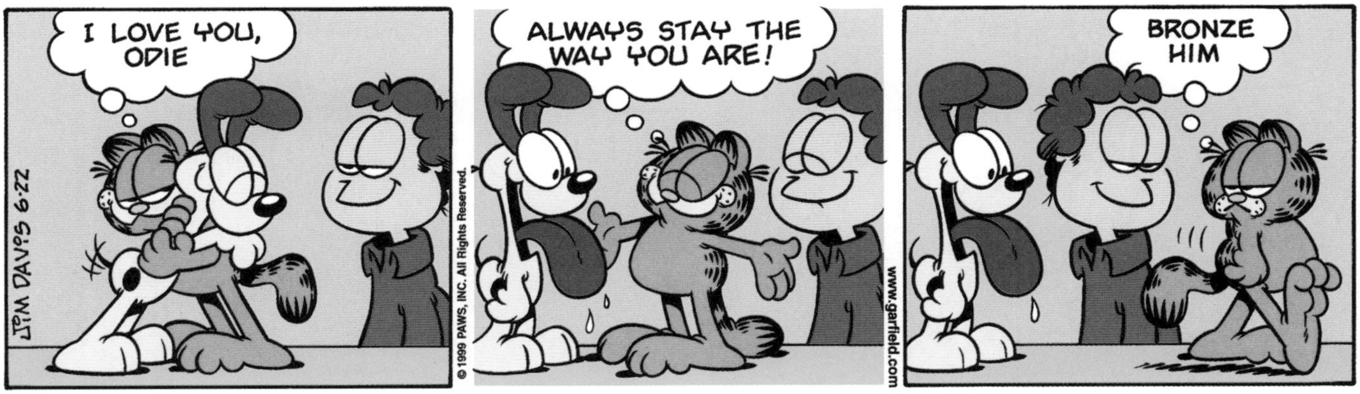
I LOVE YOU, ODIE
JIM DAVIS 6-22
© 1999 PAWS, INC. All Rights Reserved.
ALWAYS STAY THE WAY YOU ARE!
www.garfield.com
BRONZE HIM

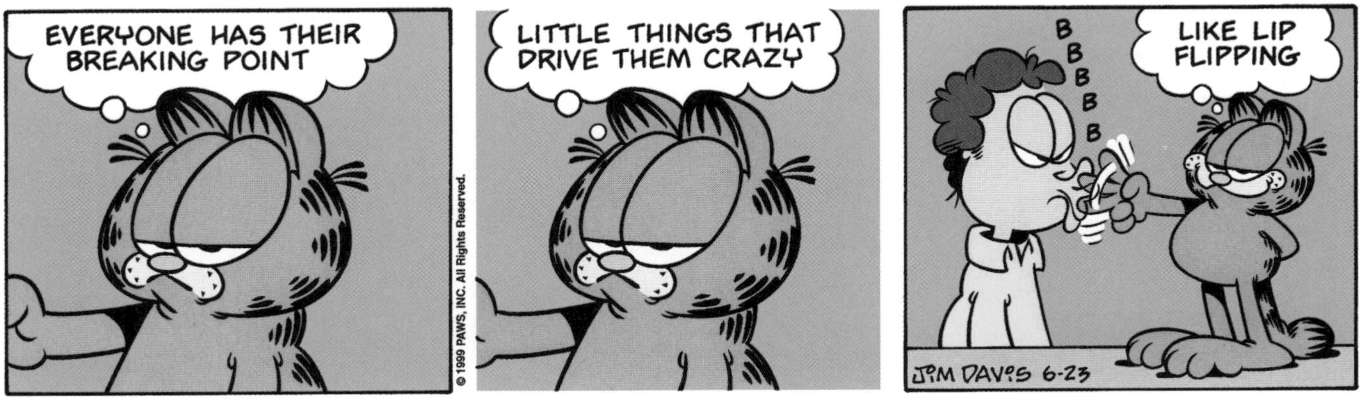
EVERYONE HAS THEIR BREAKING POINT
© 1999 PAWS, INC. All Rights Reserved.
LITTLE THINGS THAT DRIVE THEM CRAZY
B B B B B
LIKE LIP FLIPPING
JIM DAVIS 6-23

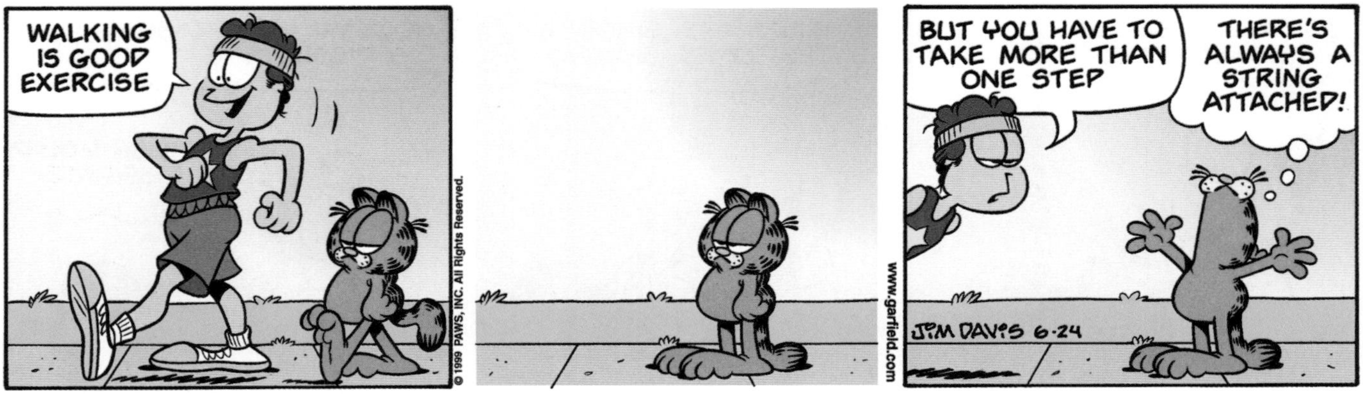
WALKING IS GOOD EXERCISE
© 1999 PAWS, INC. All Rights Reserved.
www.garfield.com
BUT YOU HAVE TO TAKE MORE THAN ONE STEP
THERE'S ALWAYS A STRING ATTACHED!
JIM DAVIS 6-24

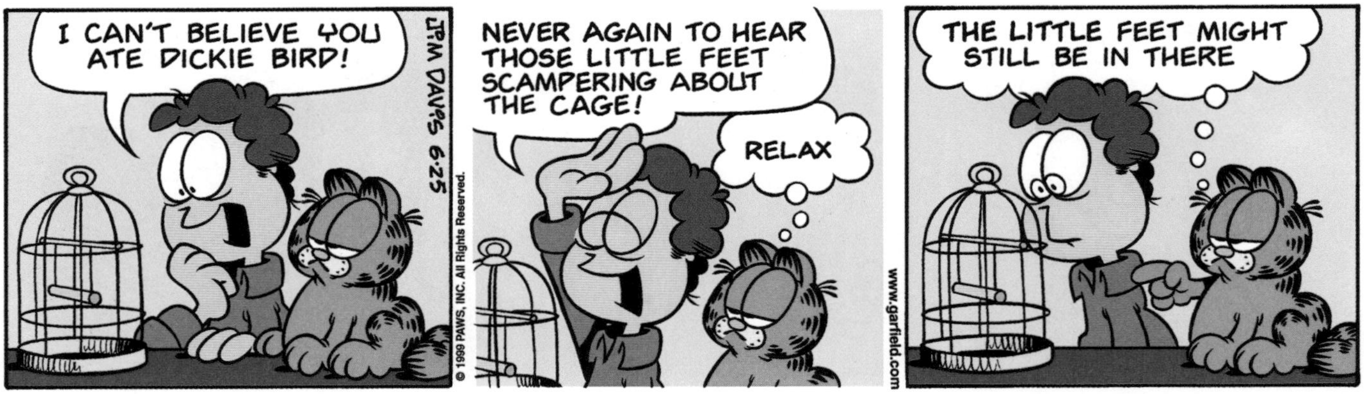
I CAN'T BELIEVE YOU ATE DICKIE BIRD!
JIM DAVIS 6-25
© 1999 PAWS, INC. All Rights Reserved.
NEVER AGAIN TO HEAR THOSE LITTLE FEET SCAMPERING ABOUT THE CAGE!
RELAX
www.garfield.com
THE LITTLE FEET MIGHT STILL BE IN THERE

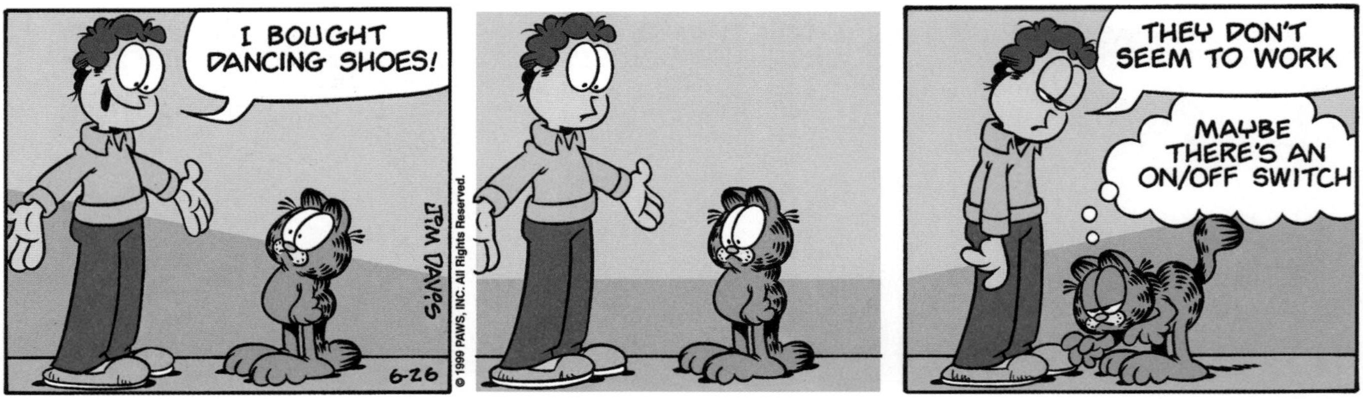
I BOUGHT DANCING SHOES!
JIM DAVIS 6-26
© 1999 PAWS, INC. All Rights Reserved.
THEY DON'T SEEM TO WORK
MAYBE THERE'S AN ON/OFF SWITCH

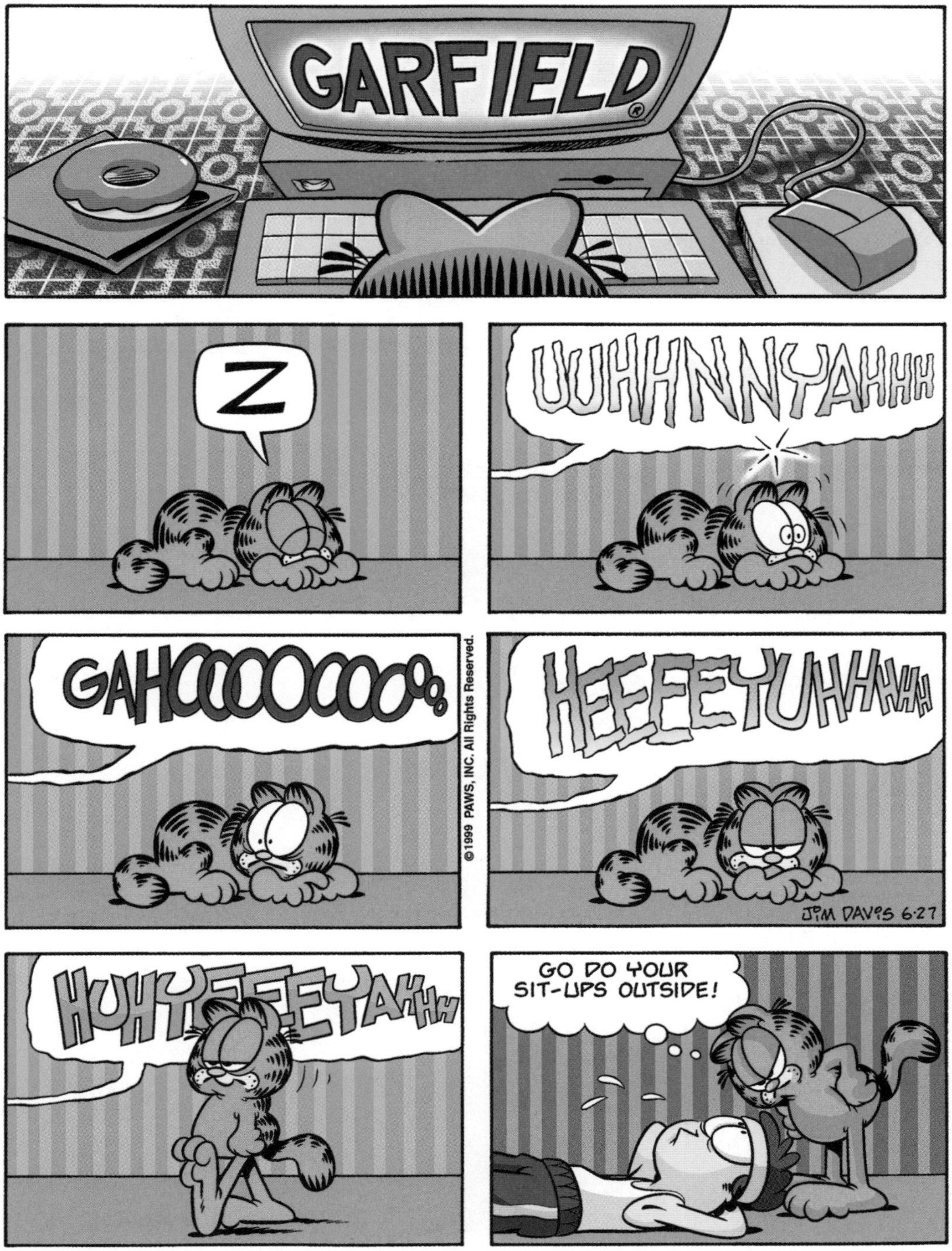
GARFIELD
Z
UUHHNNYAHHH
GAHOOOOOOOO
HEEEEEYUHHHHH
©1999 PAWS, INC. All Rights Reserved.
JIM DAVIS 6·27
HUHYEEEEYAHHH
GO DO YOUR SIT-UPS OUTSIDE!

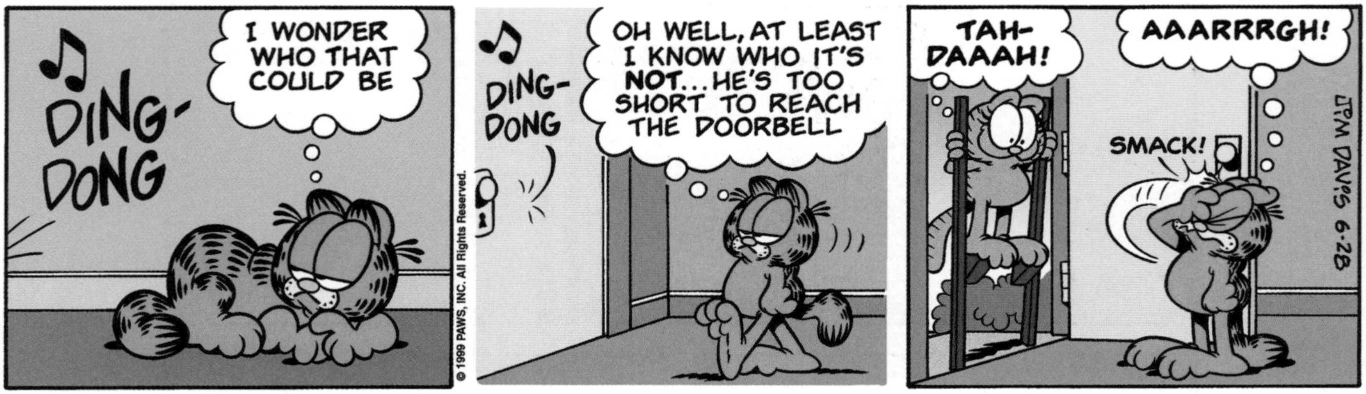
DING-DONG
I WONDER WHO THAT COULD BE
© 1999 PAWS, INC. All Rights Reserved.
DING-DONG
OH WELL, AT LEAST I KNOW WHO IT'S **NOT**... HE'S TOO SHORT TO REACH THE DOORBELL
TAH-DAAAH!
AAARRRGH!
SMACK!
JPM DAVIS 6-28

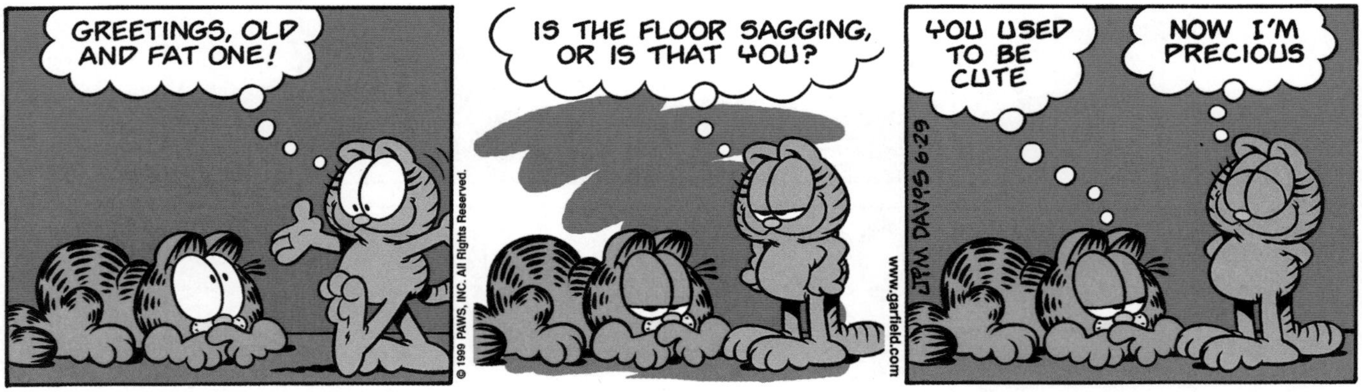
GREETINGS, OLD AND FAT ONE!
© 1999 PAWS, INC. All Rights Reserved.
IS THE FLOOR SAGGING, OR IS THAT YOU?
www.garfield.com
YOU USED TO BE CUTE
NOW I'M PRECIOUS
JPM DAVIS 6-29

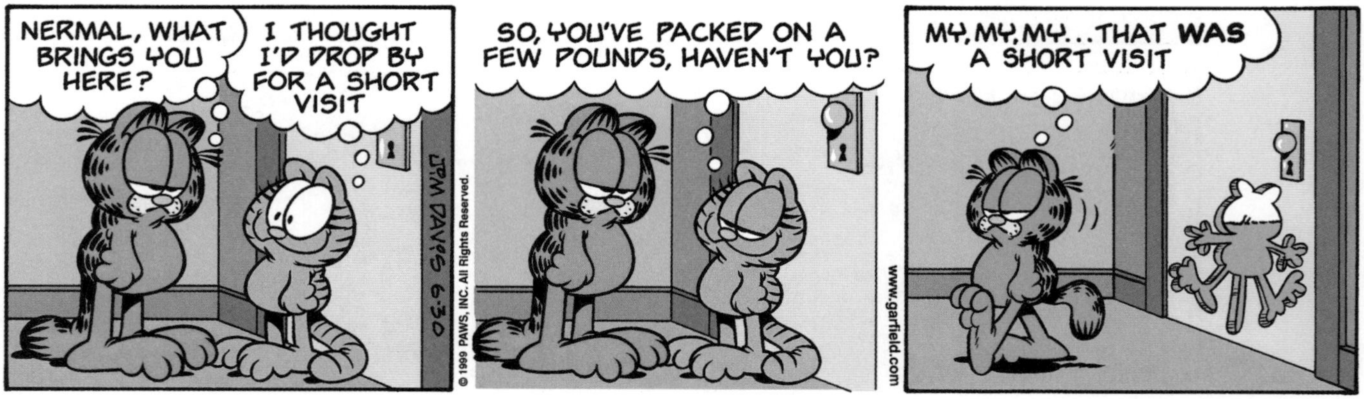
NERMAL, WHAT BRINGS YOU HERE?
I THOUGHT I'D DROP BY FOR A SHORT VISIT
JPM DAVIS 6-30
© 1999 PAWS, INC. All Rights Reserved.
SO, YOU'VE PACKED ON A FEW POUNDS, HAVEN'T YOU?
www.garfield.com
MY, MY, MY... THAT **WAS** A SHORT VISIT

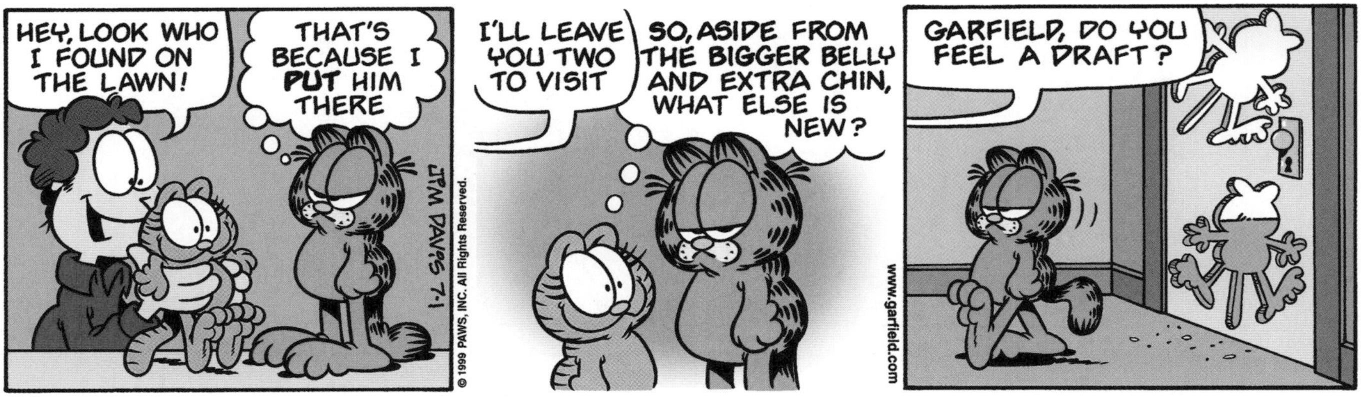
HEY, LOOK WHO I FOUND ON THE LAWN!
THAT'S BECAUSE I PUT HIM THERE
JIM DAVIS 7-1
© 1999 PAWS, INC. All Rights Reserved.
I'LL LEAVE YOU TWO TO VISIT
SO, ASIDE FROM THE BIGGER BELLY AND EXTRA CHIN, WHAT ELSE IS NEW?
www.garfield.com
GARFIELD, DO YOU FEEL A DRAFT?

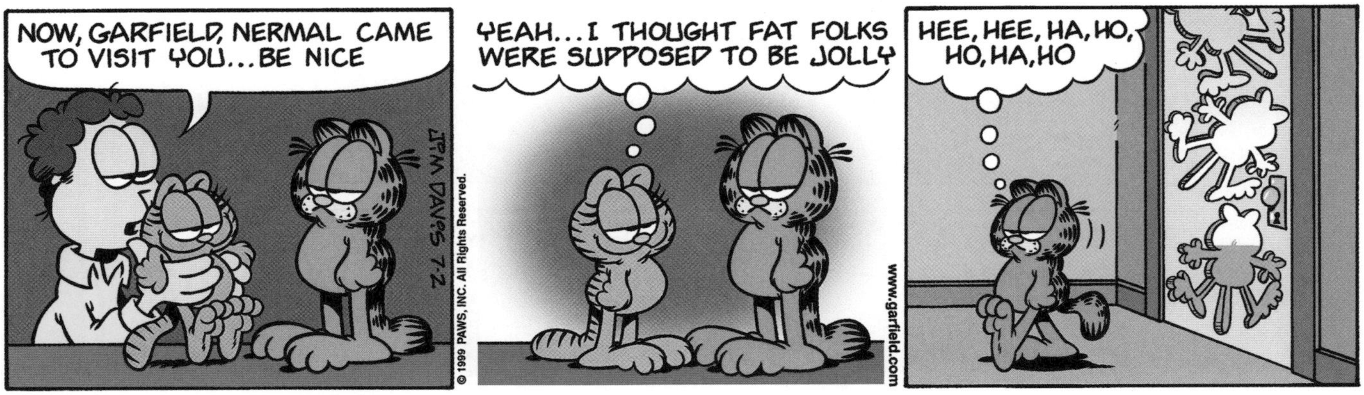
NOW, GARFIELD, NERMAL CAME TO VISIT YOU... BE NICE
JIM DAVIS 7-2
© 1999 PAWS, INC. All Rights Reserved.
YEAH... I THOUGHT FAT FOLKS WERE SUPPOSED TO BE JOLLY
www.garfield.com
HEE, HEE, HA, HO, HO, HA, HO

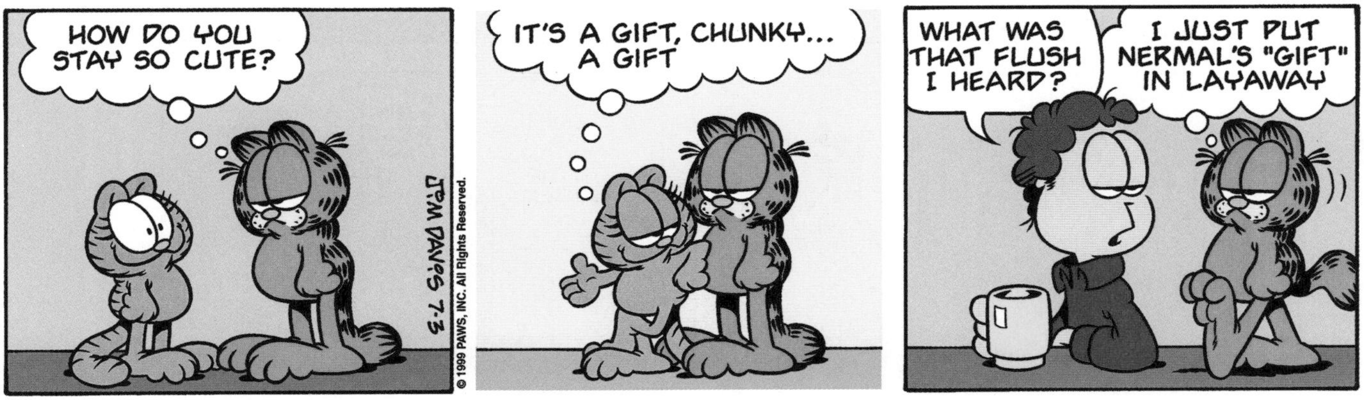
HOW DO YOU STAY SO CUTE?
JIM DAVIS 7-3
© 1999 PAWS, INC. All Rights Reserved.
IT'S A GIFT, CHUNKY... A GIFT
WHAT WAS THAT FLUSH I HEARD?
I JUST PUT NERMAL'S "GIFT" IN LAYAWAY

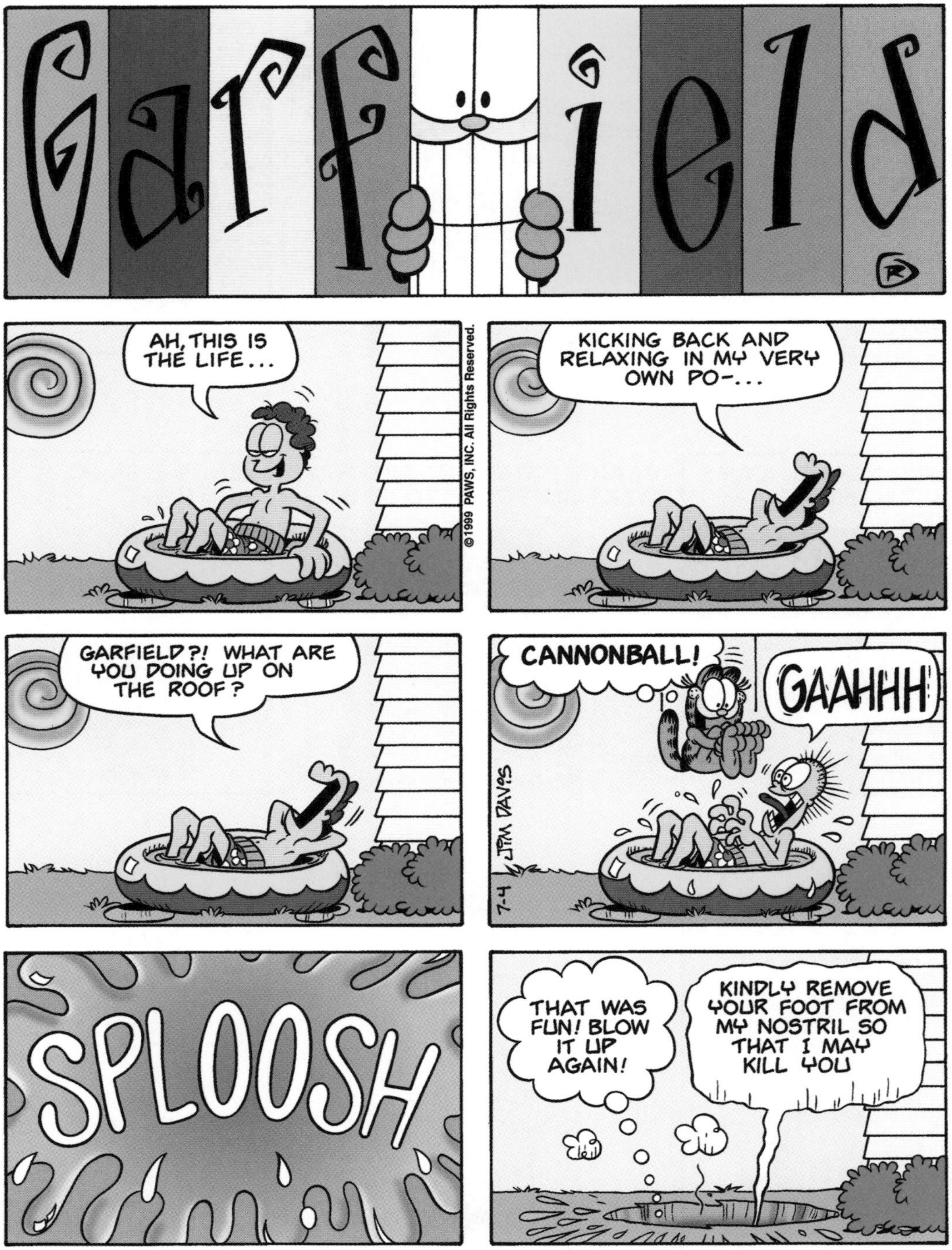

Garfield
AH, THIS IS THE LIFE...
©1999 PAWS, INC. All Rights Reserved.
KICKING BACK AND RELAXING IN MY VERY OWN PO-...
GARFIELD?! WHAT ARE YOU DOING UP ON THE ROOF?
JIM DAVIS
7-4
CANNONBALL!
GAAHHH
SPLOOSH
THAT WAS FUN! BLOW IT UP AGAIN!
KINDLY REMOVE YOUR FOOT FROM MY NOSTRIL SO THAT I MAY KILL YOU

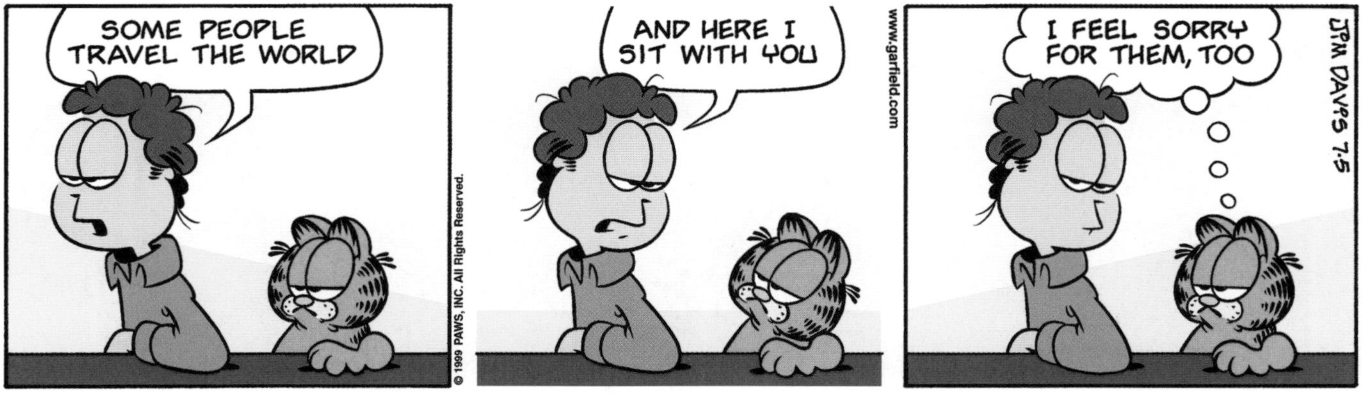
SOME PEOPLE TRAVEL THE WORLD
© 1999 PAWS, INC. All Rights Reserved.
AND HERE I SIT WITH YOU
www.garfield.com
I FEEL SORRY FOR THEM, TOO
JIM DAVIS 7-5

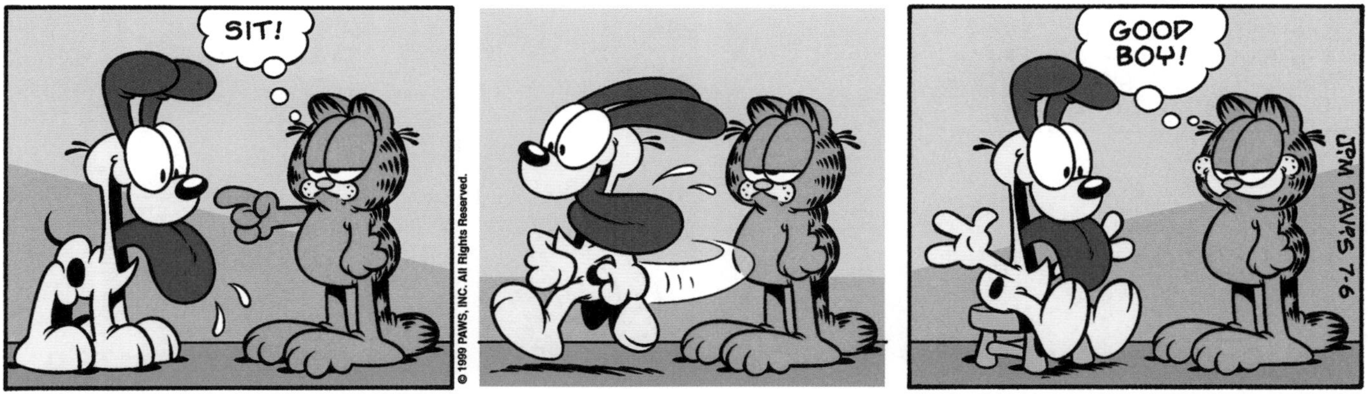
SIT!
© 1999 PAWS, INC. All Rights Reserved.
GOOD BOY!
JIM DAVIS 7-6

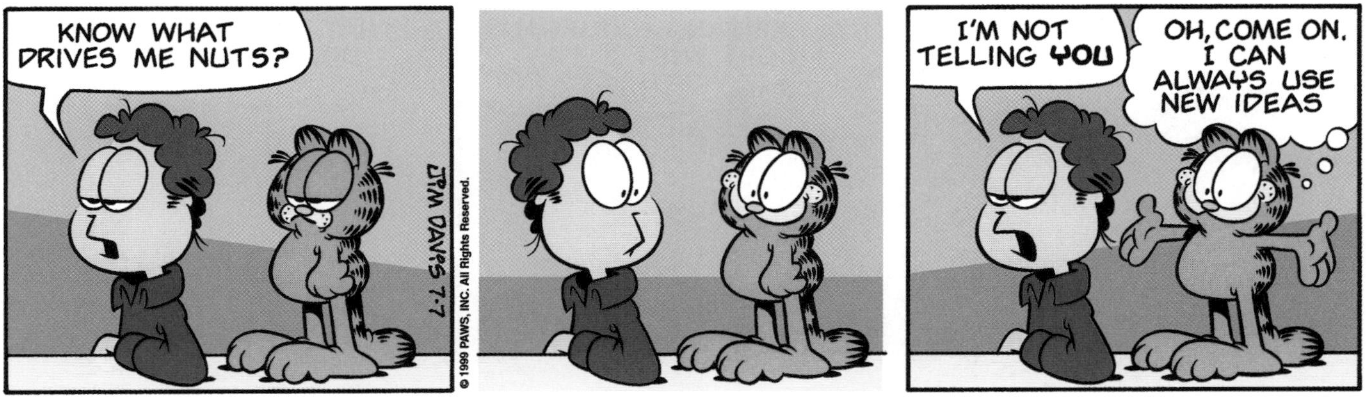
KNOW WHAT DRIVES ME NUTS?
JIM DAVIS 7-7
© 1999 PAWS, INC. All Rights Reserved.
I'M NOT TELLING **YOU**
OH, COME ON. I CAN ALWAYS USE NEW IDEAS

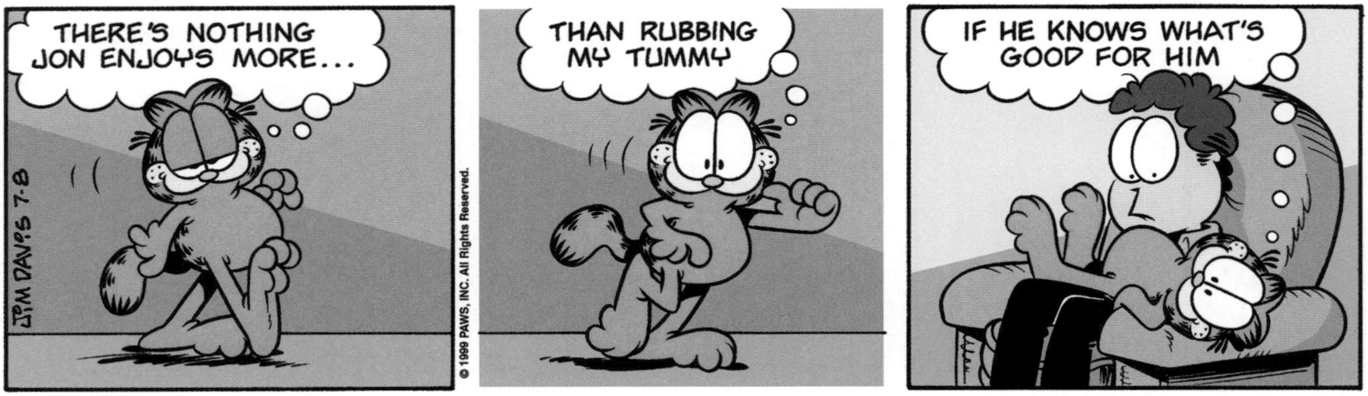
THERE'S NOTHING JON ENJOYS MORE...
THAN RUBBING MY TUMMY
IF HE KNOWS WHAT'S GOOD FOR HIM
JIM DAVIS 7-8
© 1999 PAWS, INC. All Rights Reserved.

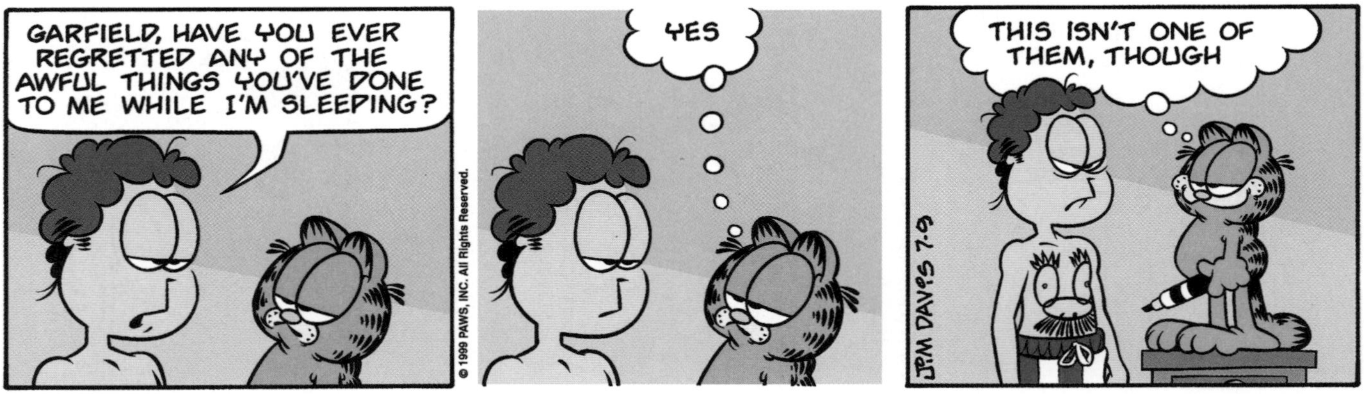
GARFIELD, HAVE YOU EVER REGRETTED ANY OF THE AWFUL THINGS YOU'VE DONE TO ME WHILE I'M SLEEPING?
YES
THIS ISN'T ONE OF THEM, THOUGH
JIM DAVIS 7-9
© 1999 PAWS, INC. All Rights Reserved.

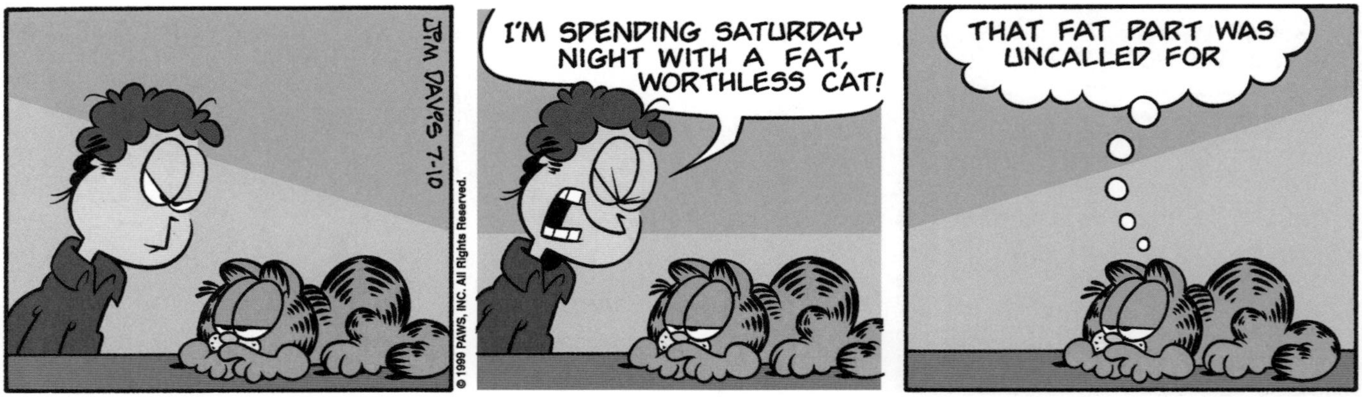
I'M SPENDING SATURDAY NIGHT WITH A FAT, WORTHLESS CAT!
THAT FAT PART WAS UNCALLED FOR
JIM DAVIS 7-10
© 1999 PAWS, INC. All Rights Reserved.

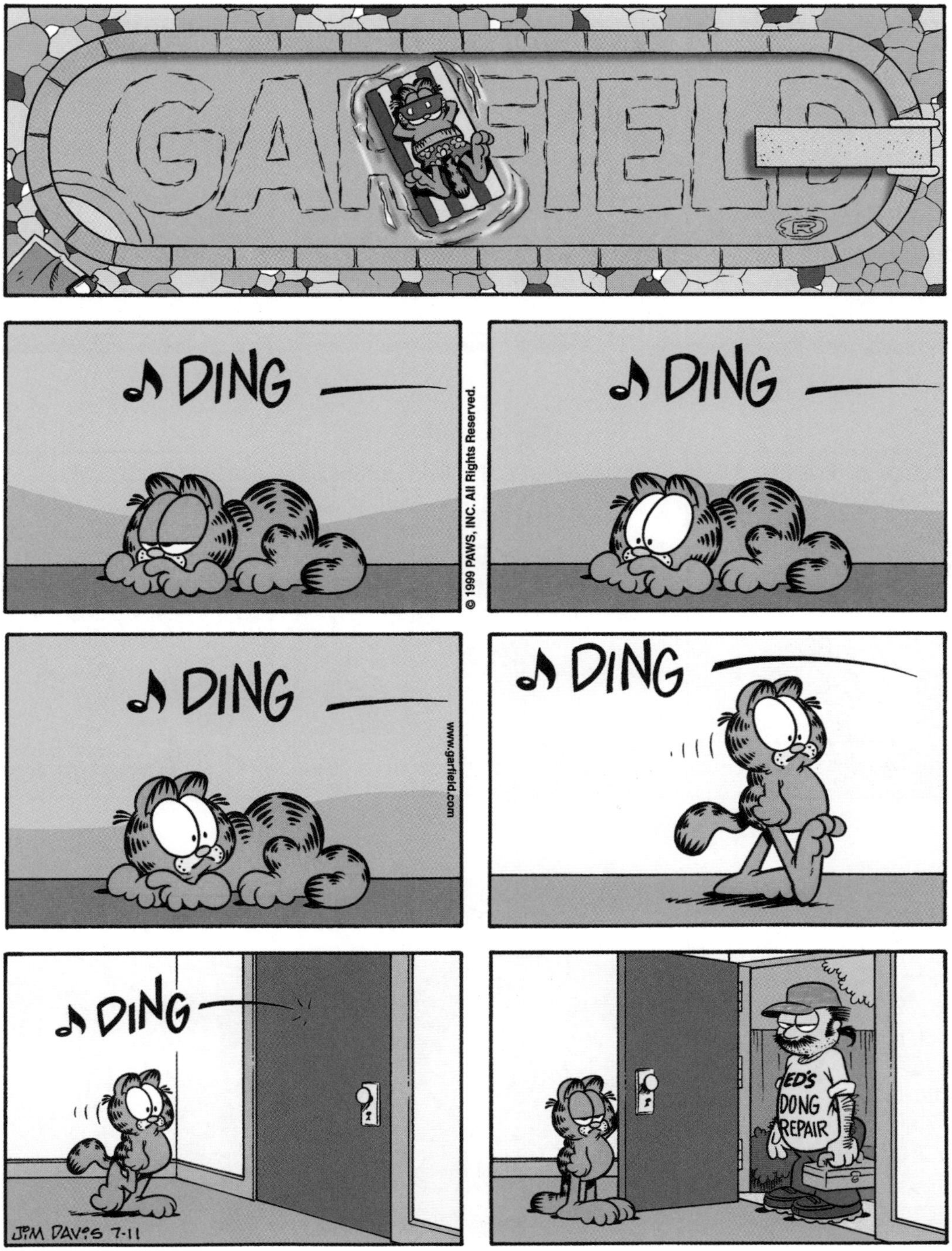
GARFIELD®
© 1999 PAWS, INC. All Rights Reserved.
www.garfield.com
♪ DING ——
♪ DING ——
♪ DING ——
♪ DING ——
♪ DING ——
JIM DAVIS 7-11
ED'S DONG REPAIR

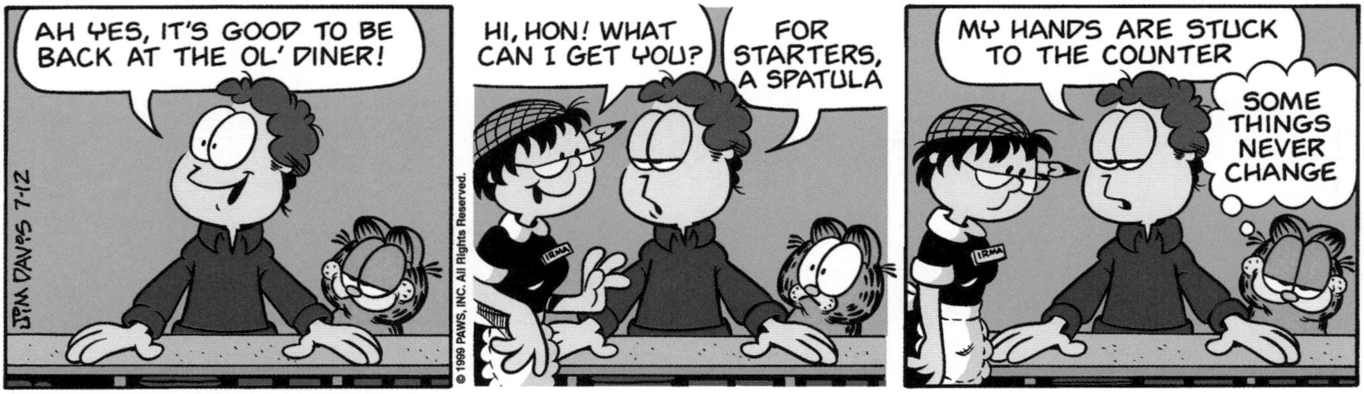
JIM DAVIS 7-12
AH YES, IT'S GOOD TO BE BACK AT THE OL' DINER!
© 1999 PAWS, INC. All Rights Reserved.
HI, HON! WHAT CAN I GET YOU?
FOR STARTERS, A SPATULA
IRMA
MY HANDS ARE STUCK TO THE COUNTER
SOME THINGS NEVER CHANGE

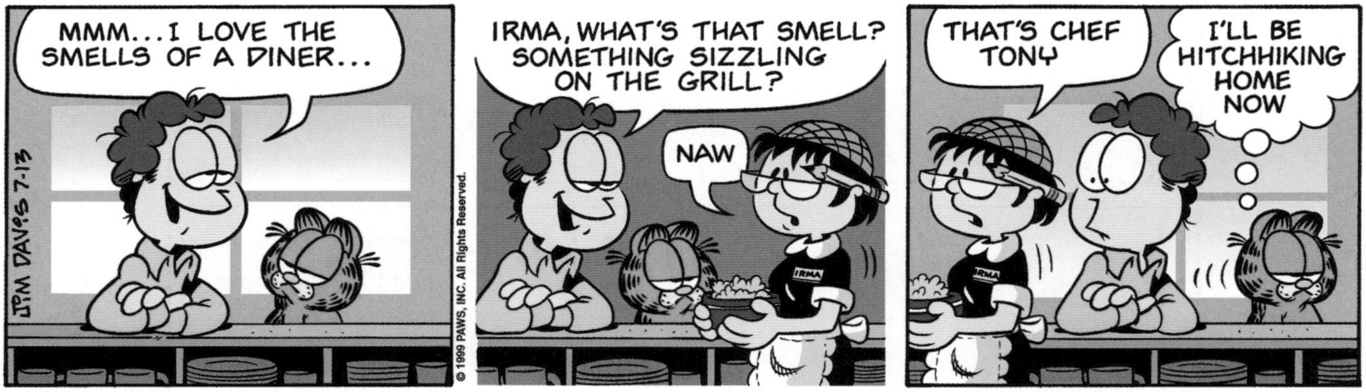
JIM DAVIS 7-13
MMM...I LOVE THE SMELLS OF A DINER...
© 1999 PAWS, INC. All Rights Reserved.
IRMA, WHAT'S THAT SMELL? SOMETHING SIZZLING ON THE GRILL?
NAW
IRMA
THAT'S CHEF TONY
I'LL BE HITCHHIKING HOME NOW

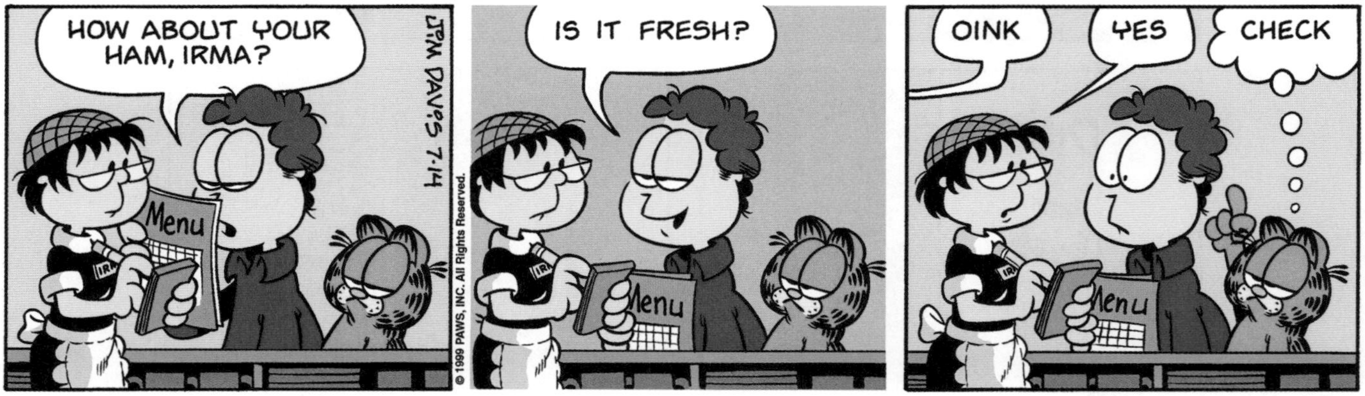
HOW ABOUT YOUR HAM, IRMA?
JIM DAVIS 7-14
Menu
© 1999 PAWS, INC. All Rights Reserved.
IS IT FRESH?
Menu
OINK
YES
CHECK
Menu

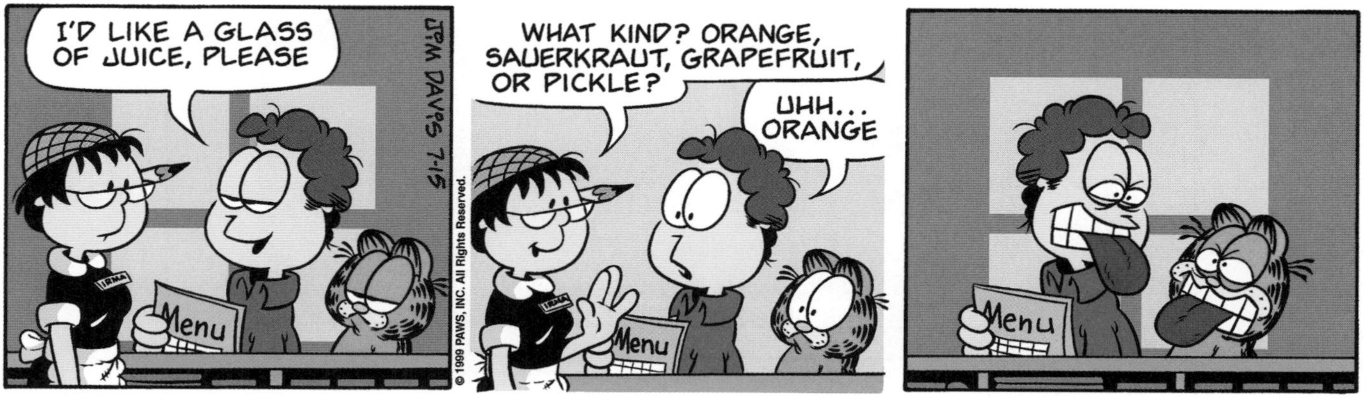
I'D LIKE A GLASS OF JUICE, PLEASE
JIM DAVIS 7-15
© 1999 PAWS, INC. All Rights Reserved.
WHAT KIND? ORANGE, SAUERKRAUT, GRAPEFRUIT, OR PICKLE?
UHH... ORANGE

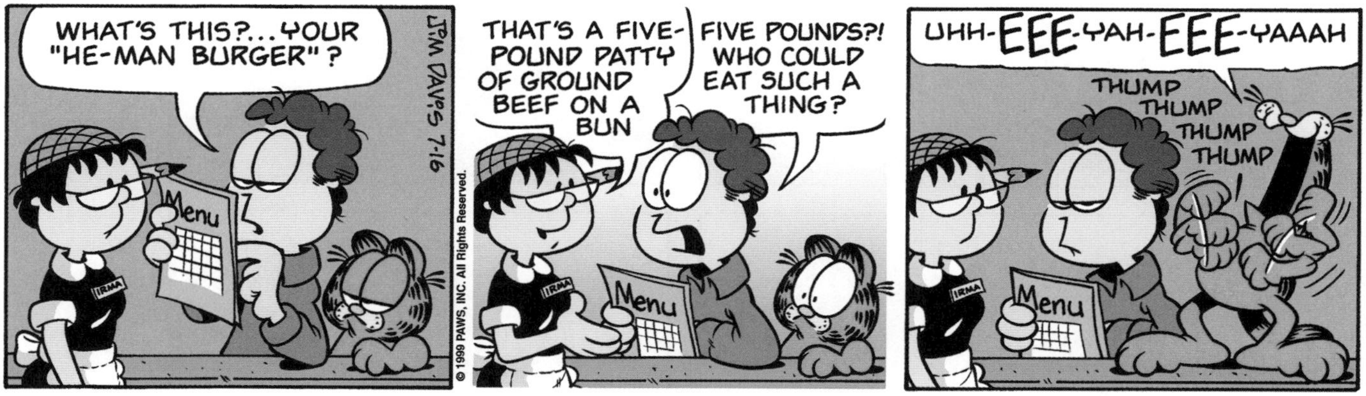
WHAT'S THIS?... YOUR "HE-MAN BURGER"?
JIM DAVIS 7-16
© 1999 PAWS, INC. All Rights Reserved.
THAT'S A FIVE-POUND PATTY OF GROUND BEEF ON A BUN
FIVE POUNDS?! WHO COULD EAT SUCH A THING?
UHH-EEE-YAH-EEE-YAAAH
THUMP THUMP THUMP THUMP

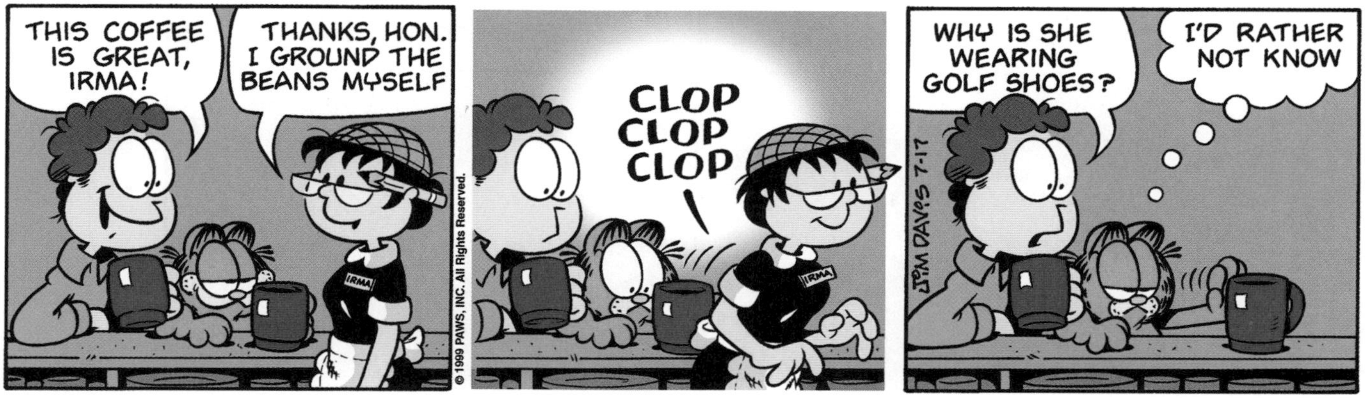
THIS COFFEE IS GREAT, IRMA!
THANKS, HON. I GROUND THE BEANS MYSELF
© 1999 PAWS, INC. All Rights Reserved.
CLOP CLOP CLOP
JIM DAVIS 7-17
WHY IS SHE WEARING GOLF SHOES?
I'D RATHER NOT KNOW

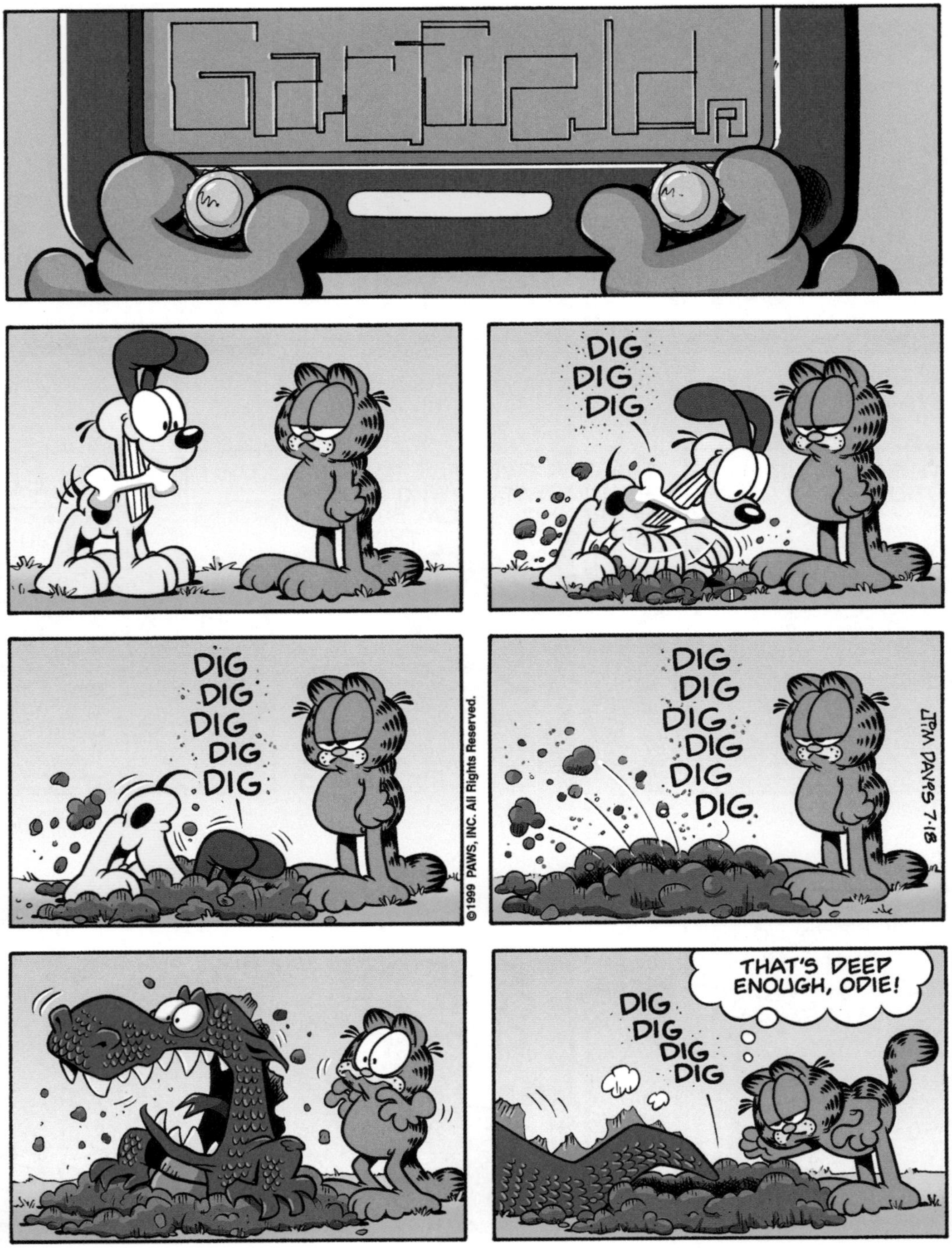
GARFIELD
DIG
DIG
DIG
DIG
DIG
DIG
DIG
DIG
©1999 PAWS, INC. All Rights Reserved.
DIG
DIG
DIG
DIG
DIG
DIG
JPM DAVIS 7-18
THAT'S DEEP ENOUGH, ODIE!
DIG
DIG
DIG
DIG

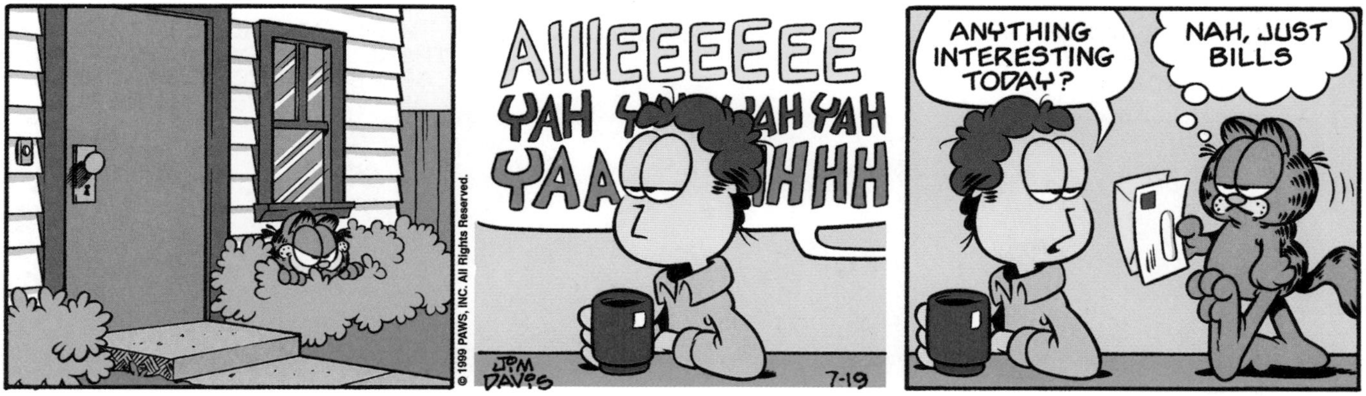
© 1999 PAWS, INC. All Rights Reserved.
AIIIEEEEEE
YAH
YAH
JIM DAVIS
7-19
ANYTHING INTERESTING TODAY?
NAH, JUST BILLS

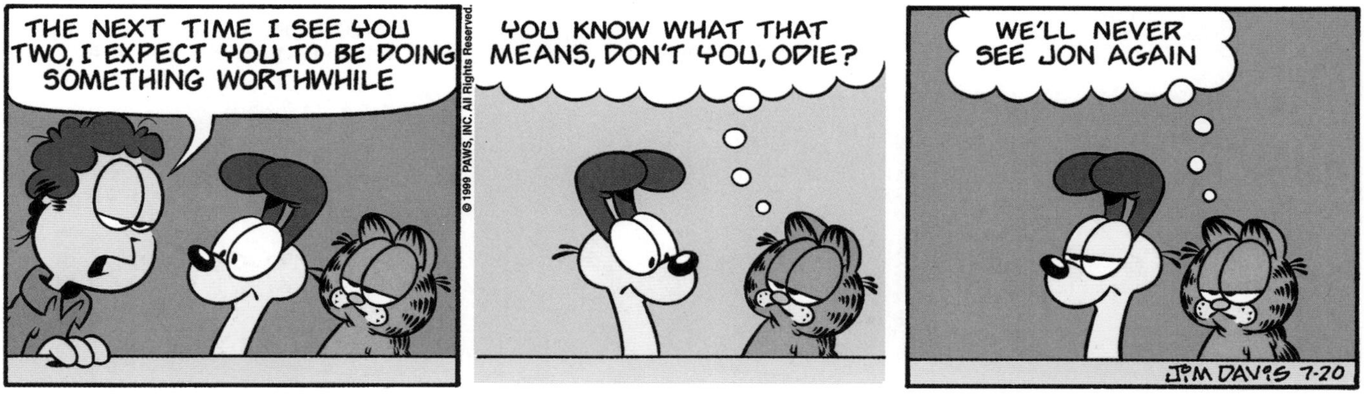
THE NEXT TIME I SEE YOU TWO, I EXPECT YOU TO BE DOING SOMETHING WORTHWHILE
© 1999 PAWS, INC. All Rights Reserved.
YOU KNOW WHAT THAT MEANS, DON'T YOU, ODIE?
WE'LL NEVER SEE JON AGAIN
JIM DAVIS 7-20

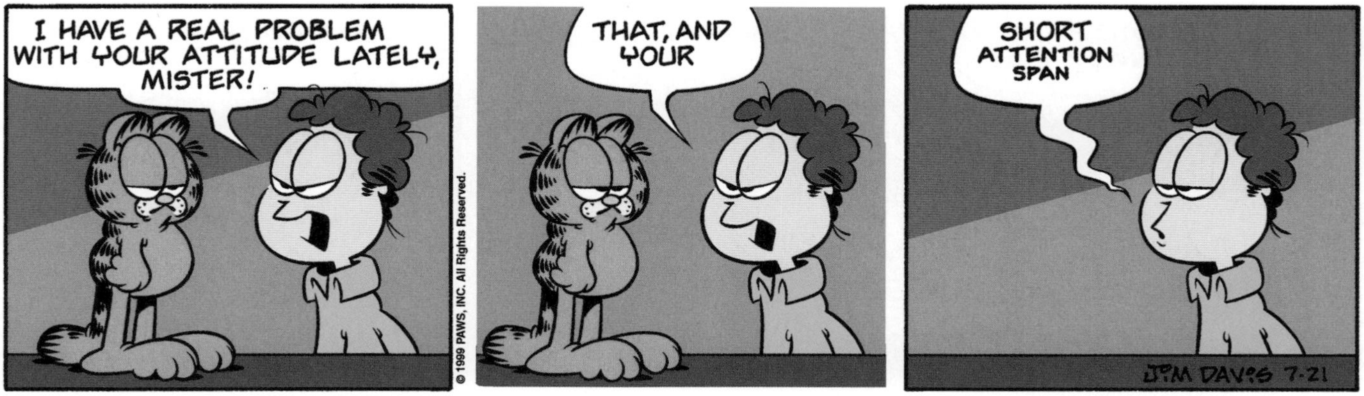
I HAVE A REAL PROBLEM WITH YOUR ATTITUDE LATELY, MISTER!
© 1999 PAWS, INC. All Rights Reserved.
THAT, AND YOUR
SHORT ATTENTION SPAN
JIM DAVIS 7-21

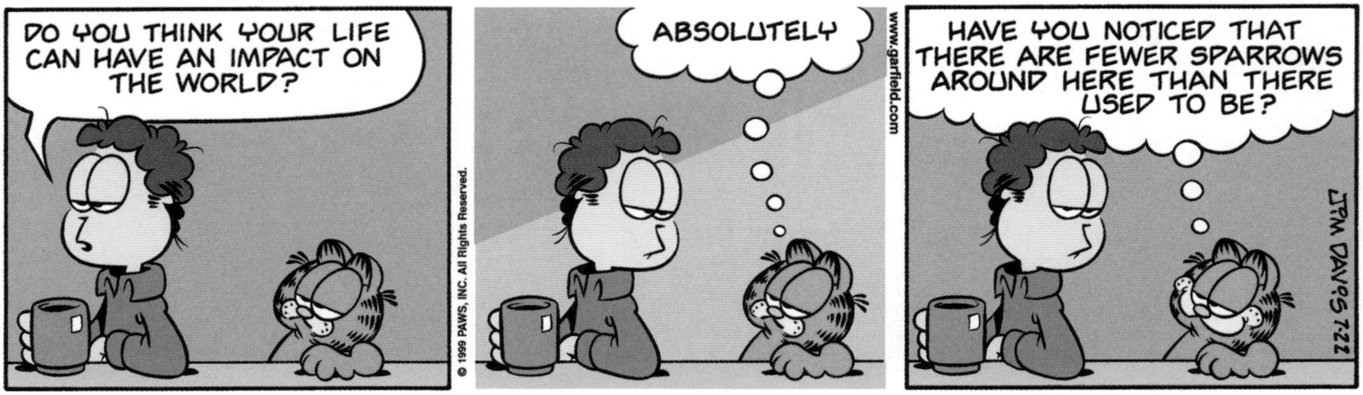
DO YOU THINK YOUR LIFE CAN HAVE AN IMPACT ON THE WORLD?
ABSOLUTELY
HAVE YOU NOTICED THAT THERE ARE FEWER SPARROWS AROUND HERE THAN THERE USED TO BE?
JIM DAVIS 7-22
© 1999 PAWS, INC. All Rights Reserved.
www.garfield.com

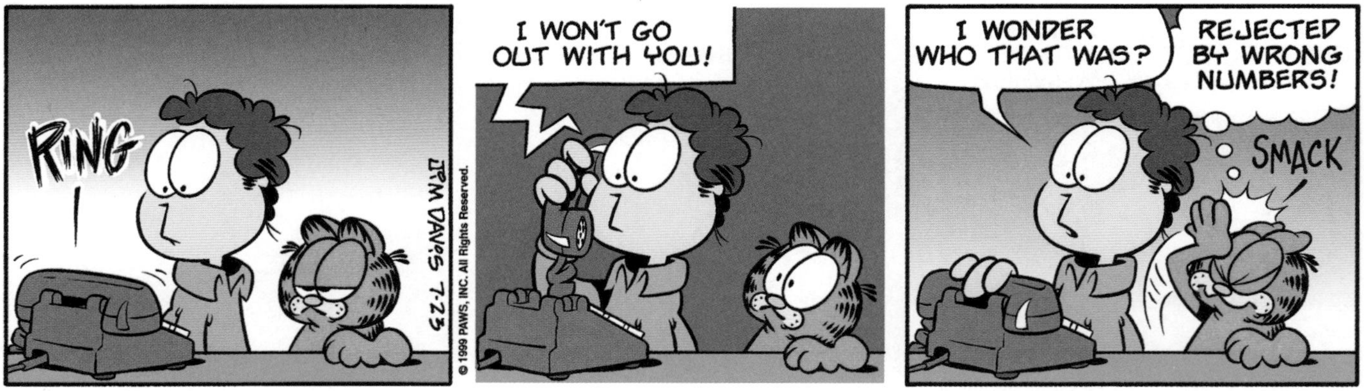
RING
JIM DAVIS 7-23
I WON'T GO OUT WITH YOU!
I WONDER WHO THAT WAS?
REJECTED BY WRONG NUMBERS!
SMACK
© 1999 PAWS, INC. All Rights Reserved.

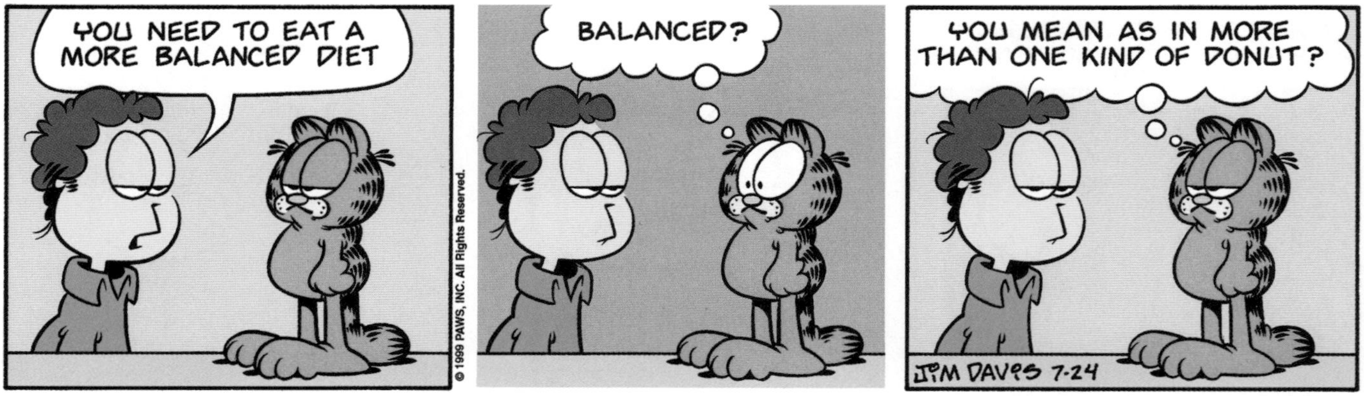
YOU NEED TO EAT A MORE BALANCED DIET
BALANCED?
YOU MEAN AS IN MORE THAN ONE KIND OF DONUT?
JIM DAVIS 7-24
© 1999 PAWS, INC. All Rights Reserved.

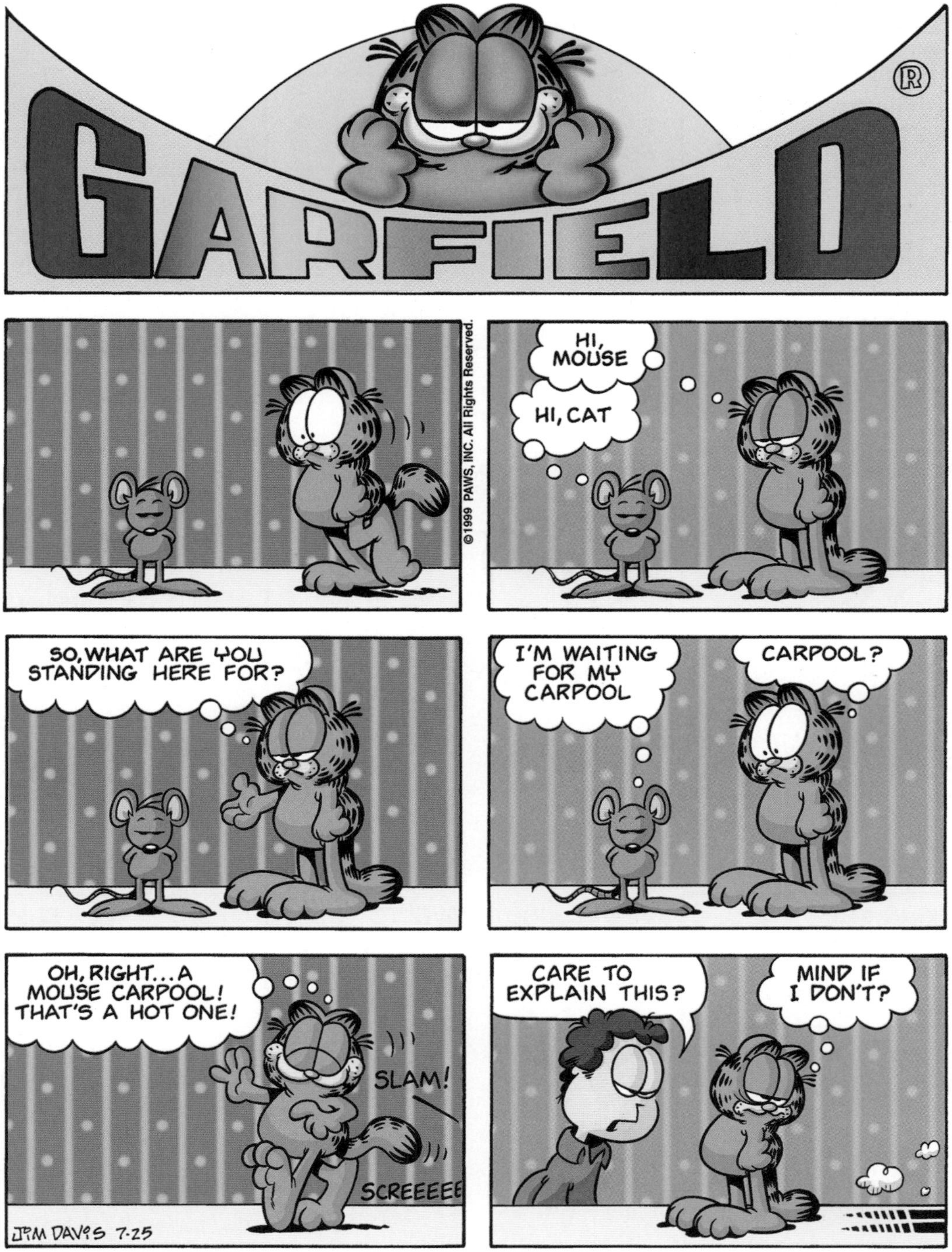
GARFIELD®
© 1999 PAWS, INC. All Rights Reserved.
HI, MOUSE
HI, CAT
SO, WHAT ARE YOU STANDING HERE FOR?
I'M WAITING FOR MY CARPOOL
CARPOOL?
OH, RIGHT... A MOUSE CARPOOL! THAT'S A HOT ONE!
SLAM!
SCREEEEEE
JIM DAVIS 7-25
CARE TO EXPLAIN THIS?
MIND IF I DON'T?

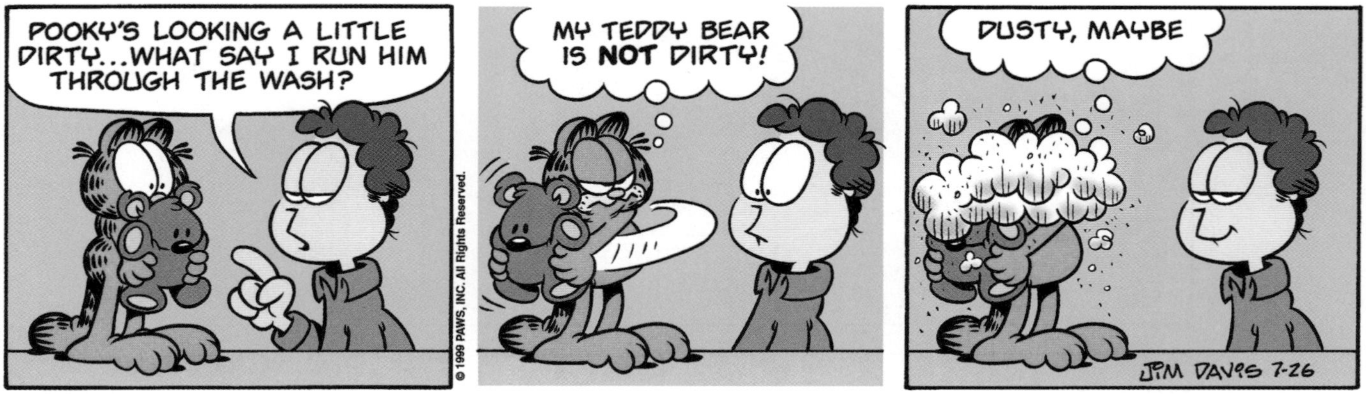
POOKY'S LOOKING A LITTLE DIRTY...WHAT SAY I RUN HIM THROUGH THE WASH?
MY TEDDY BEAR IS **NOT** DIRTY!
DUSTY, MAYBE
© 1999 PAWS, INC. All Rights Reserved.
JIM DAVIS 7-26

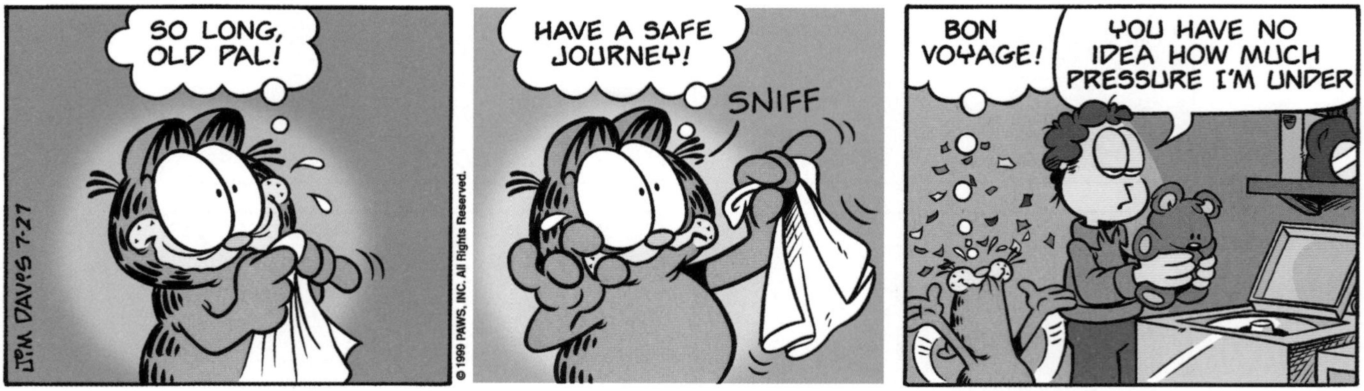
SO LONG, OLD PAL!
HAVE A SAFE JOURNEY!
SNIFF
BON VOYAGE!
YOU HAVE NO IDEA HOW MUCH PRESSURE I'M UNDER
JIM DAVIS 7-27
© 1999 PAWS, INC. All Rights Reserved.

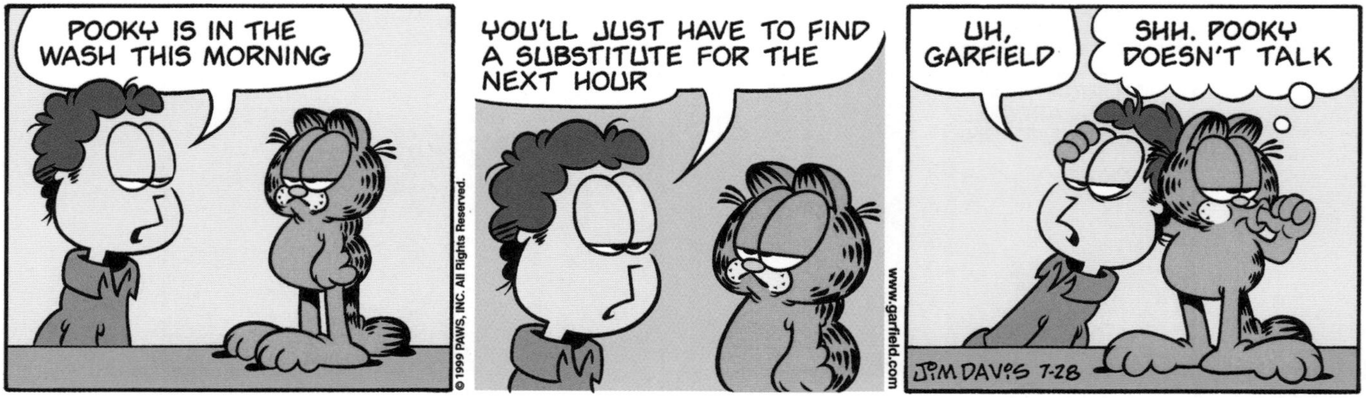
POOKY IS IN THE WASH THIS MORNING
YOU'LL JUST HAVE TO FIND A SUBSTITUTE FOR THE NEXT HOUR
UH, GARFIELD
SHH. POOKY DOESN'T TALK
© 1999 PAWS, INC. All Rights Reserved.
www.garfield.com
JIM DAVIS 7-28

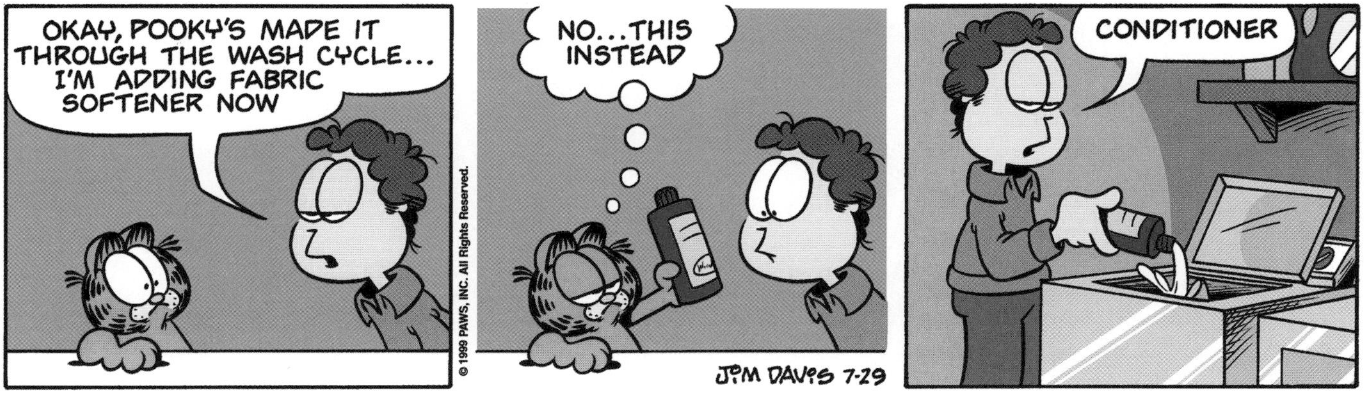
OKAY, POOKY'S MADE IT THROUGH THE WASH CYCLE... I'M ADDING FABRIC SOFTENER NOW
NO...THIS INSTEAD
CONDITIONER
© 1999 PAWS, INC. All Rights Reserved.
JIM DAVIS 7-29

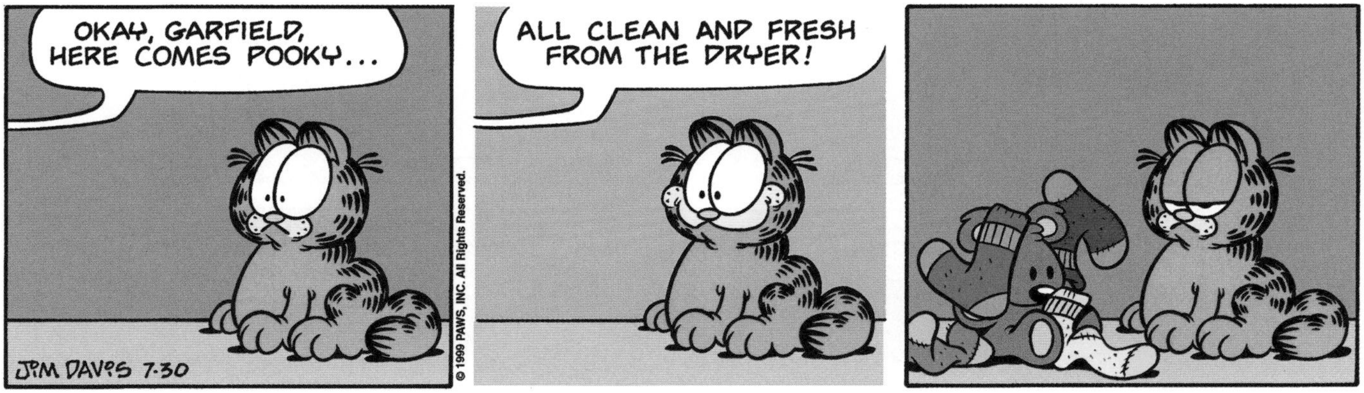
OKAY, GARFIELD, HERE COMES POOKY...
ALL CLEAN AND FRESH FROM THE DRYER!
© 1999 PAWS, INC. All Rights Reserved.
JIM DAVIS 7-30

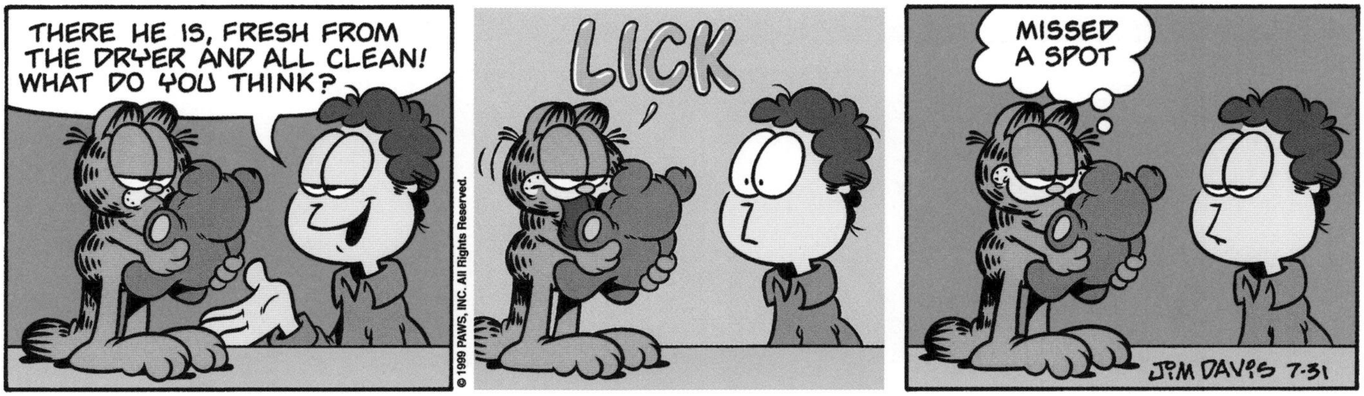
THERE HE IS, FRESH FROM THE DRYER AND ALL CLEAN! WHAT DO YOU THINK?
LICK
MISSED A SPOT
© 1999 PAWS, INC. All Rights Reserved.
JIM DAVIS 7-31

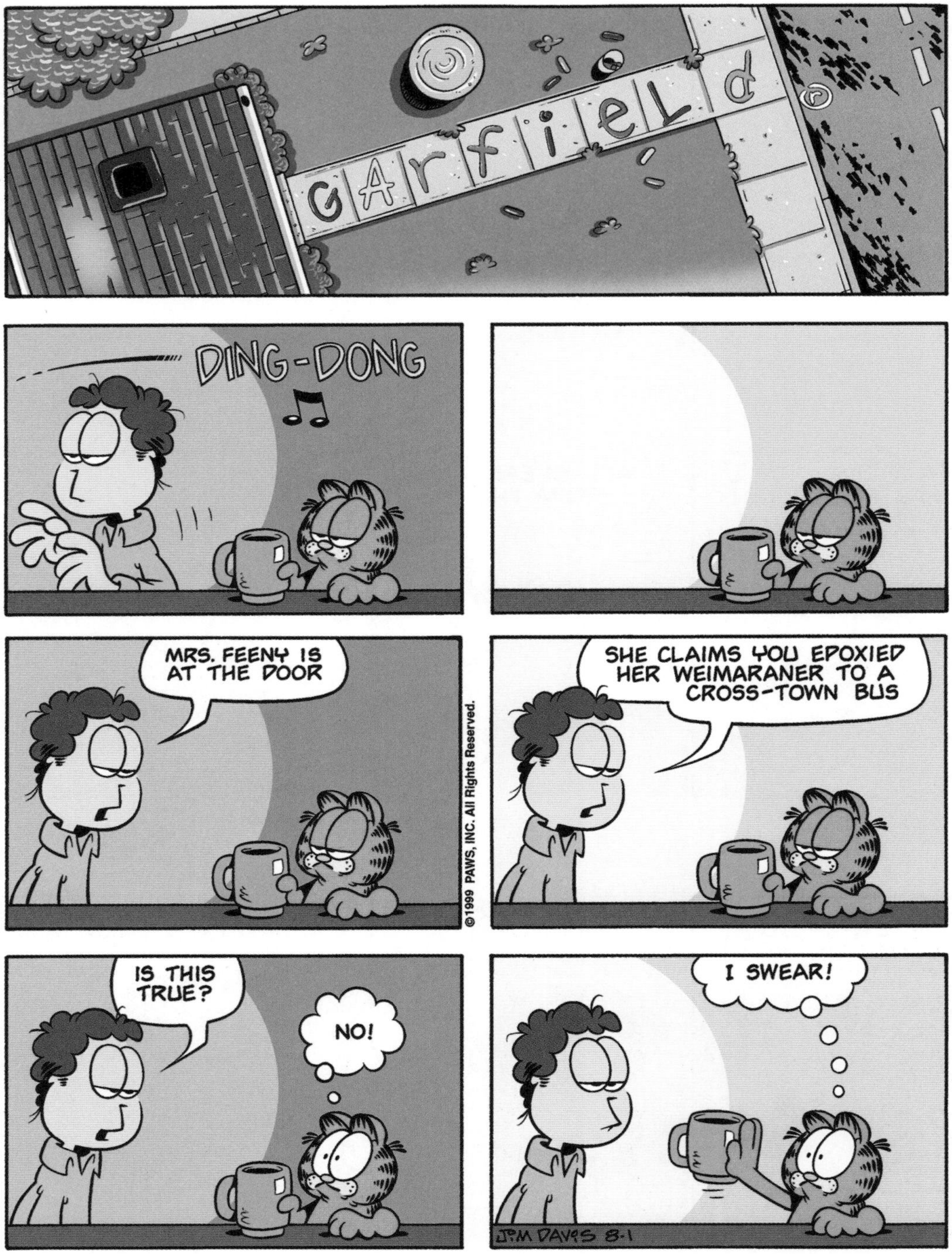
GARFIELD
DING-DONG
MRS. FEENY IS AT THE DOOR
SHE CLAIMS YOU EPOXIED HER WEIMARANER TO A CROSS-TOWN BUS
IS THIS TRUE?
NO!
I SWEAR!
JIM DAVIS 8-1

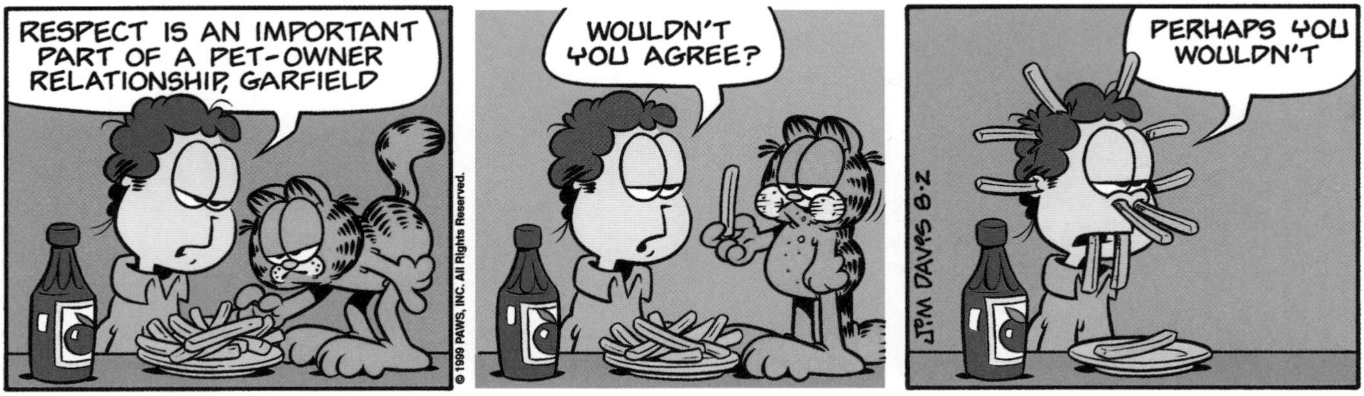
RESPECT IS AN IMPORTANT PART OF A PET-OWNER RELATIONSHIP, GARFIELD
© 1999 PAWS, INC. All Rights Reserved.
WOULDN'T YOU AGREE?
JIM DAVIS 8-2
PERHAPS YOU WOULDN'T

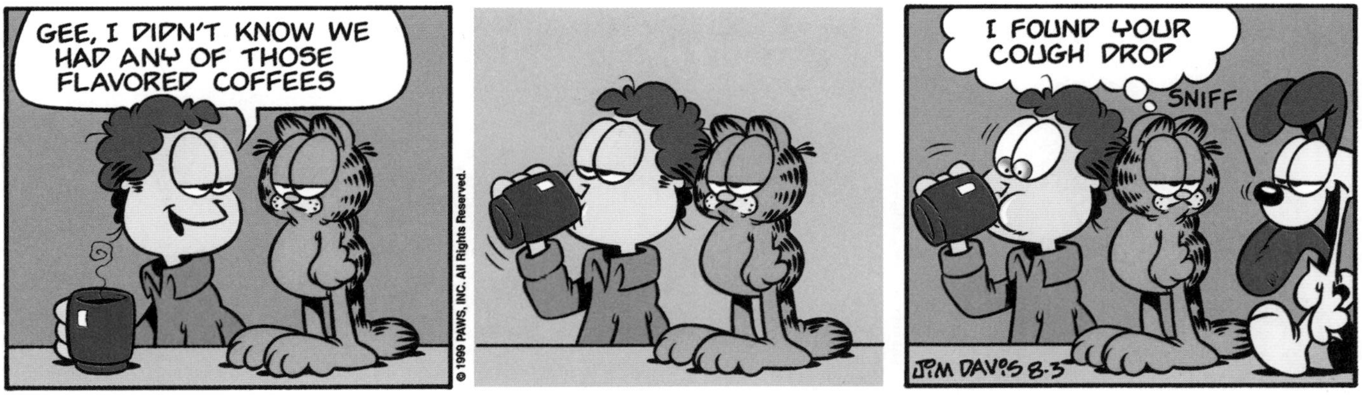
GEE, I DIDN'T KNOW WE HAD ANY OF THOSE FLAVORED COFFEES
© 1999 PAWS, INC. All Rights Reserved.
I FOUND YOUR COUGH DROP
SNIFF
JIM DAVIS 8-3

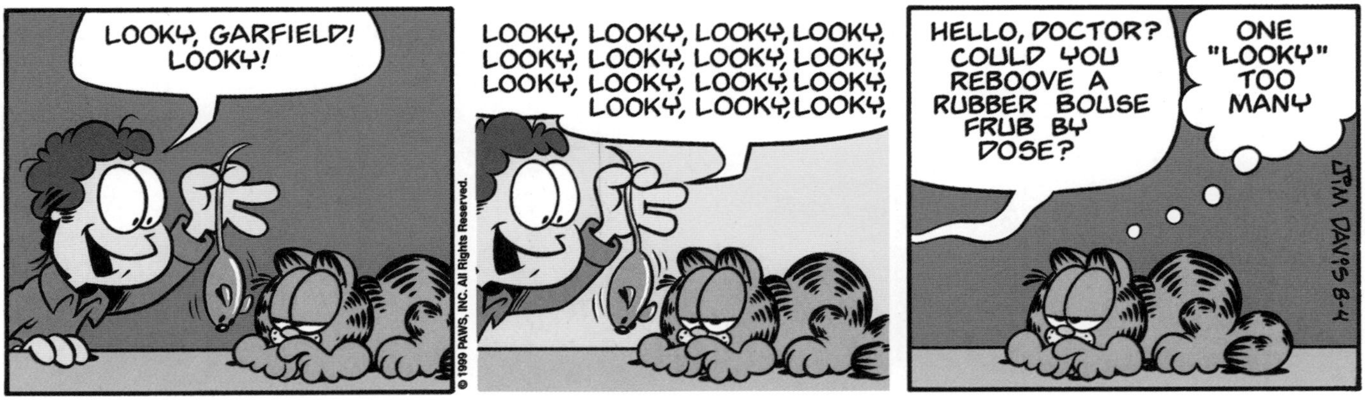
LOOKY, GARFIELD! LOOKY!
© 1999 PAWS, INC. All Rights Reserved.
LOOKY, LOOKY, LOOKY, LOOKY, LOOKY, LOOKY, LOOKY, LOOKY, LOOKY, LOOKY, LOOKY, LOOKY, LOOKY, LOOKY, LOOKY,
HELLO, DOCTOR? COULD YOU REBOOVE A RUBBER BOUSE FRUB BY DOSE?
ONE "LOOKY" TOO MANY
JIM DAVIS 8-4

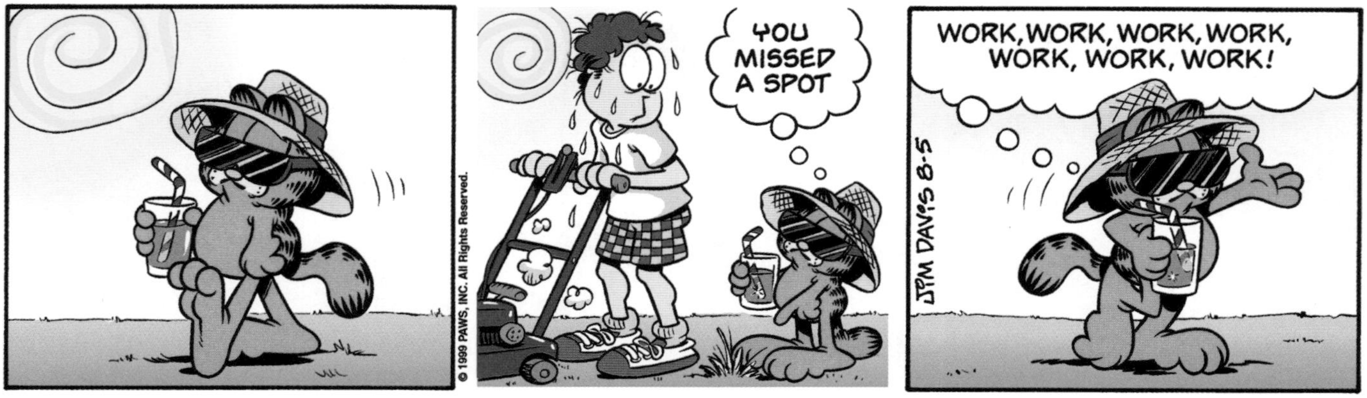
YOU MISSED A SPOT
WORK, WORK, WORK, WORK, WORK, WORK, WORK!
© 1999 PAWS, INC. All Rights Reserved.
JIM DAVIS 8-5

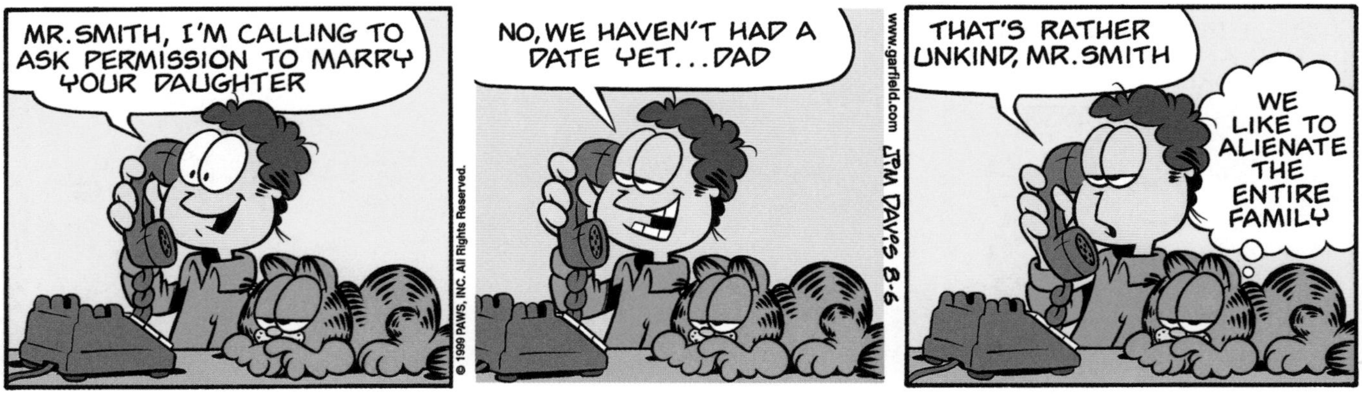
MR. SMITH, I'M CALLING TO ASK PERMISSION TO MARRY YOUR DAUGHTER
NO, WE HAVEN'T HAD A DATE YET... DAD
THAT'S RATHER UNKIND, MR. SMITH
WE LIKE TO ALIENATE THE ENTIRE FAMILY
© 1999 PAWS, INC. All Rights Reserved.
www.garfield.com
JIM DAVIS 8-6

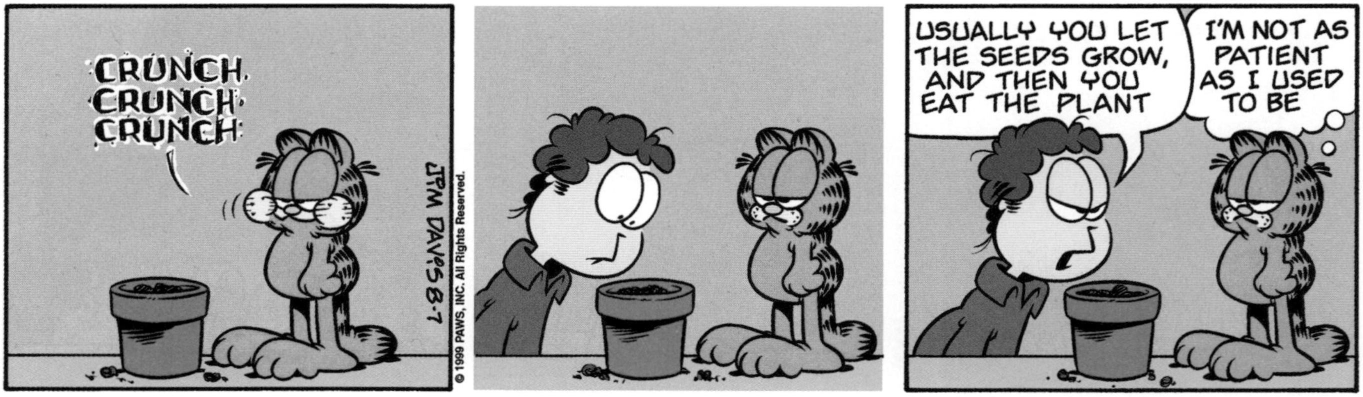
CRUNCH CRUNCH CRUNCH
USUALLY YOU LET THE SEEDS GROW, AND THEN YOU EAT THE PLANT
I'M NOT AS PATIENT AS I USED TO BE
© 1999 PAWS, INC. All Rights Reserved.
JIM DAVIS 8-7

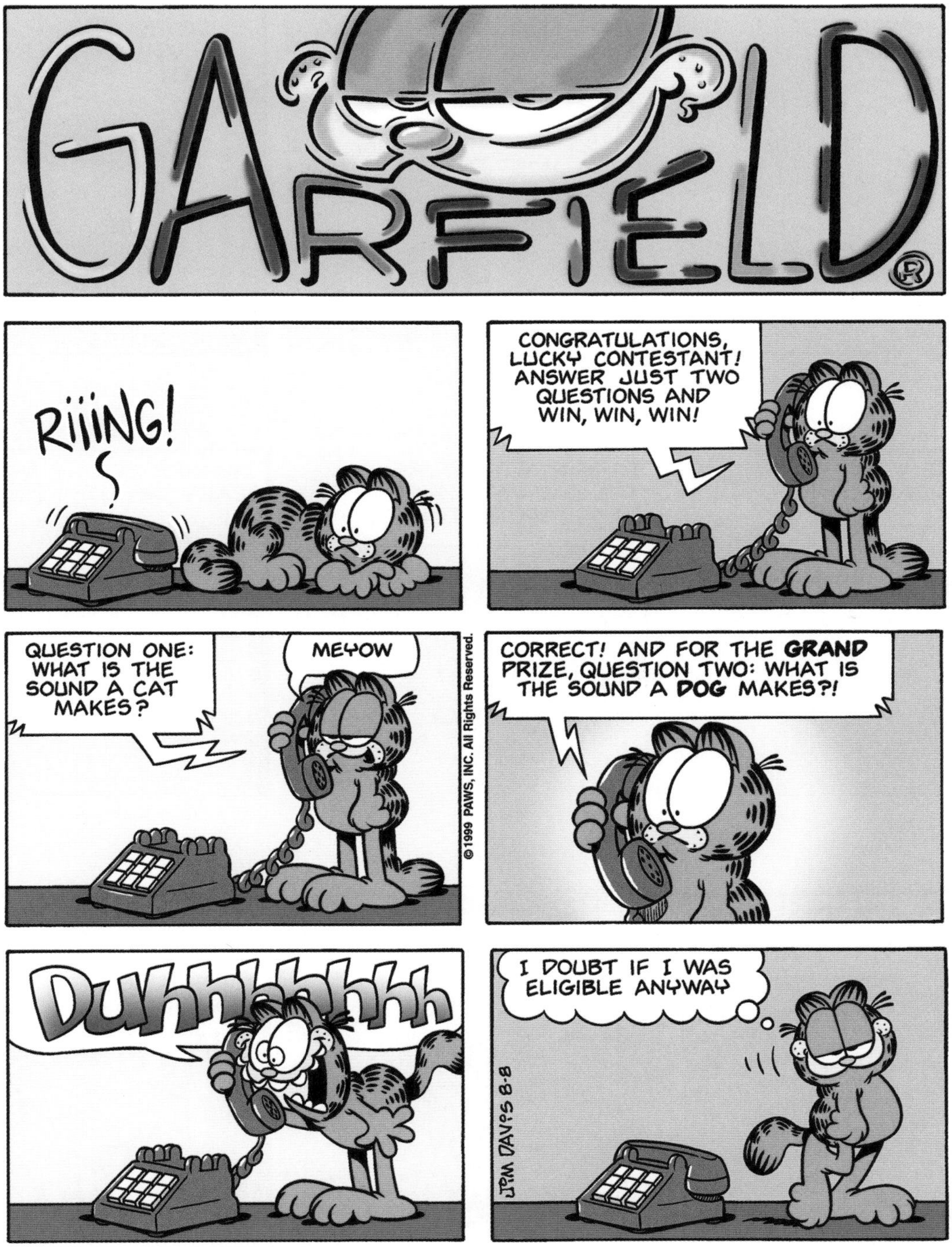
GARFIELD®
RiiiNG!
CONGRATULATIONS, LUCKY CONTESTANT! ANSWER JUST TWO QUESTIONS AND WIN, WIN, WIN!
QUESTION ONE: WHAT IS THE SOUND A CAT MAKES?
MEYOW
© 1999 PAWS, INC. All Rights Reserved.
CORRECT! AND FOR THE GRAND PRIZE, QUESTION TWO: WHAT IS THE SOUND A DOG MAKES?!
Duhhhhhhh
JPM DAVPS 8-8
I DOUBT IF I WAS ELIGIBLE ANYWAY

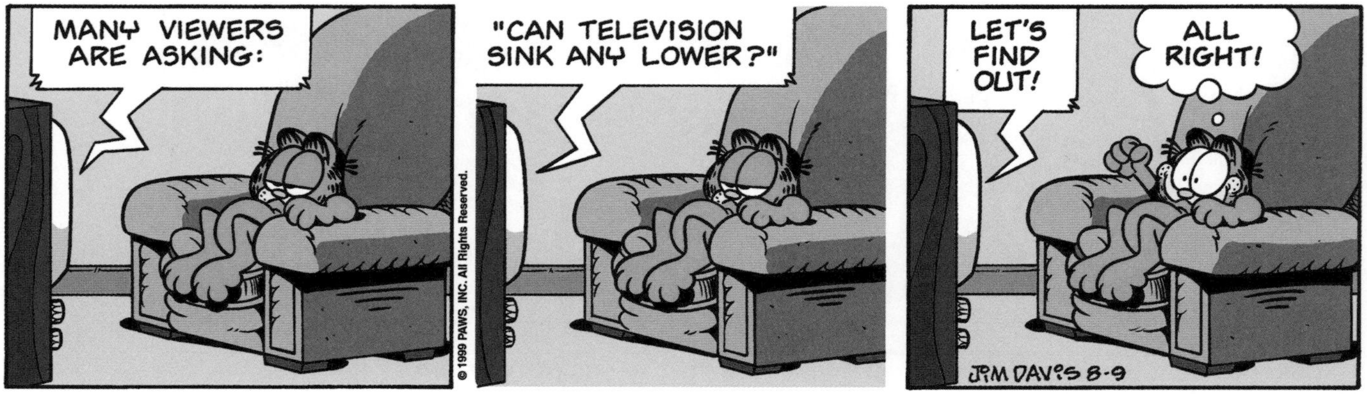
MANY VIEWERS ARE ASKING:
© 1999 PAWS, INC. All Rights Reserved.
"CAN TELEVISION SINK ANY LOWER?"
LET'S FIND OUT!
ALL RIGHT!
JIM DAVIS 8-9

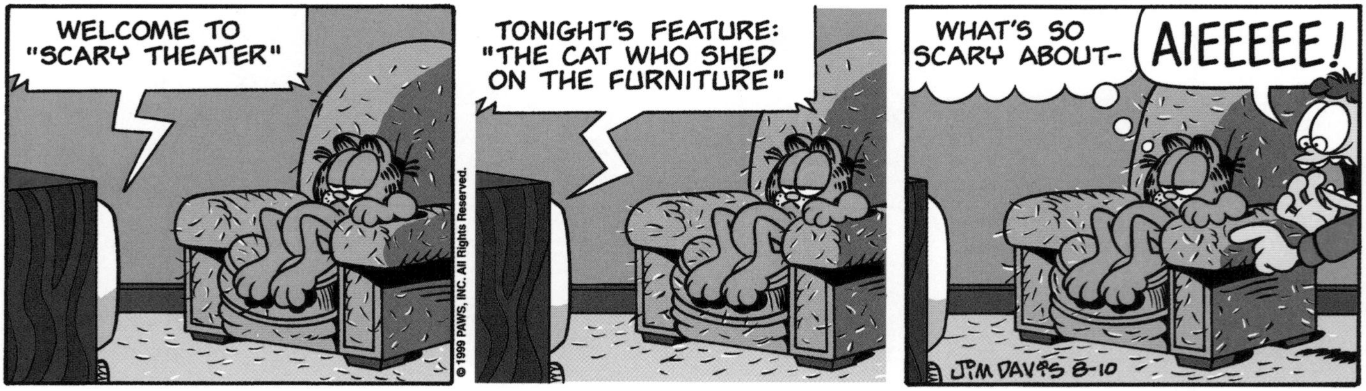
WELCOME TO "SCARY THEATER"
© 1999 PAWS, INC. All Rights Reserved.
TONIGHT'S FEATURE: "THE CAT WHO SHED ON THE FURNITURE"
WHAT'S SO SCARY ABOUT-
AIEEEEE!
JIM DAVIS 8-10

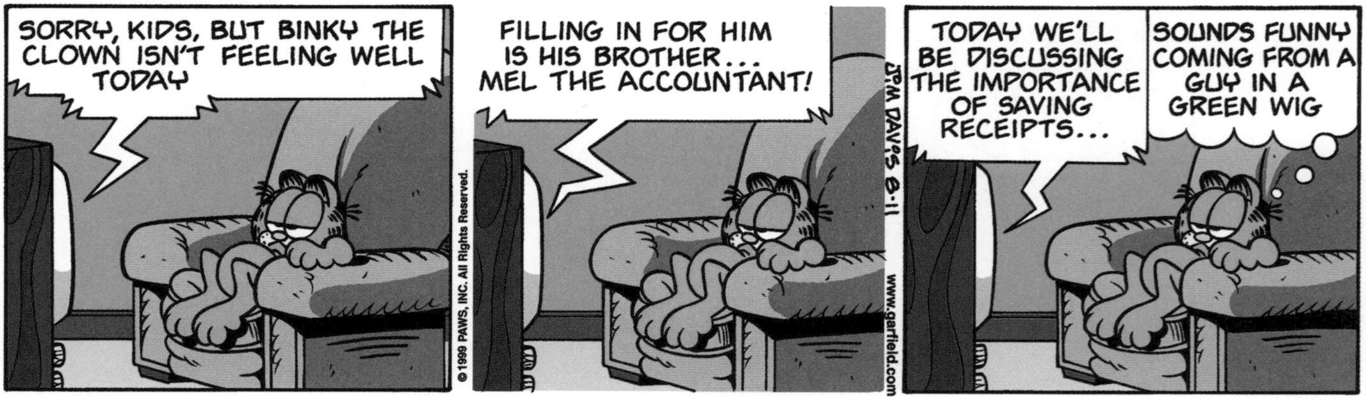
SORRY, KIDS, BUT BINKY THE CLOWN ISN'T FEELING WELL TODAY
© 1999 PAWS, INC. All Rights Reserved.
FILLING IN FOR HIM IS HIS BROTHER... MEL THE ACCOUNTANT!
JIM DAVIS 8-11
www.garfield.com
TODAY WE'LL BE DISCUSSING THE IMPORTANCE OF SAVING RECEIPTS...
SOUNDS FUNNY COMING FROM A GUY IN A GREEN WIG

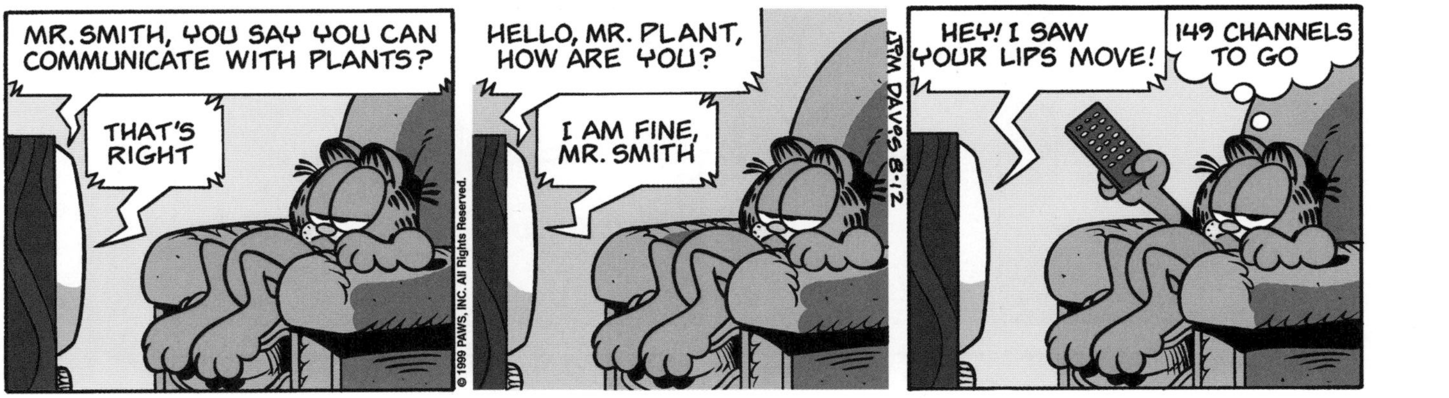
MR. SMITH, YOU SAY YOU CAN COMMUNICATE WITH PLANTS?
THAT'S RIGHT
HELLO, MR. PLANT, HOW ARE YOU?
I AM FINE, MR. SMITH
HEY! I SAW YOUR LIPS MOVE!
149 CHANNELS TO GO
© 1999 PAWS, INC. All Rights Reserved.

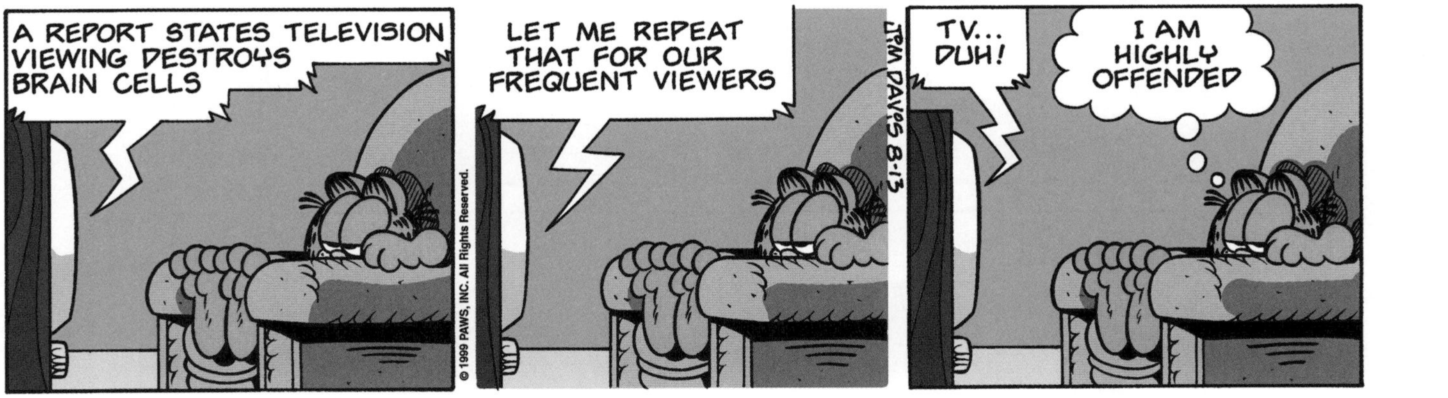
A REPORT STATES TELEVISION VIEWING DESTROYS BRAIN CELLS
LET ME REPEAT THAT FOR OUR FREQUENT VIEWERS
TV... DUH!
I AM HIGHLY OFFENDED
© 1999 PAWS, INC. All Rights Reserved.

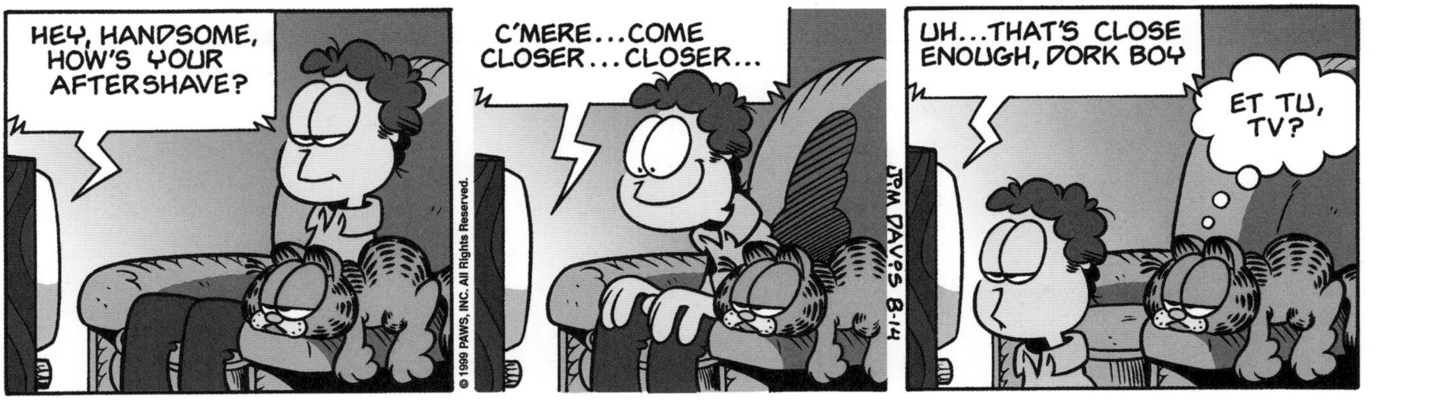
HEY, HANDSOME, HOW'S YOUR AFTERSHAVE?
C'MERE... COME CLOSER... CLOSER...
UH... THAT'S CLOSE ENOUGH, DORK BOY
ET TU, TV?
© 1999 PAWS, INC. All Rights Reserved.

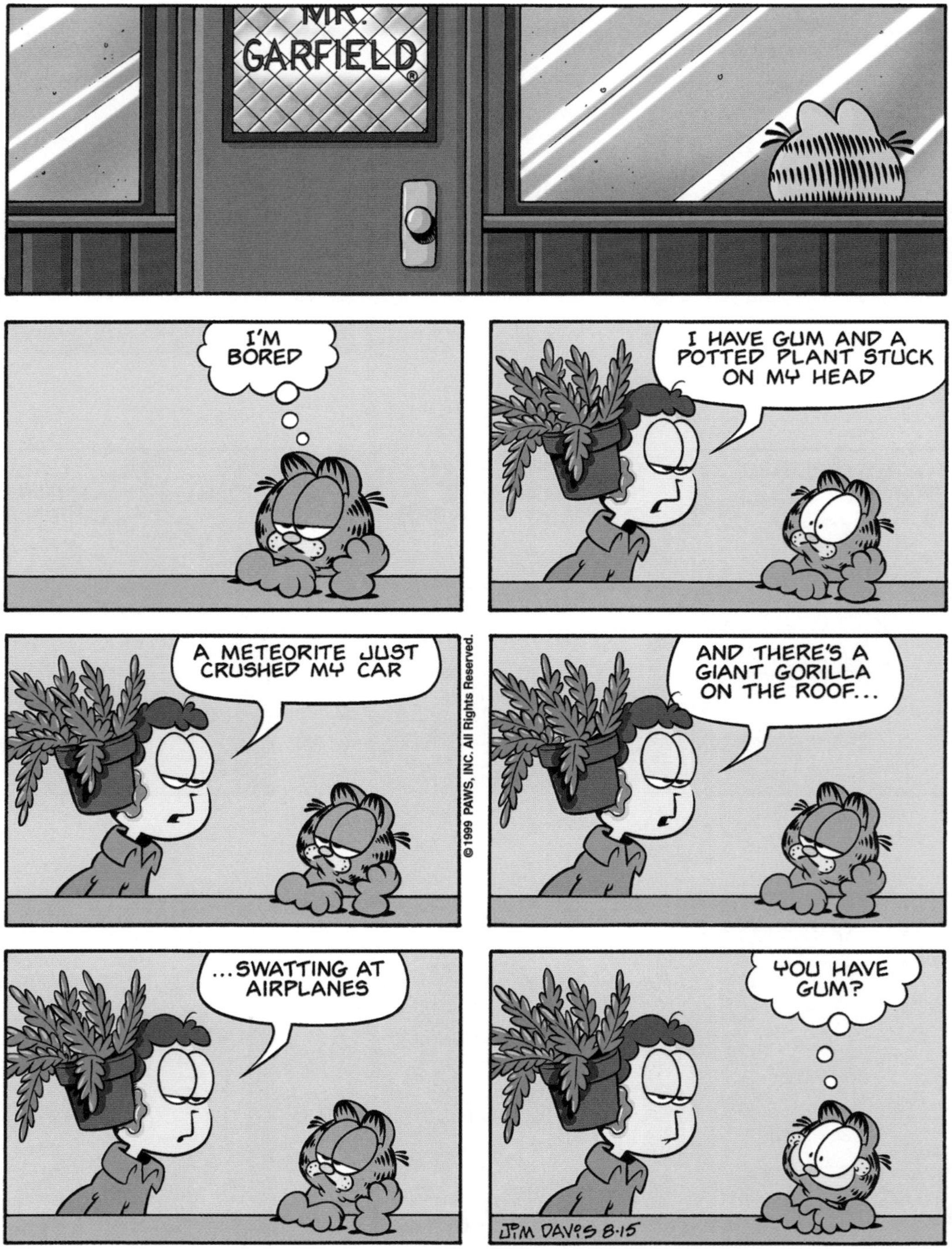
MR.
GARFIELD®
I'M BORED
I HAVE GUM AND A POTTED PLANT STUCK ON MY HEAD
A METEORITE JUST CRUSHED MY CAR
AND THERE'S A GIANT GORILLA ON THE ROOF...
...SWATTING AT AIRPLANES
YOU HAVE GUM?
JIM DAVIS 8-15

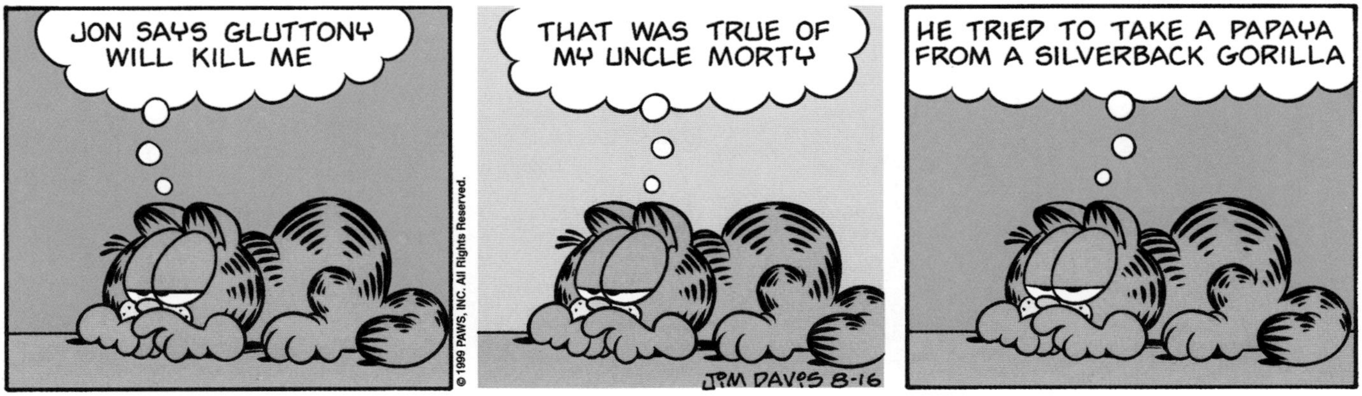
JON SAYS GLUTTONY WILL KILL ME
THAT WAS TRUE OF MY UNCLE MORTY
HE TRIED TO TAKE A PAPAYA FROM A SILVERBACK GORILLA
© 1999 PAWS, INC. All Rights Reserved.
JIM DAVIS 8-16

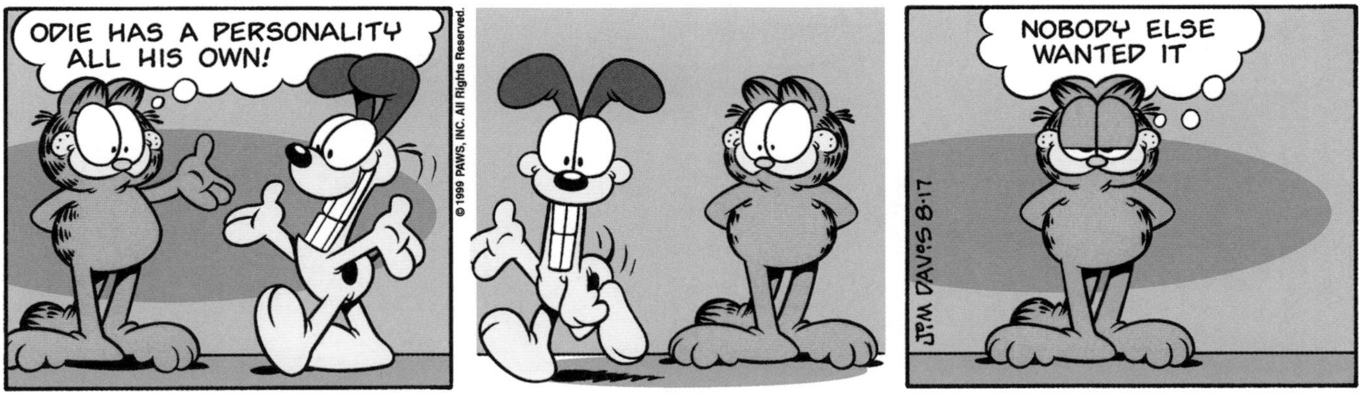
ODIE HAS A PERSONALITY ALL HIS OWN!
NOBODY ELSE WANTED IT
© 1999 PAWS, INC. All Rights Reserved.
JIM DAVIS 8-17

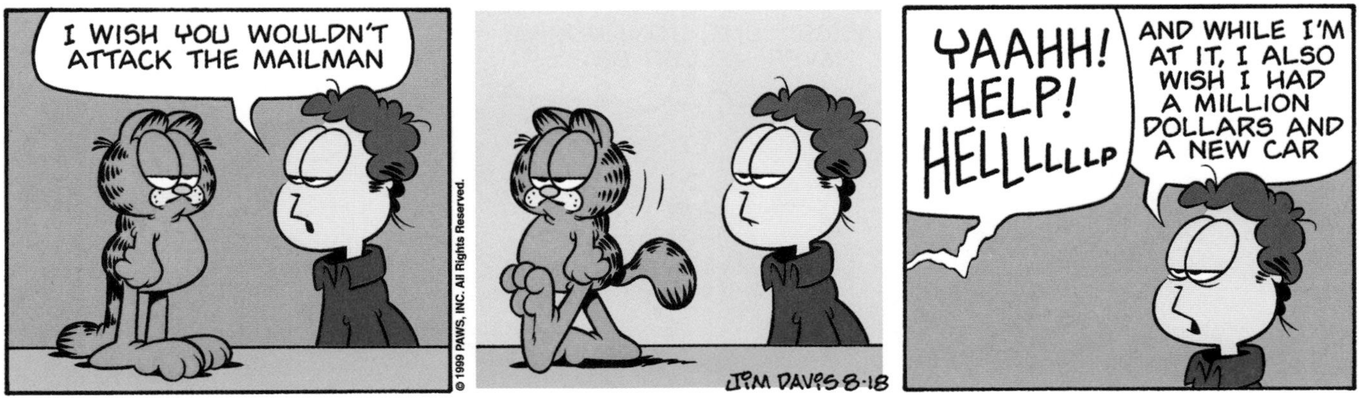
I WISH YOU WOULDN'T ATTACK THE MAILMAN
YAAHH! HELP! HELLLLLLP
AND WHILE I'M AT IT, I ALSO WISH I HAD A MILLION DOLLARS AND A NEW CAR
© 1999 PAWS, INC. All Rights Reserved.
JIM DAVIS 8-18

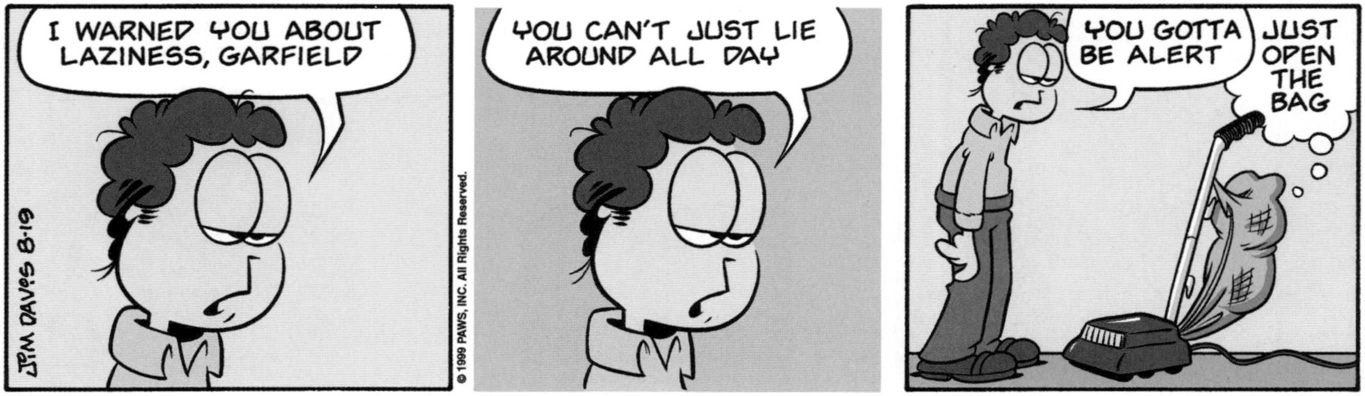
I WARNED YOU ABOUT LAZINESS, GARFIELD
JIM DAVIS 8-19
© 1999 PAWS, INC. All Rights Reserved.
YOU CAN'T JUST LIE AROUND ALL DAY
YOU GOTTA BE ALERT
JUST OPEN THE BAG

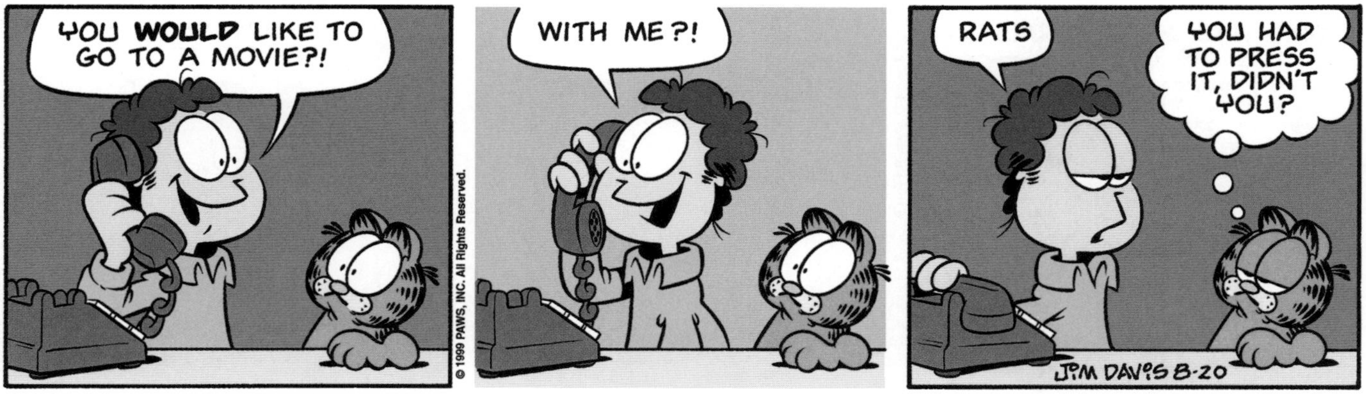
YOU **WOULD** LIKE TO GO TO A MOVIE?!
© 1999 PAWS, INC. All Rights Reserved.
WITH ME?!
RATS
YOU HAD TO PRESS IT, DIDN'T YOU?
JIM DAVIS 8-20

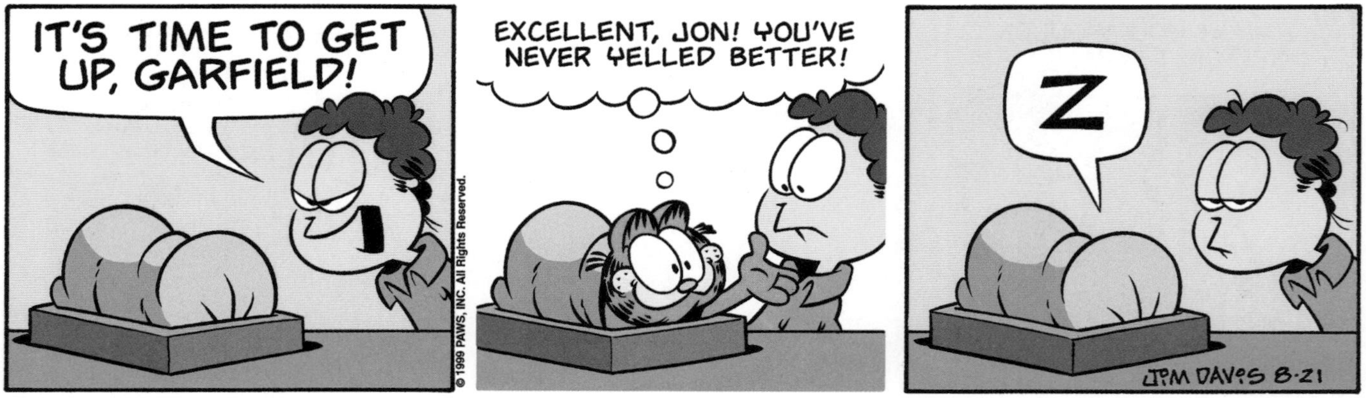
IT'S TIME TO GET UP, GARFIELD!
© 1999 PAWS, INC. All Rights Reserved.
EXCELLENT, JON! YOU'VE NEVER YELLED BETTER!
Z
JIM DAVIS 8-21

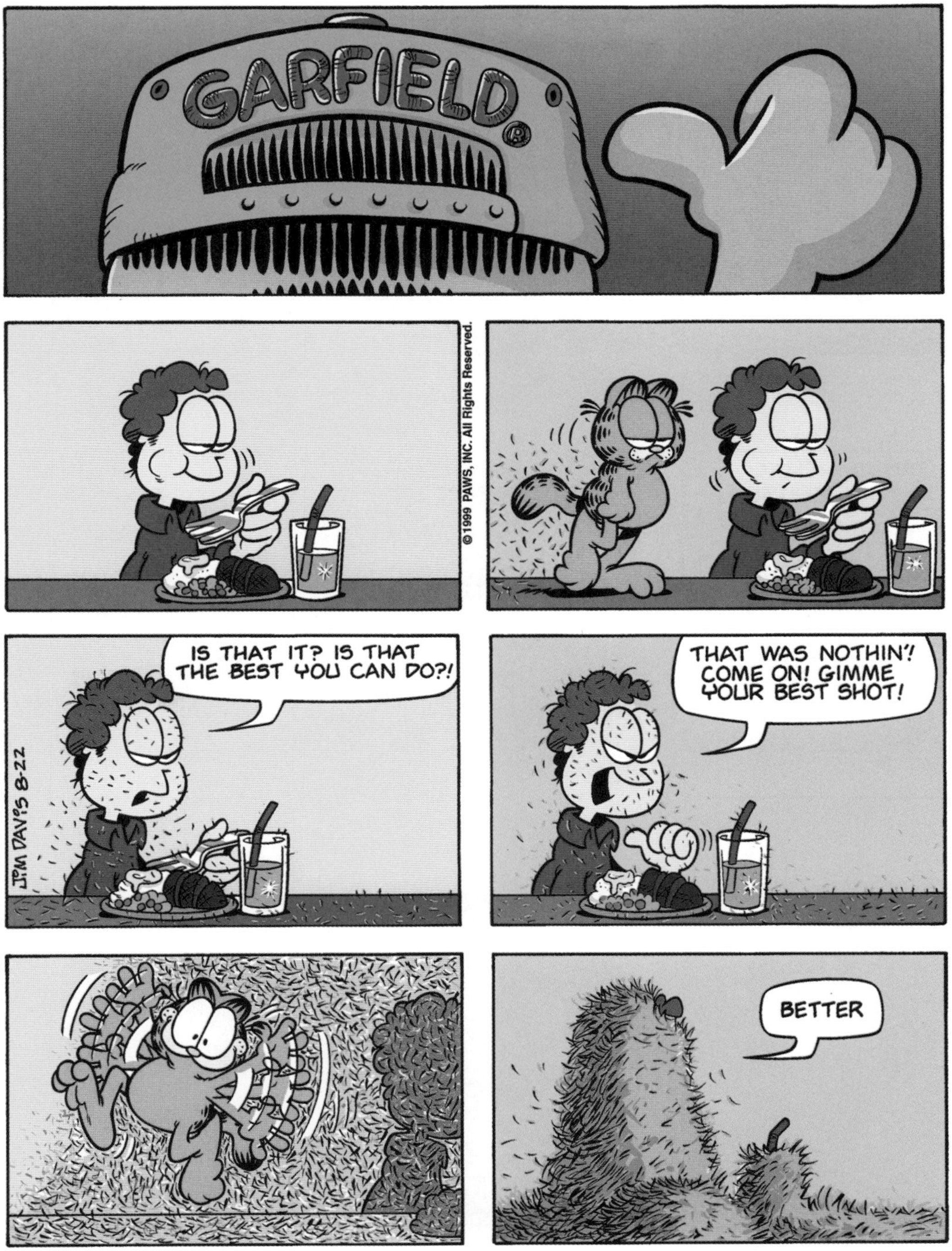
GARFIELD®
© 1999 PAWS, INC. All Rights Reserved.
JIM DAVIS 8-22
IS THAT IT? IS THAT THE BEST YOU CAN DO?!
THAT WAS NOTHIN'! COME ON! GIMME YOUR BEST SHOT!
BETTER

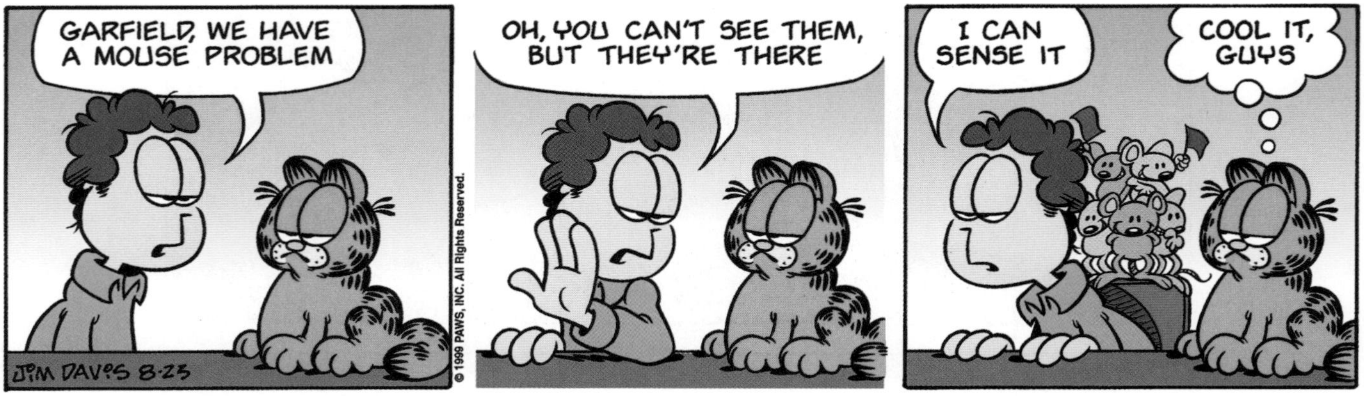
GARFIELD, WE HAVE A MOUSE PROBLEM
OH, YOU CAN'T SEE THEM, BUT THEY'RE THERE
I CAN SENSE IT
COOL IT, GUYS
JIM DAVIS 8-23

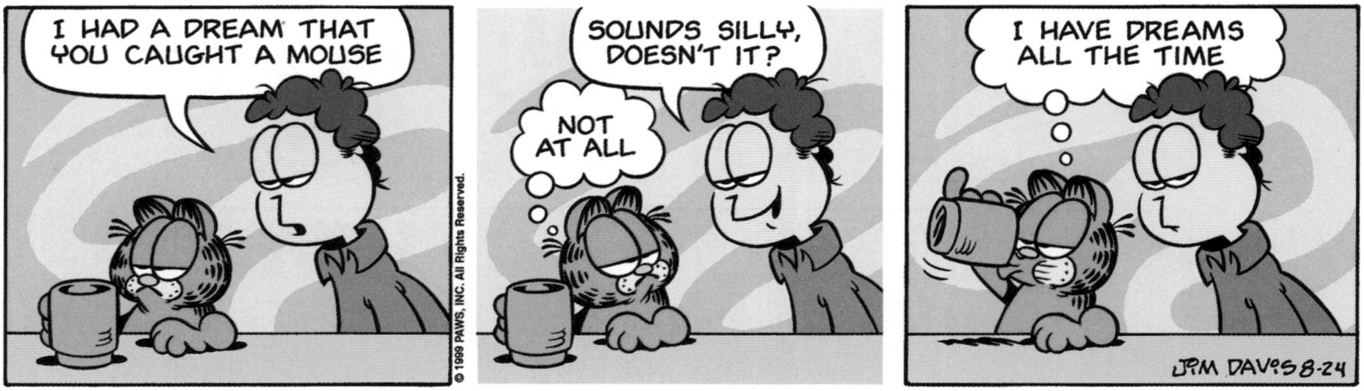
I HAD A DREAM THAT YOU CAUGHT A MOUSE
SOUNDS SILLY, DOESN'T IT?
NOT AT ALL
I HAVE DREAMS ALL THE TIME
JIM DAVIS 8-24

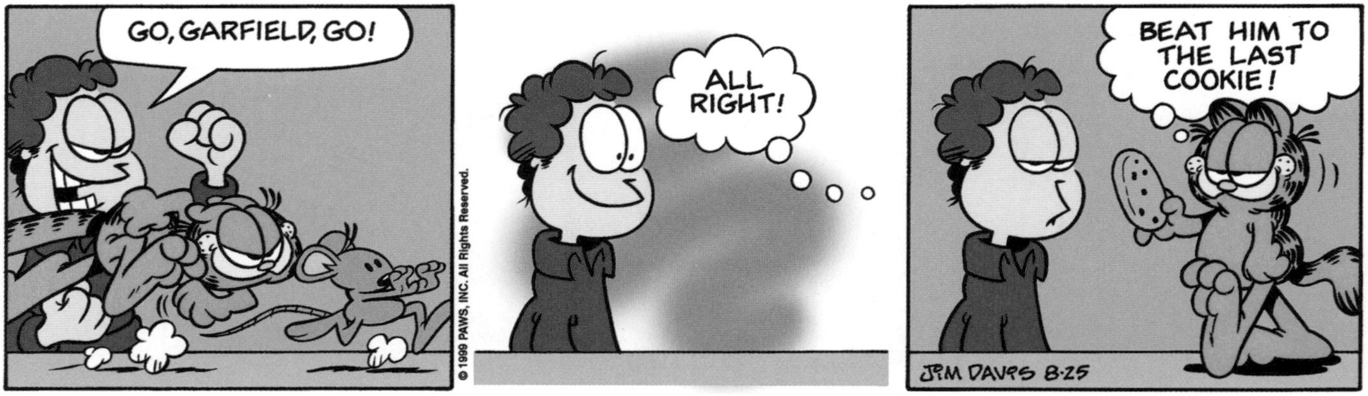
GO, GARFIELD, GO!
ALL RIGHT!
BEAT HIM TO THE LAST COOKIE!
JIM DAVIS 8-25

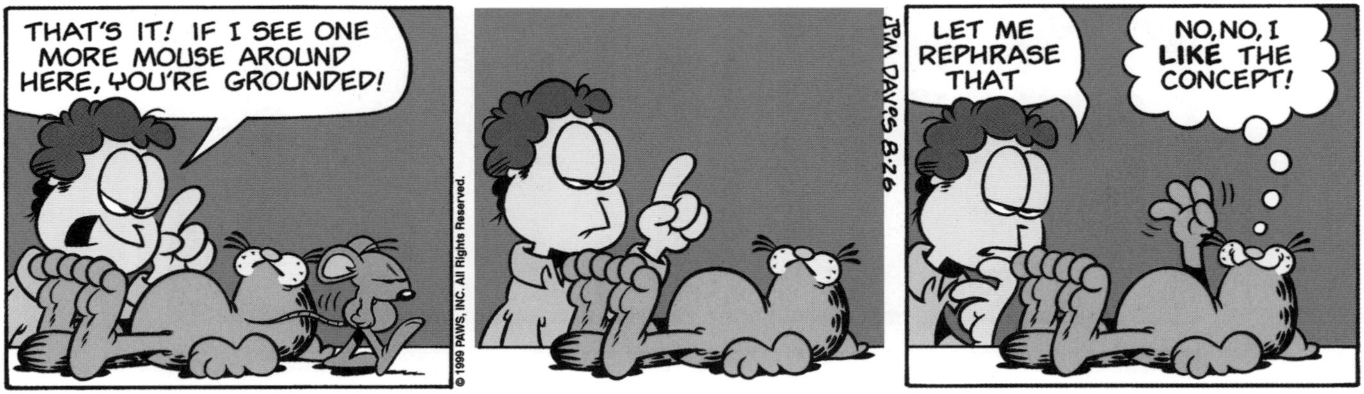
THAT'S IT! IF I SEE ONE MORE MOUSE AROUND HERE, YOU'RE GROUNDED!
© 1999 PAWS, INC. All Rights Reserved.
JIM DAVIS 8-26
LET ME REPHRASE THAT
NO, NO, I **LIKE** THE CONCEPT!

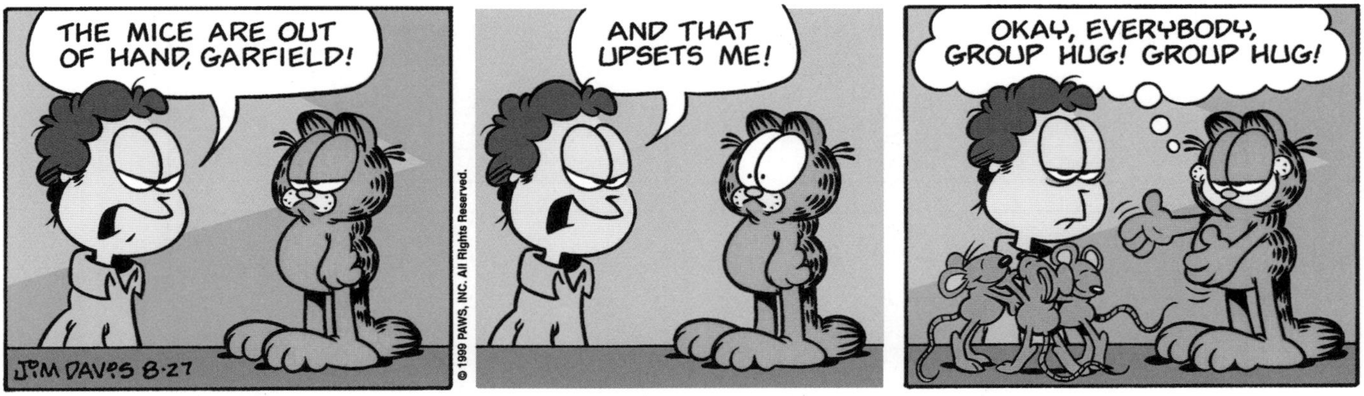
THE MICE ARE OUT OF HAND, GARFIELD!
JIM DAVIS 8-27
© 1999 PAWS, INC. All Rights Reserved.
AND THAT UPSETS ME!
OKAY, EVERYBODY, GROUP HUG! GROUP HUG!

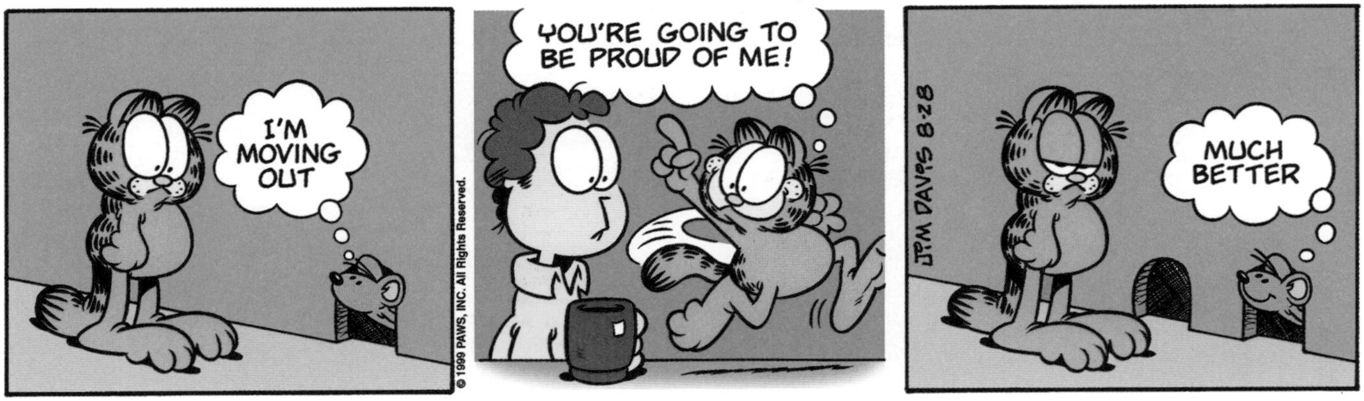
I'M MOVING OUT
© 1999 PAWS, INC. All Rights Reserved.
YOU'RE GOING TO BE PROUD OF ME!
JIM DAVIS 8-28
MUCH BETTER

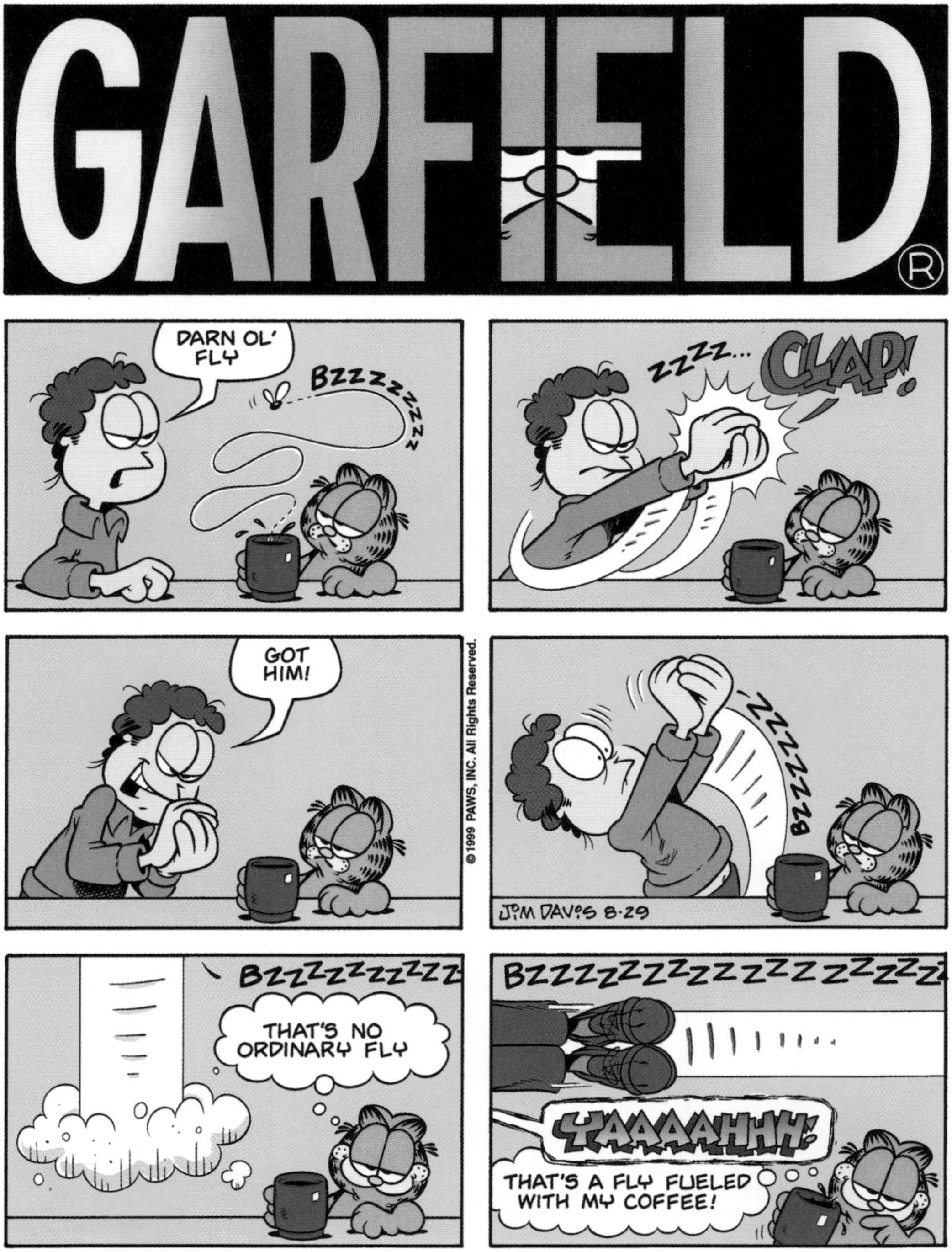
GARFIELD®
DARN OL' FLY
BZZZZZZZZZ
ZZZZ...
CLAP!
GOT HIM!
©1999 PAWS, INC. All Rights Reserved.
ZZZZZZZB
JIM DAVIS 8-29
BZZZZZZZZZZZ
THAT'S NO ORDINARY FLY
BZZZZZZZZZZZZZZZZZZ
YAAAAHHH!
THAT'S A FLY FUELED WITH MY COFFEE!

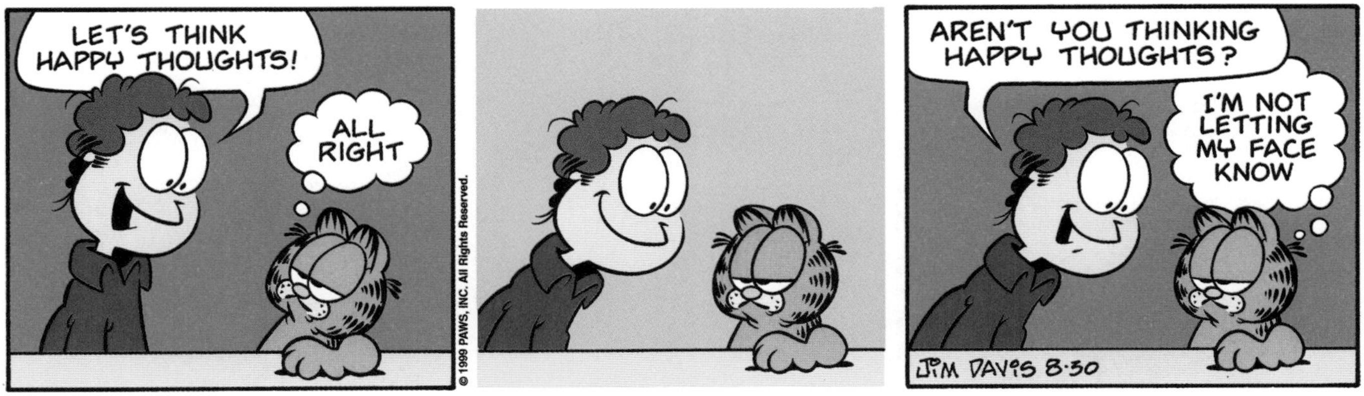
LET'S THINK HAPPY THOUGHTS!
ALL RIGHT
© 1999 PAWS, INC. All Rights Reserved.
AREN'T YOU THINKING HAPPY THOUGHTS?
I'M NOT LETTING MY FACE KNOW
JIM DAVIS 8-30

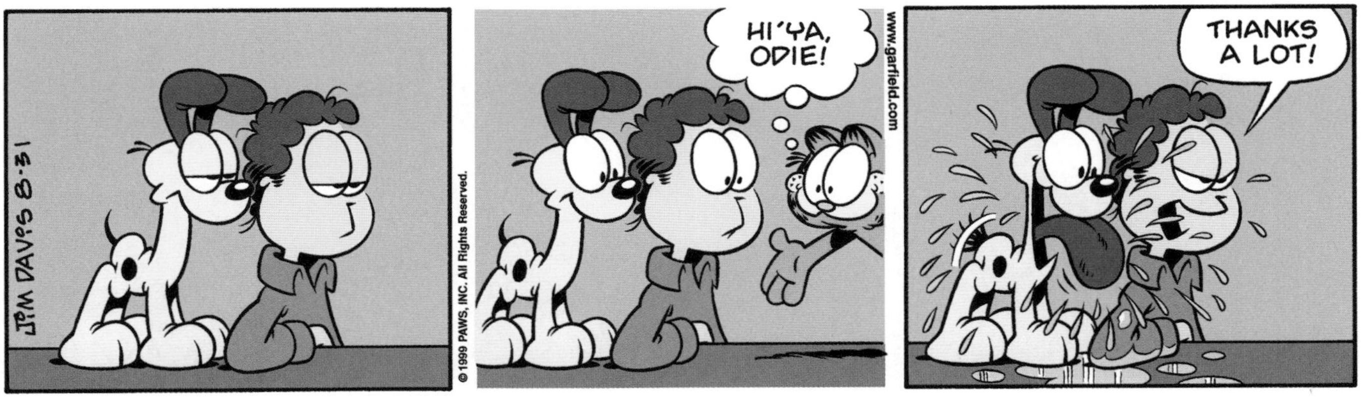
JIM DAVIS 8-31
© 1999 PAWS, INC. All Rights Reserved.
HI'YA, ODIE!
www.garfield.com
THANKS A LOT!

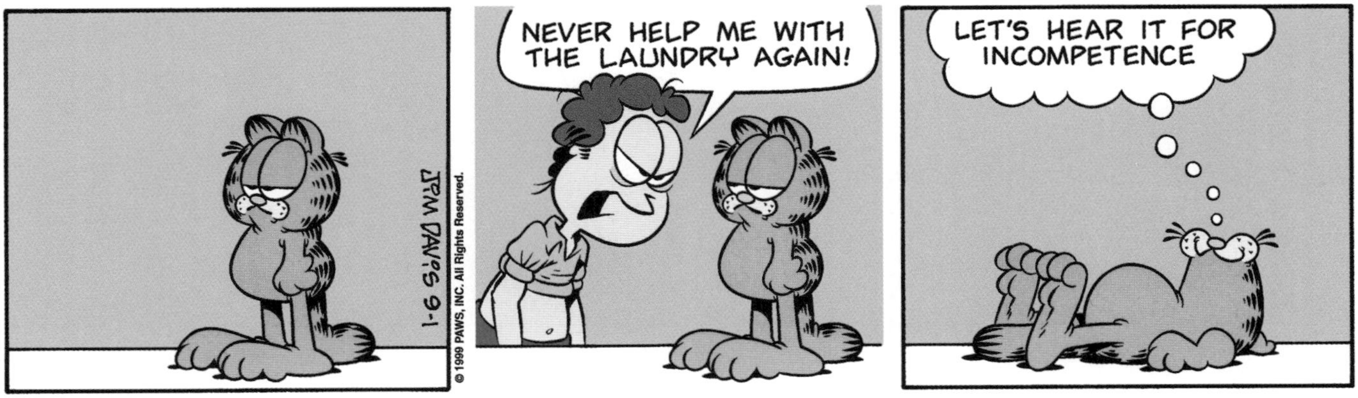
JIM DAVIS 9-1
© 1999 PAWS, INC. All Rights Reserved.
NEVER HELP ME WITH THE LAUNDRY AGAIN!
LET'S HEAR IT FOR INCOMPETENCE

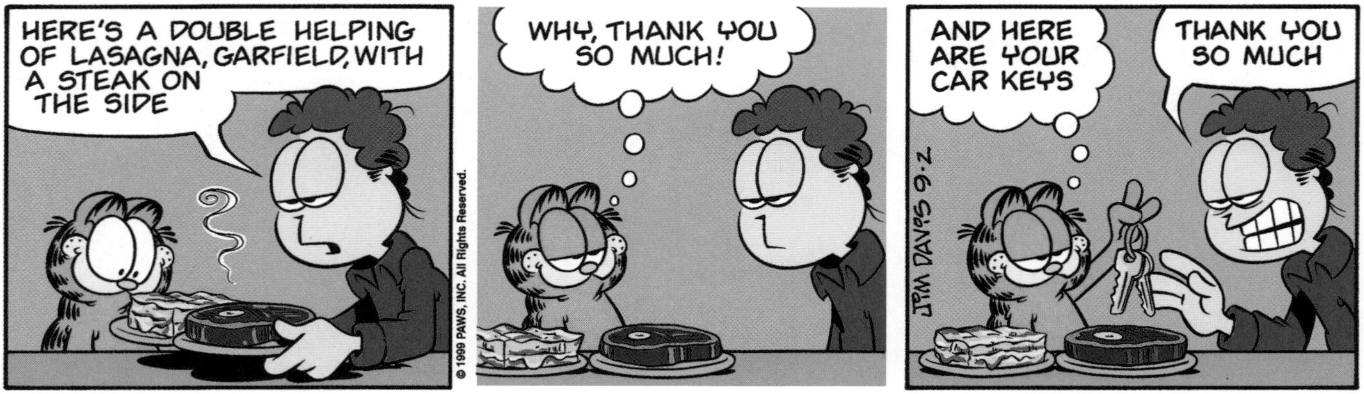
HERE'S A DOUBLE HELPING OF LASAGNA, GARFIELD, WITH A STEAK ON THE SIDE
© 1999 PAWS, INC. All Rights Reserved.
WHY, THANK YOU SO MUCH!
AND HERE ARE YOUR CAR KEYS
THANK YOU SO MUCH
JIM DAVIS 9-2

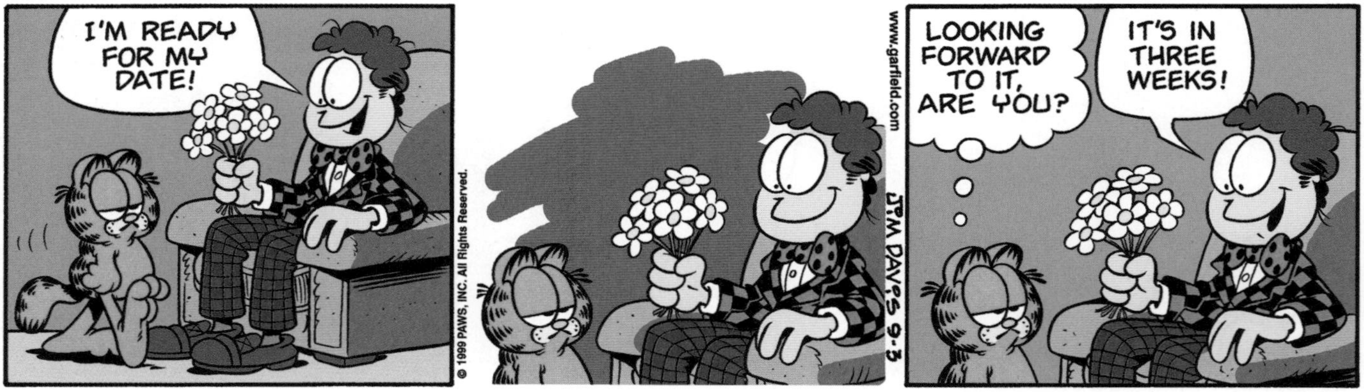
I'M READY FOR MY DATE!
© 1999 PAWS, INC. All Rights Reserved.
JIM DAVIS 9-3
www.garfield.com
LOOKING FORWARD TO IT, ARE YOU?
IT'S IN THREE WEEKS!

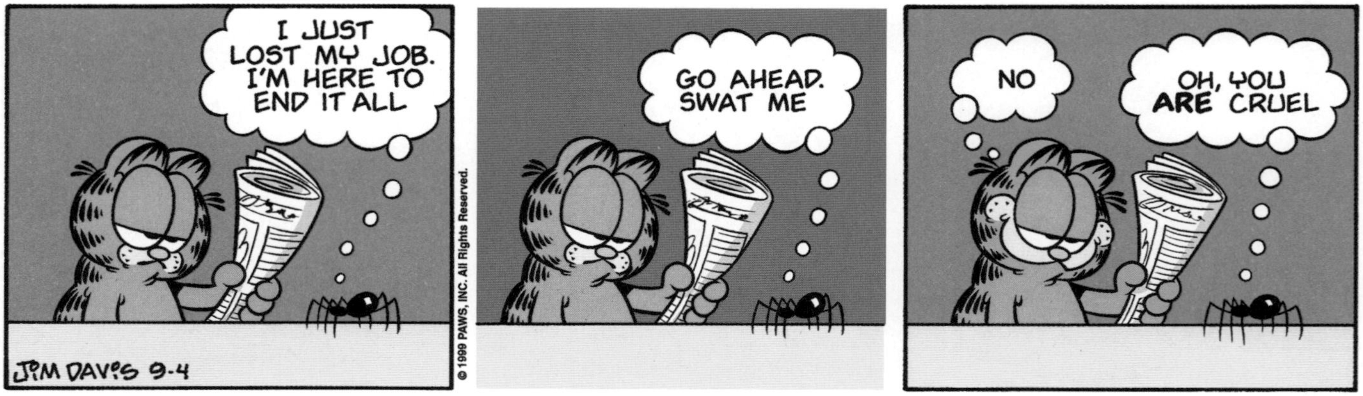
I JUST LOST MY JOB. I'M HERE TO END IT ALL
JIM DAVIS 9-4
© 1999 PAWS, INC. All Rights Reserved.
GO AHEAD. SWAT ME
NO
OH, YOU **ARE** CRUEL

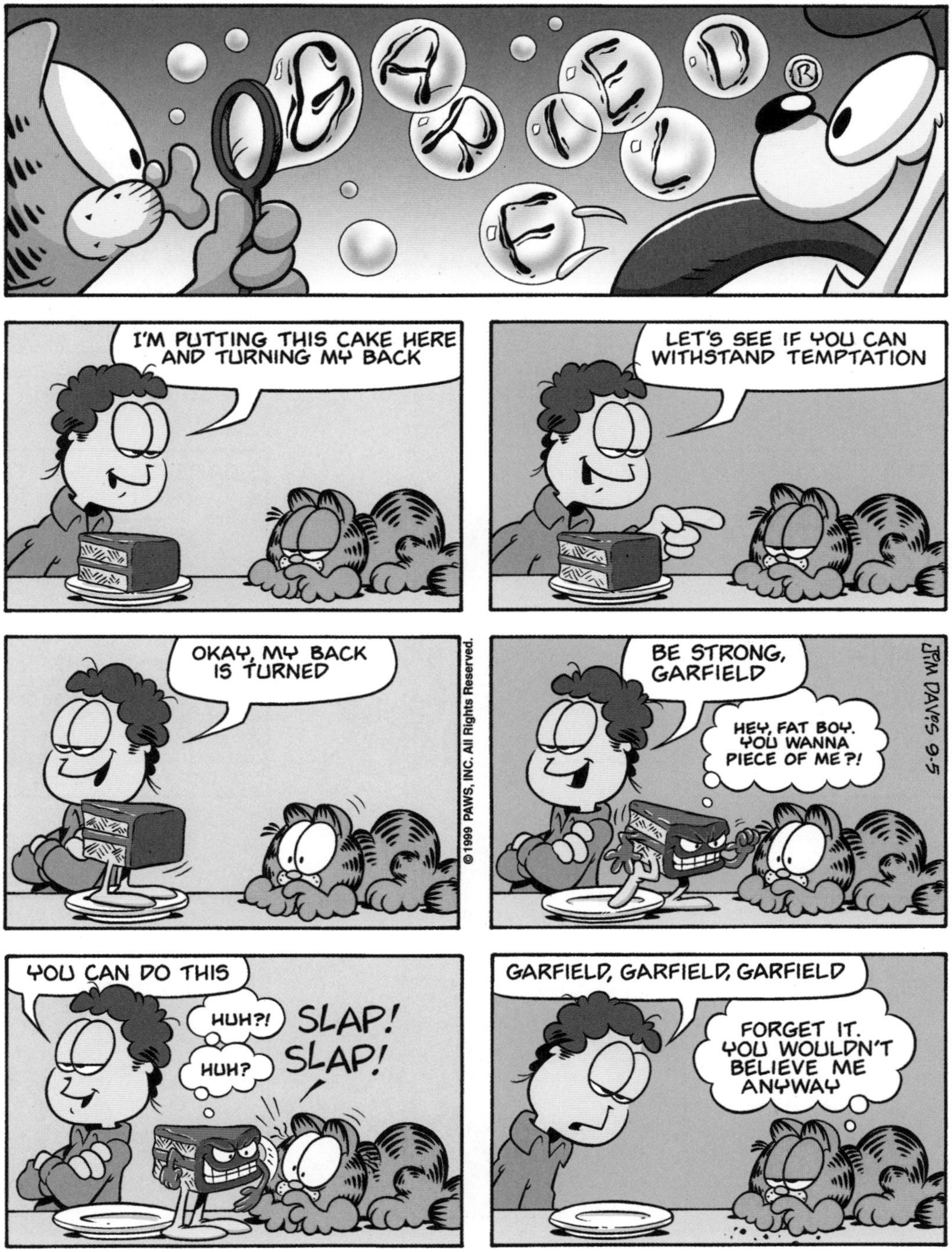
GARFIELD®
I'M PUTTING THIS CAKE HERE AND TURNING MY BACK
LET'S SEE IF YOU CAN WITHSTAND TEMPTATION
OKAY, MY BACK IS TURNED
© 1999 PAWS, INC. All Rights Reserved.
BE STRONG, GARFIELD
HEY, FAT BOY. YOU WANNA PIECE OF ME?!
JIM DAVIS 9-5
YOU CAN DO THIS
HUH?!
HUH?
SLAP! SLAP!
GARFIELD, GARFIELD, GARFIELD
FORGET IT. YOU WOULDN'T BELIEVE ME ANYWAY

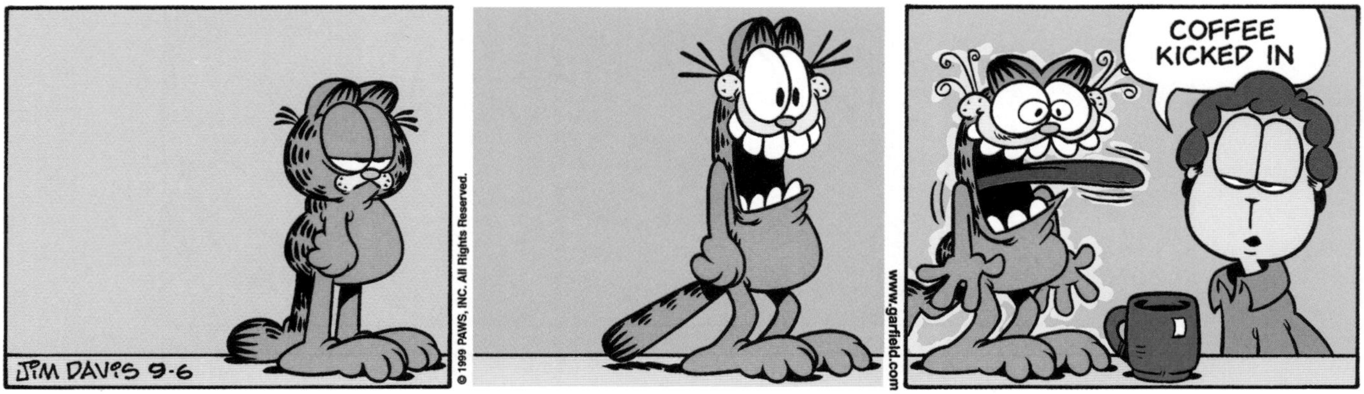
JIM DAVIS 9-6
COFFEE KICKED IN
www.garfield.com

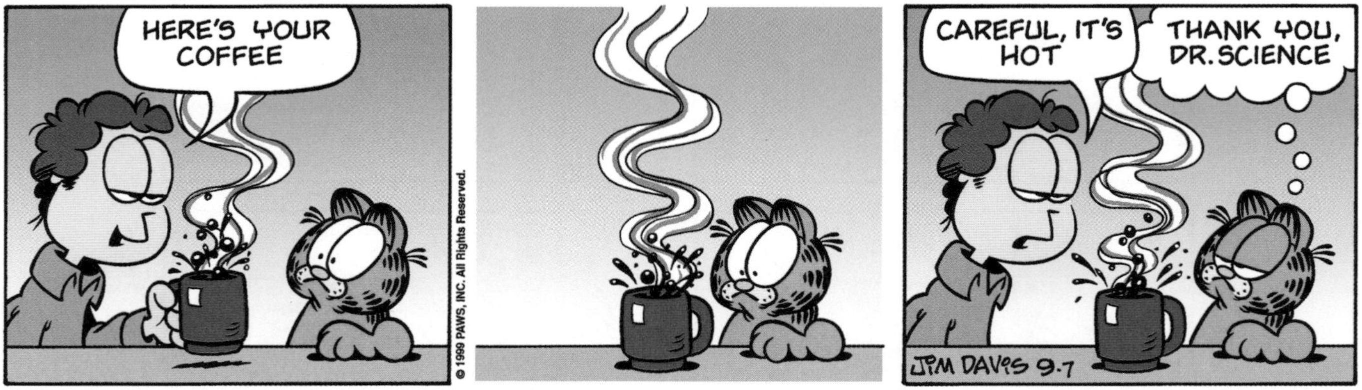
HERE'S YOUR COFFEE
CAREFUL, IT'S HOT
THANK YOU, DR. SCIENCE
JIM DAVIS 9-7

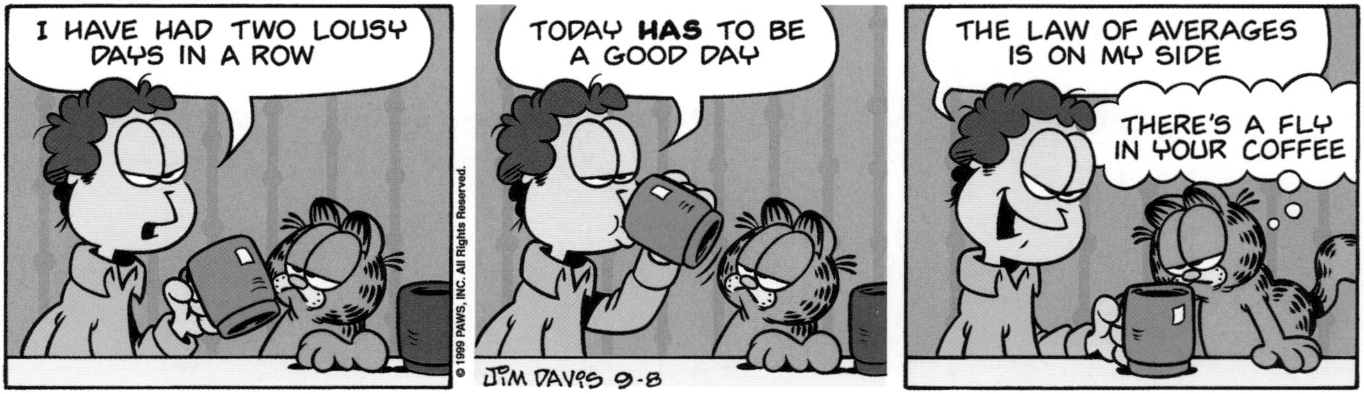
I HAVE HAD TWO LOUSY DAYS IN A ROW
TODAY **HAS** TO BE A GOOD DAY
JIM DAVIS 9-8
THE LAW OF AVERAGES IS ON MY SIDE
THERE'S A FLY IN YOUR COFFEE

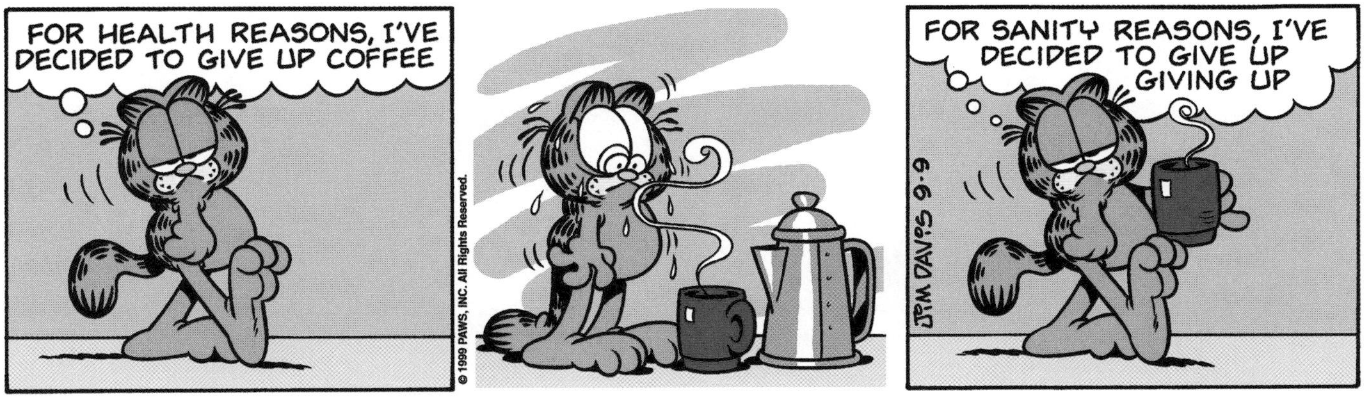
FOR HEALTH REASONS, I'VE DECIDED TO GIVE UP COFFEE
© 1999 PAWS, INC. All Rights Reserved.
JIM DAVIS 9-9
FOR SANITY REASONS, I'VE DECIDED TO GIVE UP GIVING UP

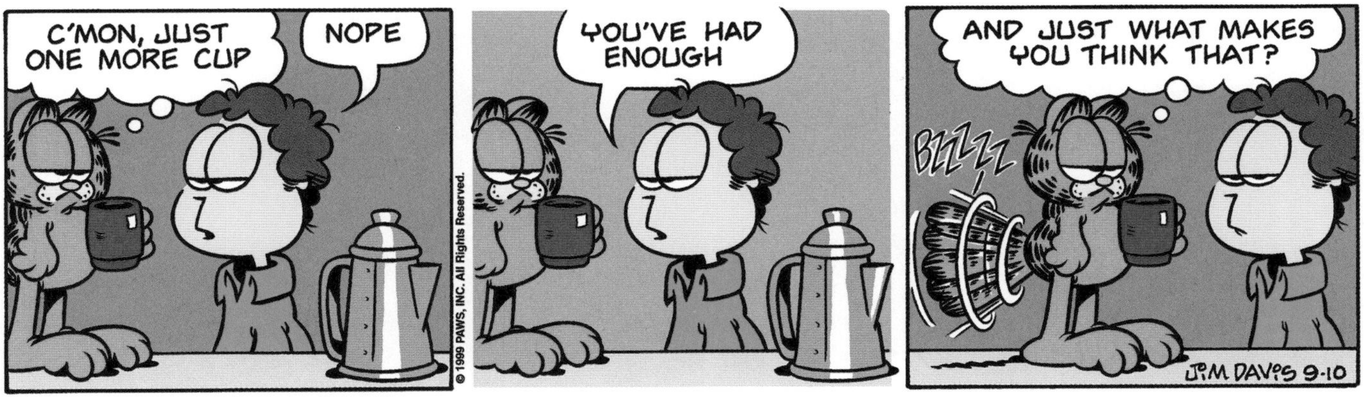
C'MON, JUST ONE MORE CUP
NOPE
© 1999 PAWS, INC. All Rights Reserved.
YOU'VE HAD ENOUGH
AND JUST WHAT MAKES YOU THINK THAT?
BZZZZZ
JIM DAVIS 9-10

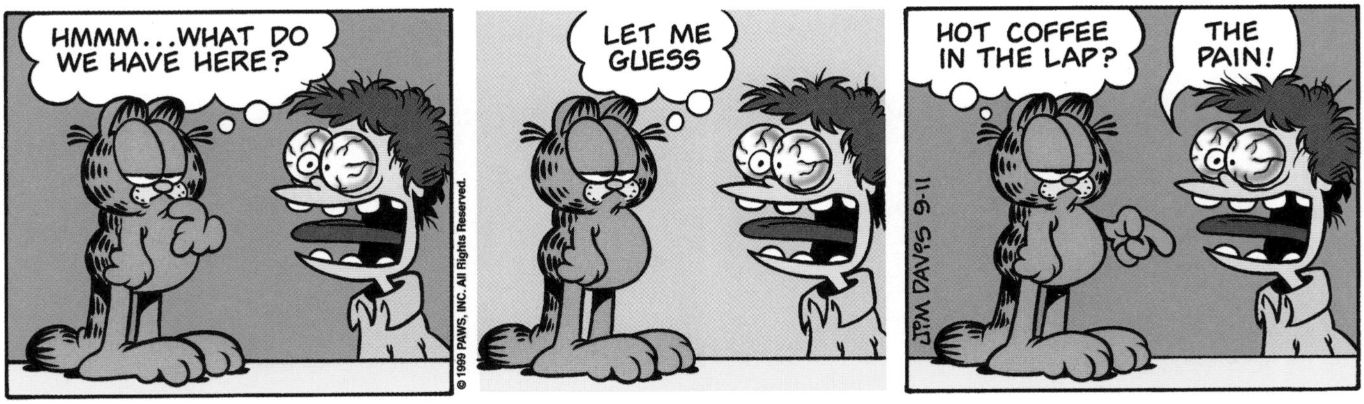
HMMM...WHAT DO WE HAVE HERE?
© 1999 PAWS, INC. All Rights Reserved.
LET ME GUESS
JIM DAVIS 9-11
HOT COFFEE IN THE LAP?
THE PAIN!

Fat Cat Classics Vol. 2

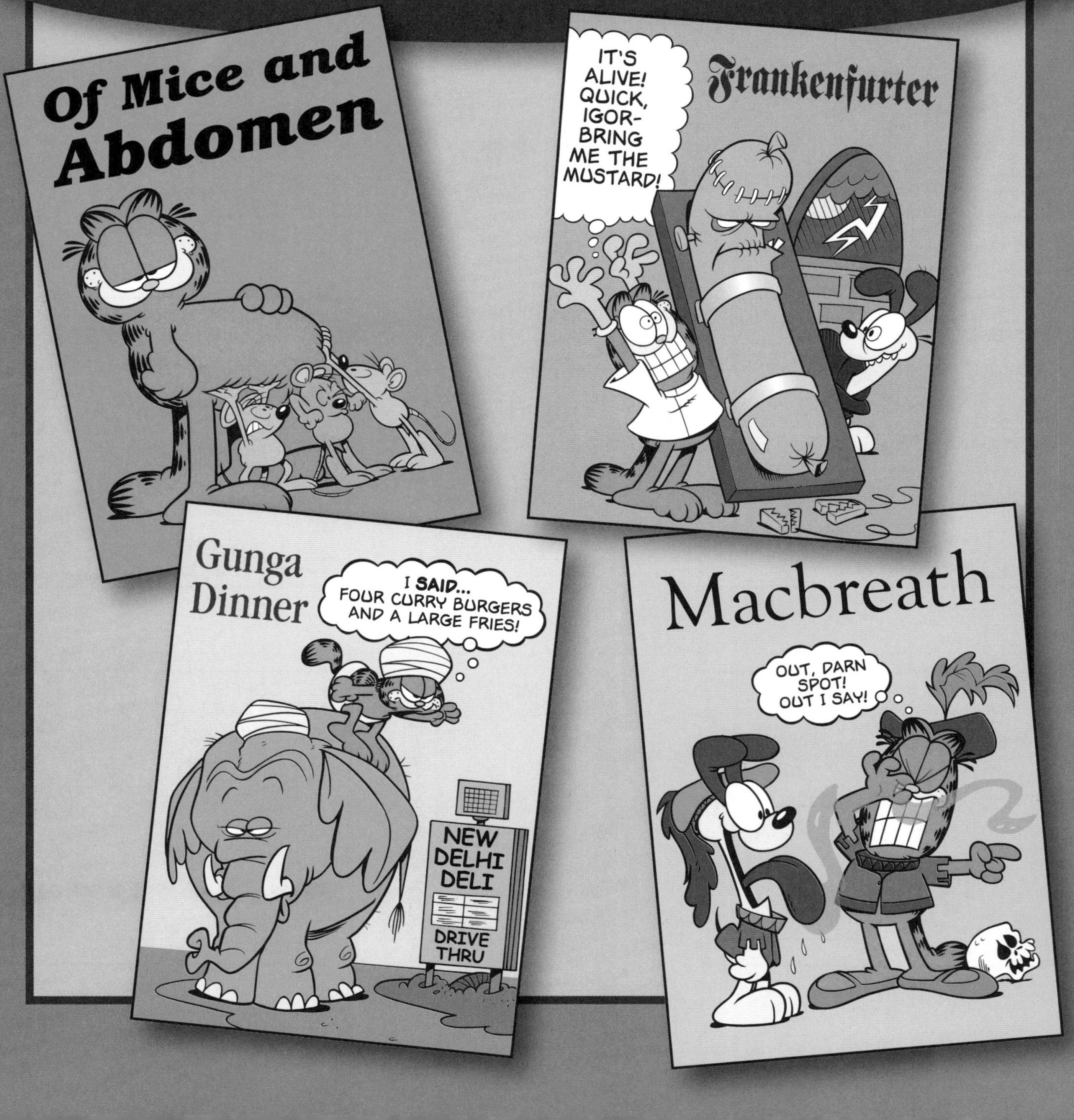
Of Mice and Abdomen
Frankenfurter
IT'S ALIVE! QUICK, IGOR-BRING ME THE MUSTARD!
Gunga Dinner
I SAID... FOUR CURRY BURGERS AND A LARGE FRIES!
NEW DELHI DELI
DRIVE THRU
Macbreath
OUT, DARN SPOT! OUT I SAY!

WATCH. READ. SHOP. PLAY.

DON'T FORGET THE SNACKS!

garfield.com

The Garfield Show

Catch Garfield and the rest of the gang on *The Garfield Show*, now airing on Cartoon Network and Boomerang!

The Comic Strip

Search & read thousands of GARFIELD® comic strips!

Garfield on Facebook & Twitter

Join millions of Garfield friends on Facebook. Get your daily dose of humor and connect with other fat cat fans!

Shop all the Garfield stores!

Original art & comic strips, books, apparel, personalized products, & more!

Play FREE online Garfield games!

Plus, check out all of the FREE Garfield apps available for your smartphone, tablet, and other mobile devices.

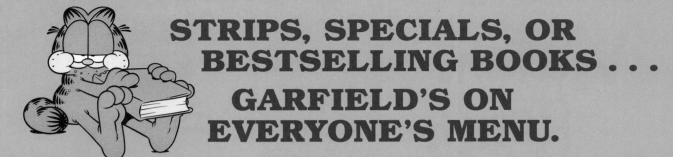

STRIPS, SPECIALS, OR BESTSELLING BOOKS . . . GARFIELD'S ON EVERYONE'S MENU.

Don't miss even one episode in the Tubby Tabby's hilarious series!

GARFIELD AT LARGE . . . (#1) 978-0-345-44382-3
GARFIELD GAINS WEIGHT . . . (#2) 978-0-345-44975-7
GARFIELD BIGGER THAN LIFE . . . (#3) 978-0-345-45027-2
GARFIELD WEIGHS IN . . . (#4) 978-0-345-45205-4
GARFIELD TAKES THE CAKE . . . (#5) 978-0-345-44978-8
GARFIELD EATS HIS HEART OUT . . . (#6) 978-0-345-46459-0
GARFIELD SITS AROUND THE HOUSE . . . (#7) 978-0-345-46463-7
GARFIELD TIPS THE SCALES . . . (#8) 978-0-345-46909-0
GARFIELD LOSES HIS FEET . . . (#9) 978-0-345-46467-5
GARFIELD MAKES IT BIG . . . (#10) 978-0-345-46468-2
GARFIELD ROLLS ON . . . (#11) 978-0-345-47561-9
GARFIELD OUT TO LUNCH . . . (#12) 978-0-345-47562-6
GARFIELD FOOD FOR THOUGHT . . . (#13) 978-0-345-47563-3
GARFIELD SWALLOWS HIS PRIDE . . . (#14) 978-0-345-91386-9
GARFIELD WORLDWIDE . . . (#15) 978-0-345-91754-6
GARFIELD ROUNDS OUT . . . (#16) 978-0-345-49169-5
GARFIELD CHEWS THE FAT . . . (#17) 978-0-345-49170-1
GARFIELD GOES TO WAIST . . . (#18) 978-0-345-49173-2
GARFIELD HANGS OUT . . . (#19) 978-0-345-49174-9
GARFIELD TAKES UP SPACE . . . (#20) 978-0-345-49178-7
GARFIELD SAYS A MOUTHFUL . . . (#21) 978-0-345-49179-4
GARFIELD BY THE POUND . . . (#22) 978-0-345-52558-1
GARFIELD KEEPS HIS CHINS UP . . . (#23) 978-0-345-52559-8
GARFIELD TAKES HIS LICKS . . . (#24) 978-0-345-52587-1
GARFIELD HITS THE BIG TIME . . . (#25) 978-0-345-52589-5
GARFIELD PULLS HIS WEIGHT . . . (#26) 978-0-345-52594-9
GARFIELD DISHES IT OUT . . . (#27) 978-0-345-52595-6
GARFIELD LIFE IN THE FAT LANE . . . (#28) 978-0-345-52600-7
GARFIELD TONS OF FUN . . . (#29) 978-0-345-52601-4
GARFIELD BIGGER AND BETTER . . . (#30) 978-0-345-52605-2
GARFIELD HAMS IT UP . . . (#31) 978-0-345-52606-9
GARFIELD THINKS BIG . . . (#32) 978-0-425-28516-9
GARFIELD THROWS HIS WEIGHT AROUND . . . (#33) 978-0-425-28559-6
GARFIELD LIFE TO THE FULLEST . . . (#34) 978-0-425-28564-0
GARFIELD FEEDS THE KITTY . . . (#35) 978-0-425-28569-5
GARFIELD HOGS THE SPOTLIGHT . . . (#36) 978-0-425-28574-9
GARFIELD BEEFS UP . . . (#37) 978-0-345-44109-6
GARFIELD GETS COOKIN' . . . (#38) 978-0-345-44582-7
GARFIELD EATS CROW . . . (#39) 978-0-345-45201-6
GARFIELD SURVIVAL OF THE FATTEST . . . (#40) 978-0-345-46458-3
GARFIELD OLDER AND WIDER . . . (#41) 978-0-345-46462-0
GARFIELD PIGS OUT . . . (#42) 978-0-345-46466-8
GARFIELD BLOTS OUT THE SUN . . . (#43) 978-0-345-46615-0
GARFIELD GOES BANANAS . . . (#44) 978-0-345-91346-3
GARFIELD LARGE & IN CHARGE . . . (#45) 978-0-345-49172-5
GARFIELD SPILLS THE BEANS . . . (#46) 978-0-345-49177-0
GARFIELD GETS HIS JUST DESSERTS . . . (#47) 978-0-345-91387-6
GARFIELD WILL EAT FOR FOOD . . . (#48) 978-0-345-49176-3
GARFIELD WEIGHS HIS OPTIONS . . . (#49) 978-0-345-49181-7
GARFIELD POTBELLY OF GOLD . . . (#50) 978-0-345-52244-3
GARFIELD SHOVELS IT IN . . . (#51) 978-0-345-52419-5
GARFIELD LARD OF THE JUNGLE . . . (#52) 978-0-345-52584-0

New larger, full-color format! (#1–#36)

GARFIELD BRINGS HOME THE BACON . . . (#53) 978-0-345-52586-4
GARFIELD GETS IN A PICKLE . . . (#54) 978-0-345-52590-1
GARFIELD SINGS FOR HIS SUPPER . . . (#55) 978-0-345-52593-2
GARFIELD CAUTION: WIDE LOAD . . . (#56) 978-0-345-52596-3
GARFIELD SOUPED UP . . . (#57) 978-0-345-52598-7
GARFIELD GOES TO HIS HAPPY PLACE . . . (#58) 978-0-345-52602-1
GARFIELD THE BIG CHEESE . . . (#59) 978-0-345-52604-5
GARFIELD CLEANS HIS PLATE . . . (#60) 978-0-345-52608-3
GARFIELD CHICKENS OUT . . . (#61) 978-0-425-28515-2
GARFIELD LISTENS TO HIS GUT . . . (#62) 978-0-425-28557-2
GARFIELD COOKS UP TROUBLE . . . (#63) 978-0-425-28562-6
GARFIELD FEEDS HIS FACE . . . (#64) 978-0-425-28567-1
GARFIELD EATS AND RUNS . . . (#65) 978-0-425-28572-5

DVD TIE-INS

GARFIELD AS HIMSELF . . . 978-0-345-47805-4
GARFIELD HOLIDAY CELEBRATIONS . . . 978-0-345-47930-3
GARFIELD TRAVEL ADVENTURES . . . 978-0-345-48087-3

AND DON'T MISS . . .

20 YEARS & STILL KICKING! . . . 978-0-345-42126-5
GARFIELD AT 25: IN DOG YEARS I'D BE DEAD . . . 978-0-345-45204-7
GARFIELD'S JOKE ZONE/INSULTS . . . 978-0-345-46263-3
GARFIELD FAT CAT 3-PACK/ VOL. 1 . . . 978-0-345-46455-2
GARFIELD FAT CAT 3-PACK/ VOL. 2 . . . 978-0-345-46465-1
GARFIELD FAT CAT 3-PACK/ VOL. 3 . . . 978-0-345-48088-0
GARFIELD FAT CAT 3-PACK/ VOL. 4 . . . 978-0-345-49171-8
GARFIELD FAT CAT 3-PACK/ VOL. 5 . . . 978-0-345-49180-8
GARFIELD FAT CAT 3-PACK/ VOL. 6 . . . 978-0-345-52420-1
GARFIELD FAT CAT 3-PACK/ VOL. 7 . . . 978-0-345-52588-8
GARFIELD FAT CAT 3-PACK/ VOL. 8 . . . 978-0-345-52599-4
GARFIELD FAT CAT 3-PACK/ VOL. 9 . . . 978-0-345-52607-6
GARFIELD FAT CAT 3-PACK/ VOL. 10 . . . 978-0-425-28558-9
GARFIELD FAT CAT 3-PACK/ VOL. 11 . . . 978-0-425-28566-4
GARFIELD FAT CAT 3-PACK/ VOL. 13 . . . 978-0-345-46460-6
GARFIELD FAT CAT 3-PACK/ VOL. 14 . . . 978-0-345-49175-6
GARFIELD FAT CAT 3-PACK/ VOL. 15 . . . 978-0-345-52585-7
GARFIELD FAT CAT 3-PACK/ VOL. 16 . . . 978-0-345-52592-5
GARFIELD FAT CAT 3-PACK/ VOL. 17 . . . 978-0-345-52603-8
GARFIELD FAT CAT 3-PACK/ VOL. 18 . . . 978-0-399-59440-3
GARFIELD FAT CAT 3-PACK/ VOL. 19 . . . 978-0-425-28561-9
GARFIELD FAT CAT 3-PACK/ VOL. 20 . . . 978-0-425-28571-8
SEASON'S EATINGS: A VERY MERRY GARFIELD CHRISTMAS . . . 978-0-345-47560-2
GARFIELD'S GUIDE TO EVERYTHING . . . 978-0-345-46461-3
ODIE UNLEASHED! . . . 978-0-345-46464-4
GARFIELD'S BOOK OF CAT NAMES . . . 978-0-345-48516-8
THE GARFIELD JOURNAL . . . 978-0-345-46469-9
LIGHTS, CAMERA, HAIRBALLS!: GARFIELD AT THE MOVIES . . . 978-0-345-49134-3
30 YEARS OF LAUGHS AND LASAGNA . . . 978-0-345-50379-4
GARFIELD MINUS GARFIELD . . . 978-0-345-51387-8
GARFIELD FROM THE TRASH BIN . . . 978-0-345-51881-1
GARFIELD LEFT SPEECHLESS . . . 978-0-345-53058-5
MY LAUGHABLE LIFE WITH GARFIELD . . . 978-0-345-52591-8
GARFIELD'S SUNDAY FINEST . . . 978-0-345-52597-0
AGE HAPPENS GARFIELD HITS THE BIG 4-0 . . . 978-0-345-52609-0